The Daily Telegraph
The Trout and I

The Daily Telegraph

The Trout and I

More Adventures in Pursuit of Wild Fish

JON BEER

AURUM PRESS

First published in Great Britain 2003 by Aurum Press Ltd
25 Bedford Avenue, London WC1B 3AT

A catalogue record for this book is available from the British Library.

ISBN 1 85410 955 3

1 2 3 4 5 6 7 8 9 10
2003 2004 2005 2006 2007

Designed by James Campus
Typeset by M Rules
Printed and bound in Great Britain by
MPG Books Ltd, Bodmin

Contents

1 𝒬

Posted to the Highlands

I started the journey with a beard – but then one thing led to another. You know how it does.

I was taking the Royal Highlander sleeper from England to Inverness. I have tried several different ways to get from Banbury to the Highlands. Flying is quicker. Driving gives you a car at the other end. But the sleeper train is far and away the most luxurious. The extra time is spent snoozing away in a private cabin or chatting in the bar as the duller bits of Britain flit unseen past the window. And besides, I didn't need a car at the other end: I would be travelling by post.

You are pampered on the sleeper. They ask you what time you would like your breakfast in bed. They ask whether you would prefer tea or coffee with your croissant. These are nice questions. Then they show you to your cabin. They give you a little Penguin novel and a complimentary wash-bag stuffed with little knick-knacks. I had had my supper in the lounge car. I had read my novel and chatted. I was tucked up in bed, rocked by the motion of the train. I woke at 5.30 the next morning. We had reached Gleneagles. From now on, the sleeper stops every twenty minutes or so, spreading travellers thinly along the line to Inverness. By Pitlochry I was wide-awake and breakfast was still an hour away. I opened my complimentary wash bag and spread the knick-knacks across the bed. By Blair Atholl I had cleaned my teeth with the travelling toothbrush. I had used the flannel and soap. By Dalwhinnie I had washed my hair and combed it with my complimentary comb. I had attached my free plastic luggage label to my rucksack. I had even tried the Shoe-Shine Wipe – not a success on waxed walking boots. As we pulled out of Newtonmore, only the complimentary razor and sachet of shaving cream remained untried. What the hell: I had scissors in my fishing bag under the bed. I could always grow another beard. I stepped onto the platform at Inverness feeling funny and fresh about the face and grateful they had packed nothing more lethal into that little bag.

The North Highland Line leaves a little later from the next platform. By lunchtime the train was pulling into the tiny station of Lairg. A red post van stood beyond the fence beside the down platform. My carriage awaited.

About this red post van: I was, I believe, the last person in the country to discover the post bus service. But if there is someone out there who has not heard of it, I will tell you now. In the remoter parts of these islands the postman delivers more that just the post. They can deliver medicines and groceries and newspapers. And me. Or you. In the Highlands these post buses go everywhere the post is delivered, and that is everywhere. The hub of this system in the Highlands is the tiny village of Lairg. The post buses wait for the train from Inverness and then potter off north and west to every glen in Sutherland.

A one-track road crosses the Highlands from Lairg in the east to the fractured coastline of the west. It may be a beautiful journey: I believe it is – but I saw nothing of it. The rain commenced to rain as we motored along the upper Oykel. Also, the only other passenger in the post bus was a stunningly beautiful woman with cascades of raven hair. Opportunities to converse with such creatures come my way very rarely these days. And I could always admire Strath Oykel some other time.

She left the post bus two hours later at Lochinver. Walter McKenzie and I pottered along the tiny road towards Drumbeg. Walter McKenzie is not stunningly beautiful. He is the postman. I looked around for the first time. The road twisted through a landscape of heather and rock. There was something vaguely nostalgic I couldn't place for a while. It was the telegraph poles. Time was when they ran along every road and railway track, telegraph poles with four or five horizontal bars at the top carrying a cat's cradle of insulators and wires. We used to put miniature ones alongside model railways to make them look realistic. I hadn't noticed the going of them until I came to Lochinver and saw them again.

Walter asked where I was staying. I didn't have an address. I had just a name: Miss Anne Gould. The joy of travelling by post was that Walter knew everyone. He dropped me at the door and waited while I introduced myself, dropped off the bulk of my rucksack and arranged for dinner that evening. I climbed back into the post bus with a rod and fishing bag and we carried on towards Drumbeg.

'You'll be looking for young Callum,' Walter said. He was right. Anyone who comes to fish the limitless lochs of North Assynt will want to find Callum Millar first.

We found Young Callum (to distinguish him from Old Callum, his father) outside his home in Drumbeg's schoolhouse. With him was the broad, cheerful figure of Bob Watson. He has reasons to be cheerful. He had recently retired from farming in Fife and now seemed to spend his time fishing hither and yon throughout the fishier bits of Scotland. He had fished and stalked amongst the hill lochs of Assynt for many years, first with Old Callum and now with Young Callum. I could not be fishing in better company than these two.

*   *   *

The North Assynt Estate is a wild and remote peninsula, a vast tract of rock and heather and water. There are large, deep, serious lochs like Loch Poll, where some of the trout can grow very large indeed, grazing on the resident char population. There are lochs of repute: some of dour days with occasional monsters, others of consistent sport. These are usually to be found close to the small road that circles the peninsula. But away from the road, down the tracks, the 'peat roads' that wander deep into the hills, there is another world. Hidden amongst the folds and outcrops lie well over a hundred lochs and lochans. The number is unknown: when a water is so fretted with peninsulas and islands it can be a single loch or a series of lochans. Most have rarely been fished. All hold trout. Most hold nuggety hill trout that average four to the pound. Some hold much larger trout. But which is which is known to no one.

It was too late in the day to head into the hills, so we strolled down to Callum's home water, Loch Drumbeg. Drumbeg is not a bad introduction to the lochs of North Assynt. The loch is studded with islands and headlands; there are narrows where a boat can scarcely thread a course that widen into basins and bays. It had been slow fishing that morning. Callum and Bob had fished hard for a dozen or so fish – which didn't sound all that slow to me, but I am used to lesser waters. The day had stilled after the rain. Callum took the oars of the comfy wooden boat and pulled us out into the loch.

We took fish. Not a vast number, but steadily that afternoon, and, creaking a little after a sumptuous meal at Anne Gould's table, we went on into the long northern gloaming. I will not describe the fishing that evening: it was just the hors d'oeuvre before the hill lochs I had come to fish.

It was raining steadily the next morning. Anne Gould runs the Cruachan guesthouse in the old manse at Stoer. When I die, if I have led a good and blameless life, I will go to somewhere a bit like Anne's guesthouse. Anne is a serious salmon fisher. She knows what a fisherman needs. We need the warmth of a big Aga to dry stuff on days like this. We need dinners that start with mushrooms in garlic cream followed by something big in the roast-beef-and-yorkshire-pud line. We need notes to say 'gone to bed – lock the door behind you' when we have staggered in from an evening's fishing and a nightcap at Callum's at 1 a.m. We need a breakfast starting with porridge and ending with coffee with fried stuff in between. And we need a labyrinth of hardly-fished trout lochs that start just across the road. And that's what you get at Anne's place.

We went across the road.

A peat road begins a few hundred yards from the house, through a gate with a sign reading, 'Man-eating sheep – please close the gate'. The road is driveable for a short distance, a granite track twisting between the chaos of rocky hummocks. Before long the track sinks beneath a bog to reappear on the far side as a shadow, two faint lines of grass through the encroaching heather. We passed small lochans to either side. Two miles from the road, the track, now barely discernible, forks and, around the next bend, ends at a loch. I could see all that on the map: we were at the western side of Loch na h-Uidhe Doimhne. It was the last time that day I had any idea where I was.

We started to fish. Bob had kept his rod set up from the previous evening and moved down to the water's edge. By the time I had renewed my leader and mounted a team of flies, he had a fish and a pull. That is about the proportion in these waters. It is embarrassing at first when a swirl appears at the end of your line and the thing twitches across the surface as a fish plucks at a fly: you strike and there is nothing there. You have struck too late. So next time you try harder, watch closer, strike quicker. It doesn't seem to make any difference. The rises are like lightning and a trout sticks or it doesn't. How a trout plucks at a wee double and swims away I cannot say, they just do in these parts.

We crossed that first loch on a shallow causeway, breasted a short rise and looked down on Loch Poll Dhaidh for the first time.

Or at least we looked down on bits of it. You do not see a loch hereabouts, not a whole loch: you see an arm or a bay and an island or a headland. The shores are steep and rocky and often involve a stiff little climb through the heather to round a point. And round the point you find that what had seemed an island is a peninsula, what seemed an isthmus is an island, and a bay has become a narrow channel to another basin, and so on. They really do have more features than they know what to do with. They lead you on. The next rocky outcrop, the next islet is just yards away, and before you know it, you are alone and lost in that tight little world of rock and water. The first time it happened I looked around for Callum and Bob. I climbed up on a headland and searched the water, but you could lose an army of fishermen in those folds and features. And I realized I had no idea where I was and which way led to the next meal. I wasn't exactly panicking but I gave a speculative, anyone-about sort of whistle. I didn't hold back: it was a loud, speculative whistle. There was no reply. I whistled again, waited and then started walking towards the nearest high point. I had not gone many yards before Callum's cap studded with wee doubles emerged from a fold in the heather to one side. Down there lay another unsuspected arm of the loch where he and Bob had been watching an otter fossicking along the shore. Until I whistled, that is.

This tortured terrain makes for fascinating fishing. On the steep shores the fish can lie within inches of the rocks, bursting up from the depths to grab at food falling from the overhanging heather. Or a fisherman's fly.

Which brings me to the fishing. I have said little or nothing about the fishing. I know that. There is little to tell. It works. In fact, it works rather well. You cast a team of traditional flies – *huge* traditional flies, mind you: take a look at Callum's recommendations. You retrieve them in the normal way, working them over and round the rocks – there are, you will have gathered, plenty of rocks. There is a swirl, a snatch and the punchy little fish is on – or it isn't. If it is, the rod dips as the fish plunges into the depths. The trout of these hill lochs are under the delusion that they weigh over a pound. They don't – mostly – but so convinced are they that for a moment the fisherman believes it too. He gives them line, which they take, until sanity returns and a boisterous little quarter-pounder is brought, kicking and protesting, to shore. It happened eighty times that day. And once I stood on a rock and took four fish in five casts fanned around me. That's all I have to tell you about the fishing.

If eighty feisty little trout between breakfast and teatime doesn't get your juices going, then, believe me, you've chosen the wrong sport.

Callum Millar's Flies for the Lochs of North Assynt

The flies that Callum suggests for the hill lochs are tried and trusted traditional patterns. What surprised me was the size. Callum recommends big flies, sizes 8–12, and often favours 'wee doubles', particularly for the point fly. Two outstanding favourites are Grouse & Claret and Cinammon & Gold. A typical team of three flies on a floating line would be selected from: Black Spider, Blae & Black, Butcher, Mallard & Claret, Zulu, Dunkeld, KeHe and Muddler.

I would like to offer one more. I think Callum would too. Before we fished that first afternoon on Drumbeg, I showed Callum a fly that had produced most of the action on a trip to the Hebrides. I did not know its name but I had copied it from a now-battered original. It has a yellow tail, a yellow/olive dubbed body with a palmered olive hackle and a front hackle of blue guinea fowl. Callum took one look at it and muttered, 'You'll no catch much with that here.' Callum is still young. Bob, at three times Callum's age, winced. He knew that, life and fishing being what they are, that garish little fly would now proceed to wipe the floor with all the others.

And so, for a time, it did. It is a Golden Olive Bumble.

2 ♌

The Duns Tew Snooker Club

I expect the MCC started small. A few blokes getting together in the car park at the back of the Marylebone Gaumont, chalking three stumps on the wall next to the dustbins and doing 'one potato, two potato' for captains. Something like that.

You may not have heard of the DTSC. The Duns Tew Snooker Club owns two trophies. A small silver eggcup that my young daughter once bought in a jumble sale is presented to the winner of an evening's play. Alice doesn't know that we have this eggcup; equally, she doesn't know that we lost it to a visitor who has never given it back. The other trophy is a huge ceramic stein of hideous design presented to the winner of the evening's highest break. The size of the break is recorded on a scroll of paper inside the stein. There are only three names on this scroll: there are only three members of the Duns Tew Snooker Club. The DTSC meets in the loft of Terry's barn around the snooker table that Terry has been storing for a bloke for the past ten years. We think the bloke may have forgotten it. The Duns Tew Snooker Club also has an annual all-members fishing outing.

We were leaving on the evening ferry. Philip and I were pretty excited when we pulled into Terry's farm that afternoon. Terry was not excited: he thought we were going the next day. It took a while to convince him this was not an elaborate joke, explain matters to his wife and lunch guests, bundle what passes for Terry's fishing tackle into the car and set off for Swansea.

The Swansea–Cork ferry is a splendid route to the south-west of Ireland. It has its surreal moments. I had expected the crew, on a ferry between Wales and Ireland, to be Welsh or, possibly, Irish. Not Polish, anyway. The ship itself has certainly seen more exotic ports than Swansea and Cork: many of the signs and labels are in Greek, while the instructions on the cabin telephone are, I think, in German. These instructions are straightforward enough: there are only two. In the case of FEUER you dial 112. You dial 110 for NOTRUF. We didn't know what NOTRUF meant, so we dialled it anyway. It was the smoothest crossing of the Irish Sea I can remember.

The sun was shining the next morning as the ferry nosed past Spike Island and on into Cork Harbour. Terry's car had started to make a Funny Noise as we had boarded the ferry in Swansea. It was not the sort of Funny Noise you would want to take with you to the west of Ireland, so we headed into the centre of Cork looking for a VW garage. While Terry was having his Funny Noise looked at, Philip and I wandered into the city centre. We crossed a handsome bridge and looked down at a handsome stretch of water. It was our first look at the River Lee. We took another look: there were three blokes in swimming trunks floating in the middle of the chilly river. They were floating very serenely on their backs with their toes up. They were bobbing a bit on the waves. And then we realized they were full-size, plastic blokes: they were ART. We knew they were art because everyone else passing by that morning was ignoring them.

Fifty miles upstream from the three plastic blokes, the River Lee rattles into life in the spectacular surroundings of Gougane Barra, a stunningly beautiful lake set in a dramatic cliff-lined cleft in the ancient mountains of the west. A small island, joined to the shore by a short causeway, has been a place of pilgrimage and prayer for well over a thousand years. It is the Holy island of St Finbar, the founder and patron saint of the city of Cork who established his first monastery here in the sixth century. Beside the island sits the Gougane Barra Hotel run by Mrs Lucey, whose family has been looking after visitors and pilgrims to this hallowed spot for four generations. And now she was to look after the Duns Tew Snooker Club annual fishing outing.

One or two members of the DTSC are, let's be frank, a bit worldly. At times they can show a lamentable lack of spirituality. I had chosen the charming hotel beside St Finbar's Holy island in the hopes, not high admittedly, that something of the saint's spiritual qualities might rub off on my fellow club members. Also, the lake is reputedly stuffed with trout, and a pair of business-like boats is kept for the convenience of visiting fishermen.

Fixing Terry's Funny Noise had set us back a bit. We had places to fish. We dropped our bags off at the hotel, climbed back in the car and headed west, through the narrow pass of Keimaneigh to the valley of the Owenbeg River and the sea.

The south-west corner of Ireland frays into the Atlantic Ocean in four great fingers. If the index finger is the Dingle Peninsula, then the middle finger is Inveragh and the Ring of Kerry. The third finger is the Beara Peninsula. The Caha mountains run down the Beara Peninsula like a spine, and in the ancient heart of these mountains are loughs. Here is what Peter O'Reilly has to say about the loughs of the Caha mountains in his *Loughs of Ireland*:

Fishing the loughs of the Cahas on the historic Beara Peninsula is an experience the angler will long remember. On a pleasant day, it can be close to paradise – or at least the Garden of Eden.

Well, you'd want a slice of that, wouldn't you?

It was early afternoon on just such a pleasant day when we reached Glengariff, squeezed between the mountains and Bantry Bay. A single-track forest road wound us up into the woods behind the town. Peter O'Reilly describes three routes into the Cahas: this is none of them. After two miles or so, the road emerges from the trees and meets the little Coomarkane River. The secret little world of the Coomarkane valley in May was having a fair stab at impersonating the Garden of Eden. Outrageous tumbles of pink rhododendron crowded a lane punctuated by the deeper red of wild fuchsia. Honeysuckle was occurring as well. Also yellow gorse. Above this heady mixture the steep walls of the valley rose in a series of polished cliffs like fresh-mined anthracite. A path led between the rhododendrons and up into that wall of cliffs.

We were heading for Lough Derreenadarodia. Strange name: it sounds like a fourteen-year-old eastern European gymnast. Not half as strange, however, as the little lough that lies in the crags above. I have no idea what Lough Eekenohoolikeaghaun sounds like because I have never managed to pronounce it all in one go. I have to take a run at the thing but it falls out from under me just over halfway through. I love places like this. I will travel to fish them for their name alone. There is a place in the Shetlands I am determined to fish. It is the Loch of Northouse – close to the village of Twatt.

We climbed on. I like almost everything about fishing on these mountain loughs, lochs, llyns or lakes, but there is one magical moment that stands out if only because it comes first. It is the moment when a lough, loch, llyn or lake first comes into view, the first glint of water as you crest a ridge or climb a waterfall and the thing opens in front of you. In that moment you take in the character of the place. It can be a forbidding bowl of a place or a soft pattern of islands or a wind-raked cleft in the rocks. It is always exciting, particularly the first one of a visit to the mountains.

Lough Derreenadarodia lay before us. We sort of sidled apart, unpacking rods and reels as we each edged towards a different bit of shoreline. That is another thing about high mountain loughs. The remoter ones are fished so seldom that they are still something to be explored and discovered: there is always excitement in waiting for the first rise, the first tug, the first fish to show what the water holds. We fished Lough Derreenadarodia for well over an hour without a sniff of a rise, a tug, let alone a fish. The excitement was wearing a bit thin. To be honest, we explorers had discovered all we really wanted to discover about Lough Derreenadarodia. A small stream runs into the lough on the far side. We made our way round and followed the trickling water upstream.

Lough Eekenohoolikeaghaun was a different kettle of fish. On the skyline the rock strata lay like the ribs of a gigantic carcass. One of these rock ribs extended through the lough to form a natural pier reaching out towards the middle. A bed of reeds in an impossible shade of green ringed the far shore and in the fringes of those reeds a fish rose. Terry is the best snooker player in the Duns Tew Snooker Club and certainly the least experienced fisherman, but you couldn't have guessed that from the casually deceptive turn of speed he put on to arrive first at the point where the fish had risen. You would think he had been fishing with friends for years. And sure enough, in the way of these things, it was Terry who took the first trout of the DTSC annual fishing outing. It was one of the smallest trout Philip and I had ever seen. We told him so. I believe that the truth will set you free.

It was a start. We spread out around the coast of little Lough Eekenohoolikeaghaun and fish began to come steadily. They were the usual fish of the mountains at three or four to the pound and everything about the place was just about right. The sun shone. Terry and I collected dry heather stalks washed ashore in stormier times and brewed tea in the Kelly Kettle. Philip carried on fishing and then drank the tea. Philip believes in the division of labour. The sun was still shining as we made our way down past from Eekenohoolikeaghaun, past Derreenadarodia and down the hill path to Hellofalotofrhododendron and the car.

Dinner in the Gougane Barra Hotel takes place a few yards from the lakeside. It was all but still that evening and the surface of the lake beyond the glass was pocked with rising trout. It is a cruel and unnatural form of torture. I was eating the best steak I can remember and hoping it wouldn't last too long in case the rise finished before the coffee. They were still at it when we fetched the oars in the twilight and rowed out around St Finbar's island for a few casts.

The next day we headed back to the Caha mountains. This time we would approach them from the west. Peter O'Reilly describes the place:

As can be seen from a glance at the contour lines on an Ordnance Survey map of the area, these are true mountain loughs, accessible only to the fit and agile.

'Fit and agile' are almost the exact words to describe the Duns Tew Snooker Club – a result, I believe, of having the snooker table in the loft of Terry's barn, up a pretty steep flight of steps.

Peter O'Reilly suggests that you:

. . . set out from Adrigole village for Glen Lough and then make the steep climb up the left side of the waterfall towards Glenkeel Lough.

I don't know what I had expected from a 'steep climb'. Porlock Hill in Somerset is a steep climb; the zig-zag West Cliff path up from the seafront in Bournemouth is a steep climb. But neither of these requires pitons. The thing was vertical. The stream we were to follow runs down the smooth face of a series of small cliffs that climbed from the car to Glenkeel Lough, 800 feet above us. The stream had not managed to carve a comfortable route down these cliffs: it just slid down each rock face and bounced on to the next. I knew how it felt: there were times I thought we might end up doing the same. And so we climbed and scrambled and crawled to the top and when we looked back where we had come from it was all worthwhile.

Glenkeel Lough and its neighbours are quite different from the loughs-of-the-long-names we had fished the day before. They are almost twice as high for a start. The whole place has a more serious countenance. You wouldn't find these loughs tarting themselves up with a lot of rhododendron blossom. Life is stern up here. There seemed to be a lot more rock about the place. Glenkeel Lough has been dammed and deepened to provide a water supply to the farms far below: what was once the outflow stream has become a long, narrow arm of the lough. To the eye of the experienced mountain lough fisher, this narrow channel looked barren and unpromising. Philip and I passed it by. Terry is not an experienced mountain lough fisher, so he strode up to the thing and cast and caught a fish. And then he caught another.

We fished our way along the length of the lough, taking hard-fighting little fish from the rocky shore. The map showed a stream flowing from Lough Shanoge, higher and further into the fastness of the Caha Mountains. It started to rain. I like a bit of rain up in the mountains: the sun is nice, too, but it is hard to feel very intrepid on a balmy day. In a driving rain you can feel the elemental battle of man against an unforgiving environment. Which is quite nice in short doses. It had also got colder. The south-westerly wind that was driving the rain had been at our backs along Loughs Glenkeel and Shanoge. It would be in our faces for the journey back. At the far end of Shanoge we found a small lee behind a bank of heather and brewed a kettle of tea. Actually, Terry and I brewed the tea while Philip kept fishing. I was a bit fed up with feeling the elemental battle of man against an unforgiving environment. The only consolation in that driving rain was that it was too windy for any chance of fog. What you don't want in these mountains is fog. Peter O'Reilly had been pretty clear about this in his description of the Cahas:

Cloud and fog are hazards encountered from time to time at this altitude. The correct procedure in the event of such weather is to remain on the mountain and wait until it disperses, no matter how long this may take. To do otherwise is extremely dangerous and attempts to follow streams etc., can have disastrous consequences because of the numerous sheer cliff faces all over this range of mountains.

At this point we heard a cry from Philip. He had caught another fish – a better one, he thought. We looked out from behind the lee of the heather. Sure enough, his rod was bent into a fish. But beyond this figure on the lough shore everything was disappearing into a dense fog rolling in from the south-west.

Oh, bugger.

Now it had reached us, blotting out everything beyond a few paces. Within that little circle of visibility stood the entire membership of the Duns Tew Snooker Club.

Look: I am old enough to remember 1958, Busby's Babes and the Munich Air Disaster. A team of sportsmen at the peak of their sporting powers was lost in a tragic accident resulting from bad weather. The resemblance was uncanny.

I don't know who it was that suggested we head off across the tops to find Lough Moredoolig. And I don't know why the other two agreed. It was madness. We got out the map and the compass and decided that Moredoolig lay somewhere over there in the fog. We fixed on the furthest thing we could see in that direction and made for that. And so on until we came to the edge of a cliff. Just about everywhere you go in the Cahas you come to the edge of a cliff. We were not the first to find the edge of this cliff. On a ledge below us, just visible down through the mist, was the crumpled shape of a lamb, bleating feebly. It was barely alive. It had broken both front legs in the fall onto the ledge and, unable to suckle from its mother, it was no more than skin and bones. Terry is a farmer. He said we would have to do something: the lamb could not be left to suffer. Philip and I though this was probably a job for a farmer and we talked fairly loudly to each other and looked off in another direction whilst Terry climbed down and settled the matter with a large rock. It was a sobering moment. We were a sombre little party as we climbed down through the crags and fished our way back to Glenkeel. Terry had a funny sort of look in his eye and Philip and I were being very, very careful not to slip and break a leg on the long descent back down to the car. We were cold and wet and tired. We retreated to Gougane Barra: St Finbar used to do much the same, by all accounts.

As we tucked into huge and succulent steaks, the trout began to rise on the lake outside the window. We had tried for these trout for an hour before breakfast. And we had tried for them on the morning and evening of the day before and we had caught some. But very few and very small.

Now, I do not object to catching very few, very small trout if that is what the water holds. Quite a lot of the waters I get to fish hold very few, very small trout. But Gougane Barra has lots of fish: we could see them rising across the lake. And not all of them were small. Besides, there was a sort of something about the fish we did catch that felt like the purest fluke. I am no stranger to flukes: they are an integral part of my snooker – any break in double figures usually contains one or more. Flukes are always welcome. And so were these small fish, but in each case it felt as if the fish had made a mistake rather than that we had cracked the problem of presenting the right fly in the right place. There were lots of half-hearted plucks and lost fish, and those that stuck were often hooked in a fin or tail when the fish had turned away from the fly at the last minute.

We did the usual sorts of thing. There is a familiar ritual to this situation. You consider the behaviour of the fish, the evidence of any flies on the surface and suddenly everything is clear. They are taking buzzers. It is all so obvious it is amazing you hadn't spotted it from the start. So you tie on a buzzer and send it out. And that doesn't work either. Or if it does, it only works once and feels just as fluky as the rest. And so you think it all out again until the next solution hits you. And so on, until it is too dark.

It was our last day. Breda Lucey was on the case. She told us of a lough, just over the hill from Gougane Barra. You will find Lough Nambrackdergs all over Ireland: there is another one just east of Gougane Barra and there are several (or something very similar) in Peter O'Reilly's book. This is none of them. The name apparently means 'lake of the speckled trout'. It was about three miles away across the hill, but as that hill rises over 1000 feet in one big cliff, we chose the roundabout route with a drive of 25 miles. Lough

Nambrackderg is a spectacular bowl of rock, a classic corrie lake hanging above the valley of the Coomhola river. We went there. We fished. We caught trout. They were speckled. I have nothing more to add. We drove back for lunch. We were determined to spend our last afternoon cracking the case of the fastidious little trout of Gougane Barra.

The breeze was fitful after lunch as we pulled the boats past Finbar's island with its stone oratory. A group of coaches from a cruise-liner anchored in Bantry Bay had just delivered 150 Americans. Breda was busy conjuring up 150 Irish coffees. The trout were still rising sporadically and ignoring our wet-flies, nymphs, goldheads, buzzers and emergers just as assiduously. There was one trick we had not tried. When all else fails, it is often worth trying something so huge that the trout feel they must grab or live with regret for the rest of their lives. Last Christmas I was buying my turkey from a farmer in the next village when I noticed a sign on his gate announcing that he sold ducks as well. He showed me a shed full of mallards waiting to be plucked. I asked if I might have a few feathers from around the bum. He said I could help myself. That was how I came to be in possession of the European Cul-de-canard Mountain. I had fashioned myself a sedge. I wound the hackle from two magnificent grizzle hackles with the stripped stalks left long for antennae. The wing was formed with dense bunches of cul-de-canard feathers tied into the length of a seal's fur body. About four ducks went into that wing.

There is really only one way to deliver a fly like this. It must arrive with dignity: it must be dapped. I was fishing with Terry. He had never seen a dapping rod before. It spoke to him. There is something about the massive heft of a dapping rod, the butt-section like a down-pipe and rings like basketball hoops: it appeals to the agricultural mind. This was Terry's sort of rod and never mind your poncy progressive tapers and fancy fol-de-rol. I set up the rod and let the breeze waft the super-sedge away from the boat. The response from the fish was sudden and spectacular. Within a minute a trout launched itself through the surface to get at the thing. This was Terry's sort of fly. This was a fly the fish could see – this was a fly anyone could see from about a hundred yards. He took the dapping rod from me and we drifted down towards a small bay opposite Finbar's island where the odd fish was rising. A few yards from the rocky shore the huge fly disappeared in a swirl. And for once it was a proper fish. Up to this point our average Gougane Barra trout was six inches. This was more than double that. Not a huge fish but a decent fish. And ten minutes later he had another a little bigger that leapt from the surface to grab the fly as it rode up on the breeze.

This was Terry's sort of fishing: you did it sitting on your backside with almost no effort and the fish jumped out of the water to get at the thing. It was like watching Nureyev pull on his first pair of tights: Terry had found his destiny.

Spirituality comes in some very curious forms.

3 𝒬

Size Matters

Try this for size: think of a one-pound trout. Hold your hands apart, the length of the fish, go to the bottom of this opened book and mark the length there. You'll see why later.

We have arrived at the end of the trout season and I have not caught a one-pound trout. I haven't even come close. One or two might possibly have reached 12 ounces. Of course, I have caught lots of fish that were 'a good three-quarters of a pound', but that is not quite the same thing. These trout are declared to be 'a good three-quarters of a pound' by the friend you are fishing with, in much the same spirit as he might concede a three-foot putt. You will catch a lot of these fish when fishing an Irish lough with a local boatman. In fact, it is quite hard to catch an Irish lough trout that isn't 'a good three-quarters of a pound'. And you catch quite a few when you are fishing alone. Before you go on, mark the length of a good three-quarter pound trout along the bottom of the opened book

In my experience, a good-three-quarter-pound-trout weighs about 8 ounces.

Does it matter? Surely fishermen are notorious fibbers anyway? Well, I think it might. We may be getting a ludicrously distorted notion of a good fish and good fishing, and this can have serious consequences in the management of fisheries. At the very least it can lead to disappointment. If everything you have read or heard or remembered about the fishing on a river or a loch leads you to expect fish of a pound or more and you are catching things in ounces, then you are apt to get gloomy. You are apt to think that the old hand and eye have lost their cunning: you are not the wily trout-hound that once you were. You are apt to think that the water has been stricken down: poachers have vacuumed the river or netted the lake and only the tiddlers were able to slip through the mesh. Or perhaps someone, sometime, has been fibbing.

The Tweed and its tributaries have always had some fine trouting: a century and a half ago Thomas Stoddart, in just four hours around noon, 'managed to encreel three dozen and five fish, the largest of which was a three-pounder, and there were at least twelve others that weighed a pound apiece'. Now this is indeed powerful fishing, with one fish every six minutes. Around the same time and place W.C. Stewart recalls catching on a minnow, 'twenty trout, the whole we got that day which weighed fifteen pounds, and we never got such a large average size of trout in any of the other tributaries of the Tweed, or even in Tweed itself'. Other authors on the nearby Clyde report similar catches, so perhaps there were just more, and bigger, trout in the rivers of those days.

And then, in September 1993, a fascinating piece of reseach was reported in *Trout and Salmon*. William Miller had come across the records of the West of Scotland Angling Club in Glasgow's Mitchell Library. Here were the records of angling competitions on these same waters. The catches were certainly impressive, with the winners basketing several dozen trout: in one the winner caught a staggering 359 fish. But then Mr Williams points out the total weight of these catches. The average sizes of trout in these competitions were remarkable similar – around *two ounces*.

'Where are the three pounders?' asked William Miller. 'In some competitions prizes were awarded for the best half-dozen trout but it is rare for the total weight of the best six even to approach 3lb.'

So on the fine trout streams of the border, in the golden days of the last century, an angler might reckon to catch some fish around the half-pound with some a little smaller and most something less than two ounces. Although, of course, these might not be the weights he records in his diary.

The deception need not be deliberate. We forget the tiddlers and blank days in averages and in fact it is surprisingly hard to judge the size of an 8-ounce fish. Try it yourself. Mark its length along the bottom of this book. Look: fishermen and fishing magazines and books all talk glibly of fish being 'pounders' or '12-ounce fish', as if each fish we catch is carefully weighed. They aren't. Few of us carry scales and even fewer use them, so these descriptions may be wildly inaccurate. And probably optimistic. Just how optimistic we shall see now.

Those marks on the bottom of the page: the one-pound fish should be the same width as this opened book, covers and all – just over 13 inches. The three-quarter pounder is only a little shorter at 12 inches. An 8-ounce trout measures 10$\frac{1}{2}$ inches – from the edge of one page to the end of the writing on the other page. And in case your estimate was nearer 9 inches – that is a trout of just *four ounces*.

Isn't it time we switched to measuring and describing our fish by length. And have an inch-scale penned on your rod by an obliging rod-maker. I have.

4 ❧

Another Season, Another Reason, For Makin' Whoopee

A trout fishing season doesn't just happen, you know. Time passes after the New Year, the days get longer and sometime around Easter you start to go trout fishing: you go trout fishing through the spring and summer and then, sometime around the end of September, you stop going trout fishing. That's not a trout fishing season.

A trout fishing season is a thing of beauty. It has light and shade, it has yin and yang. All this does not just occur. It must be composed like a symphony, and like a symphony, it must have a story: a beginning, a middle and an end.

The beginning is in Wales. It's not a bad place for beginnings: a land of mystery and legends – and with a trout season that opens on 3 March. It can be cold in Wales at the beginning of March. It can also be dry, but that's not very likely. The rivers will probably be big. I like to start on the River Usk, which has traditionally been an early river. The great Oliver Kite used to start his season an hour or so further west, on the River Teifi.

Tricky business, fishing a trout river in March. Now, there are two possible approaches to March. Both can work but they are diametrically opposite: you must decide which one suits you and don't mess with Mr In-between. The first is the Professional. If, anywhere on your fishing gear, you have a badge saying 'Team Diawa' or similar; if you have ever found yourself saying, 'When the going gets tough, the tough get going'; if any piece of your fishing apparel is camouflaged; if you are now, or have ever been, American – then this is the approach for you.

In March the waters of the Usk are cold and coloured. I do not mean they are flood-brown (they can be that as well): the colour is a steely grey-green and reluctant to transmit light. Perhaps there's just not much to transmit. You know there are fish down there but you can't see them. They are lying deep, close to the bottom where stones and hollows give a little shelter from the press of the cold current. These fish do not move much and I don't blame them. You will be told that there can be hatches of flies on these early rivers. This is very true. Big flies, too: the Large Dark Olive is often over when the fishing starts elsewhere, but it will be seen sailing down in March. Kite devised his Imperial to imitate the thing on the Teifi. The March Brown is bigger still and can hatch in impressive bursts: the trouble is that more often than not the trout are not impressed by such hatches. And nor is the Professional.

The Professional gets down to the fish. He has fast sink lines with sinking leaders. And he has a team of flies in which every member pulls its weight or, by heavens, it's dropped and finds itself back on the bench. And he works. He casts and mends. He covers the ground systematically and, by golly, he catches trout or he stays there till he does.

But there is another approach to trout fishing in March. This is the Dilettante. The secret of this approach is to pretend, even to yourself, that you are not fishing at all but doing something else. This something else can be just a brisk walk on a brisk March day or something vague like 'reconnaissance'. The vital point is that you do not intend to fish at all. The Dilettante does not carry any tackle – he is not going fishing. He may, of course, have a fly-box in his pocket where he left it last season. Possibly even a reel. But his rod is not made up. He walks along the river breathing deeply. Anon, he may notice a hatch of flies on the water – as he has noticed the primroses nestling along the bank. He may stop to admire a fine bend in the river where, look, the hatching flies are drifting out of the main current. He is not looking for feeding fish – last thing on his mind – but a movement catches his eye, as it will when one is drinking in the beauties of nature. In the same spirit of natural inquiry he observes that the movement is repeated at the same spot in a regular pattern. Could it be a feeding fish, possibly of the genus Salmo? It would be gratifying to confirm the suspicion. If only he had thought to bring along a rod or something but it's not as if he had been planning to fish . . . Hang on, though! Wasn't there a rod back in the car? It wouldn't take a minute to pop back for it and then, if the fish were still feeding, he could try a fly over it before resuming this splendid and invigorating walk.

The Professional and the Dilettante avoid heartache in different ways. The stakes are high in March fishing. It has been a long time since you last cast at a trout. The joys of trout fishing, forbidden for five months, have billowed in the imagination. The new fly you created in February – it looked irresistible in the vice – don't use it in March, it's not that sort of month. You are over-ripe for disillusion and March is just the man to give it to you.

You will, of course, take no notice of this advice. You will do what I used to do. I would arrive at the river eager, full of zip and hope, believing that March is just like any other month, only earlier. Hours later I would retreat, a broken man: cold, baffled and determined not to fish again until May.

All the trout waters are open by the first week in April and I shall not try to suggest a region to explore. For those who started their trouting in March the pressure is off. They have survived, either by catching fish come-what-may or by taking enough invigorating riverside walks until something catchable presented itself. Or they have not survived and have taken up golf. For those who do not start until April the pressure is mounting. Things have changed. The invigorating-walk-by-the-river stuff won't really wash in April. No one, not even the fisherman himself, will be taken in by that hogwash in April. Now that all the waters are open, you will not have to go off to Wales (3 March), the North West or the South West (15 March). The best bet for the first week or so is to stick to a local water where, through long experience and a practised eye, you know where the fish are lurking at this time of year – particularly if you helped to put them there a week ago in the pre-season club work-party in charge of restocking.

I had a memorable, if short, first day's fishing on such a water many years ago. It was a small stocked stillwater. We knew the fish were there: we put them there. I was allowed to fish three days in any week but I had the boat on Thursday. I resisted the temptation to start the season until my Thursday rolled around. Father and I drove down to the small fishing hut. We had not fished there for six months and we were a touch excited. It looked about perfect. We tackled up at the hut and laid our rods carefully in the small boat. We rowed out into the centre of the lake beside the small island. We were in position. It was the sixth day of the season. The sun shone. A fish rose. I picked up my rod and drove the hook in its keeper ring firmly into my thumb. Right to the bend. We rowed back to the hut. We got into the car and drove back down the track and off to the cottage hospital.

These things are behind us in May and June. By now we are back into the swing of the trout fishing and each day the river gets better and better. This is the time to explore. The countryside is at its best. All those things that ought to have happened in April – buds bursting and greening the trees, bluebells and birdsong and so forth – they all actually happen in May. The things that ought to happen in May – mayflies, for instance – they happen in June. It's probably something to do with the Julian Calendar. This is the time to take a day or two in a small country hotel with a mile or so of its own water on a trout stream. In May and June you don't need a lifetime's local knowledge to know where the trout like to lie: you can see them. Take an invigorating riverside walk by all means, but make sure you take a rod with you. It's invidious to pick out a few of these places: there are so many I have never tried and probably the best I have never heard of. No matter, I'll do it anyway, all waters I have visited in May and June. The Bull at Fairford has a stretch of the River Coln, and if you'd like to see what mayfly on a chalk stream was like before corporate entertaining, go to the Bull at the end of May. It is unstocked and catch-and-release, and so it has wild fish of sensible sizes and a lot of them. The Inn at Whitewell has the Hodder and everything, including sea trout, a little later on in the season. Further north, on the skirts of the Lake District, there is a hidden gem, a private estate that has miles of idyllic trouting with bed and breakfast in a manor house of the softest pink sandstone: Hornby Hall on the River Eamont.

By July the rivers that were at their peak in spring may be getting a bit blowsy. And there are school holidays. One is often required to be the Genial Family Man during large portions of the day; one is not required to slope off on little fishing holidays of one's own. And so the Good Lord invented sea trout. Now, I firmly believe that sea trout are caught by people who live next to a sea trout river. But the rest of us can at least go sea trout fishing. Sea trout fishing is the perfect occupation for a Genial Family Man on holiday. It is often carried on close to the seaside, the natural habitat of a GFM. It takes place during the short summer nights when even the most dedicated GFM can be considered off-duty for an hour or so. And an hour or so is often enough to tell if tonight is to be one of those magical nights when the sea trout are taking. There is, of course, a price to pay. For the duration of the holiday the GFM must never once exhibit even a hint of tiredness during the long days under a blazing summer sun. There are some charming rivers for summer sea trouting just near the beaches of the south-west. The Devon Avon has a modest run on a modest weekly ticket before the salmon arrive in September. At Budleigh Salterton there is a short stretch of free fishing on the river Otter before it joins the tide, and if you can't tell the difference between sea trout and grey mullet in the peaty depths before the light fades, you can get very excited indeed; but there *are* sea trout to be had after the picnickers have left at dusk.

If you actually wish to catch fish (rather than go sea trout fishing), July is the time to visit the River Eden in Cumbria. Here, in the long, deep pools above the town of Appleby, July and early August is the time of the Bustard fishing. The technique is similar to sea trout fishing but the quarry is the large resident brown trout that rest during the long hot days of summer and come out to mop up the large sedges and moths that take up a surprising amount of the Cumbrian airspace after dark.

By late August the lowland rivers that sparkled in the spring can become comatose in the summer heat. So have the fishermen. This is the time to head for the hills and the high streams. Up on the Northern fells, in the mountains of Wales and on the high moors of the West Country there are tiny becks draining the boggy uplands. Up here the water is still cool and the fact that the hatches of aquatic flies have all but finished for the season hardly matters: most of the food up here blows in off the moorland. This is Dilettante Country. A small fly box, a tiny rod and a good pair of boots are what is required, and you are going to get that invigorating walk whether you like it or not – if the wind gets up, just standing still can be invigorating enough. There is a bonus in the high streams of autumn. Some of the large fish from the lowland rivers will be making their way up into the headwaters before spawning. Each year the best fish from the Eamont system comes, not from the beautiful lower reaches around Hornby Hall, but from a tiny beck that runs down from the fellside village of Dacre and trickles past Dalemain House to join the Eamont a mile or so below Ullswater. Many of these upland becks have reservoirs high up in the hills, near their source. In September the large fish that have fed in the richer waters of the reservoir start to nose up into the tiny becks. And then these tiny September streams can give you the best fish of the season.

I started the season on the Usk, on a big river in March between Brecon and Abergavenny. Years ago I ended the season on the same river, away to the west where it rises high on the Black Mountain, above the Usk reservoir. Here it is a tiny trickle across a bleak moor, hardly enough to cover the back of a two-pound brown trout that had taken a small black fly bouncing down the thin current. Have fun.

5

Two Cheers for OFFSTED

It cannot have escaped your notice that the Office for Standards in Education (OFFSTED) is the most reviled body since the Spanish Inquisition finally hung up its thumbscrews in 1834. But I will not hear a word against it. If it were not for OFFSTED, I would not have met Luciano and watched an artist at work, nor visited the magical, trouty little world of the Silisia.

Here's how it happened.

My wife is a teacher in a small village school in Oxfordshire. The dreaded OFFSTED inspection was imminent. (I have just asked Judi how to spell OFFSTED. It turns out to be OFSTED. 'There's only one Ef-in OFSTED,' she said: that's a teachers' joke, apparently.) These inspections are quite daunting. The day starts off in the early hours of the morning when a column of armoured vehicles pulls up in the darkened streets and a jack-booted officer kicks your door in. He makes way for a sinister blond bloke wearing a long black leather coat, wire-rimmed glasses and a jagged duelling scar on his cheek. He has black leather gloves and a riding crop. The first bloke ties you to a chair and they stand around sneering and looking sinister and smoking cigarettes and not letting you have one. Then they shine the angle-poise lamp into your face and ask you some very tricky questions about Literacy Hour and the provision of PE for the under 5s. Not nice at all.

People of the right age will tell you that in the worst days of the London Blitz there was a blossoming of comradeship in the face of imminent invasion. It was the same in the staffroom of Judi's school. They did not actually get as far as singing Vera Lynn songs, but they got close. They bonded. One afternoon in the dark days before the inspection, the ladies on the school staff promised themselves that, if they came through the other side of OFSTED alive, they would all go on holiday together. They were so bucked at the thought of this that they went and booked the thing the same day. And so, last spring, there it was: wife and mother off on the razzle to the island of

Gozo, husband and eleven-year-old daughter left behind and feeling, if not exactly disgruntled, then a long way from being gruntled. Daughter and I had a bit of a confab and decided to go somewhere ourselves.

I asked her where she fancied. She said 'Venice'. I was rather impressed: given a choice, Beers do not usually plump for Culture. We tend to shy away from the stuff like startled deer. And then she reminded me that Eliana lived near Venice. Eliana had been Alice's best friend in the village until her father had been posted back to Florida and then to Italy. They had not seen each other for five years – half a lifetime when you are eleven. So Venice is where we went.

Eliana does not live in Venice. No one, as far as I can see, lives in Venice. She lives in the village of Cavasso Nuovo, somewhere to the north and east, across the vast flood plain that separates the Alps and the Adriatic. As we bowled along the autostrada towards Trieste, the distant wall of the Alps kept pace with us, jeering 'Come over here if you think you're hard enough.' So we did. At Portogruaro we turned north. The terrain here is perfectly flat, a vast wash of pebbles flushed out of the mountains by flood and snow melt, stretching 40km to the foot of the mountains. These rise in a sheer wall. If you kept your foot down, you would smash your radiator against them, and when you climbed from the wreckage, you would have arrived in Cavasso Nuovo. Houses here have flat front gardens and a mountain starting at the back door.

There was much rejoicing and killing of the fatted tagliatelle that lunchtime, and in the afternoon we set out to climb the mountain. It was a stiff climb up through woods of towering sweet chestnuts, along tracks clinging to the slope until we reached the ruins of a castle on the top. It was a staggering sight. What I had taken as an alp was just a first lowly ridge. Before us the Alps rose, ridge after ridge, crest after crest, each higher than the one before like waves before a stiff onshore breeze. Below our feet the trees fell away into a tight valley where, far below, a stream sparkled. It was spring, a time when a young man's fancy turns to love and a bloke of my age thinks about trout.

It was not a fishing trip, I had brought no tackle. I had thought Venice about as safe from the temptations of trout as a man can get, and yet there were these streams dashing through the limestone gorges at the fag-end of the Dolomites, not an hour or so from the Grand Canal. Over dinner that evening I asked if they knew of any trout fishermen in the village. Which was how I came to meet Luciano.

Luciano lives across the road with his wife and son and his goats and chickens and rabbits and heaven knows what else and two of the largest dogs I have ever seen. They dwarf Luciano, who is a little nugget of a man. He lives as a man ought to live, surrounded by sheds and outhouses full of bits and pieces and gizmos hanging from the rafters by hairy string. He took me into one of his sheds to show me his rods and tackle. Luciano does not go fly-fishing or spin-fishing or bait-fishing: Luciano goes trout fishing and he catches trout any way he thinks might work, and quite right, too. Luciano just loves to commit fishing. Would he take me with him? *Si*. We arranged to meet at dawn the morning after next. Luciano is a dawn sort of fisherman.

That night there were flashing lights in the street. Luciano's wife, Lida, was taken into hospital with the abdominal agony of Crohn's disease. The next day he came back from the hospital: Lida was weak but stable. He said he would not be able to fish at dawn the next morning: he had to visit Lida in the hospital. I had forgotten about the fishing. I assured him it didn't matter – perhaps we could fish together on my next visit. I had got the wrong end of the stick. He did not mean we couldn't fish *tomorrow*, only that we couldn't fish at *dawn*. We *must* fish tomorrow: the only food Lida could eat in her condition, it seems, was the sweet wild trout Luciano caught in the mountain streams.

The River Meduna breaks out of the mountains between Cavasso Nuovo and Meduno and immediately celebrates its release from confinement by dividing into half a dozen channels and wandering about all over the plain. You can't blame it: since birth the waters had been hemmed into gorges and valleys or trapped behind towering hydro dams. We crossed the river at the first of these. The valley sides are so precipitous that the little lakeside road drills through several tunnels on its way to the village of Chievolis. We turned up the valley of the Silisia, climbing in hairpins above the vertical sides of its gorge. There is something about these twisting mountain roads with a wall of limestone on one side and a vertical drop on the other – they scare me spitless. We climbed higher, and at a point where the road hung crazily out over the gorge, we stopped. I thought we were admiring the view: it was stunning – if a little scary. Then Luciano got a rucksack out of the car, shrugged it on, slung a large binocular case across his shoulder and disappeared over the edge of the cliff.

So I followed. We may have been following a goat track but it must have been a particularly agile or foolhardy goat. About a third of the way down I remembered that Luciano had been an Alpini in his youth, one of the elite corps of mountain troops. And I hadn't. Also I remembered that it was cursed OFSTED's fault that I was sliding down this goat track in the first place.

There was a crashing sound as we neared the bottom. I checked: it wasn't me. It was the little River Silisia.

Limestone does something to a river. You know those sunglasses that make the world look yellow? Credulous fishermen wear them in the belief that things must be brighter. That is silly. Glasses can only reduce the amount of light. But limestone does something similar to water. The blue-green clarity looks more transparent, the bottom clearer, than if there were no water at all. But I still couldn't see any trout as we stood beside a river of the stuff that filled the little gap between the walls of the gorge.

Luciano commenced to fish. He popped the lid from the large binocular case. It was not a binocular case: it was a live-bait carrier. He scooped out a tiny silver fish, dispatched it with the flick of a fingernail and threaded the little corpse onto a baiting needle. The shank of the hook was wrapped in lead foil to sink the bait. Another weight was threaded up the line. Luciano makes these weights by winding lead wire around a thin plastic tube. They are slid up the line above a swivel or slipped onto a dropper that snaps off if the weight jams in the rocky bottom. He cast the little bait upstream where the crystal current convulsed between the rocks. The trick is to swim the bait just above the bottom. Although it was late spring down on the plain, in these deep mountain gorges the water was still icy cold and the trout were not up to frolicking at the surface. Luciano swam the little fish back down the current, varying the retrieve to search the eddies and hollows of the river bed. There was no float but I could follow what was happening under water by the changing expressions on Luciano's wrinkled features as he felt the attentions of a trout. When the fish was hooked, his face lost all expression: Luciano likes to look as cool as the next fisherman. The trout danced about the stream until swung unceremoniously into hand.

It was not a big trout and there was no trace of the broad stripes typical of the *zebrée* trout you find in the limestone rivers of France and Spain. This little fish with its bold spots could have come from any highland beck or burn in Britain. Luciano measured this first fish meticulously, dispatched it and tucked it away in the rucksack. I hoped Lida didn't have a big appetite. From the rucksack he dug out a pen and a small book. It was a Friulan Fishing Licence.

We were fishing in Friuli, the mountainous corner of north-east Italy between Austria and Slovenia. Friuli has its own lore, its own language – Friulan – and its own fishing licensing as part of the autonomous region of Friuli-Venezia Giulia. Let's start with the easy bit about fishing in Friuli: you can fish anywhere – except for the bits where you can't. These are usually some headwaters and sidestreams that are reserved as *Zone di Ripopolamento* – spawning areas – and quite right, too. You cannot pretend you missed the signs: they are red and very obvious – DIVIETO DI PESCA – fishing forbidden. Anywhere else you can fish if you have a licence. And you can use any method legal in Britain: there are a few stretches where no bait fishing is allowed – SOLO ESCHE ARTIFICIALI – and a very, very few reserved for fly-only, catch-and-release – NO KILL.

'No kill' is not a comfortable concept to the hunter-gatherers of Friuli. There is hardly a fungus, plant or creature safe in its season from a Friulan: he will have it dried or bottled before you can say Giacomo Robinson. The law makers are well aware of this weakness and have drafted laws to protect the Friulans from themselves. Also to protect the fungi, plants and creatures. A fisherman may only fish on sixteen days each month. That would be more than enough for most of us, but a Friulan fisherman must be saved from himself. Before he fishes, he must write the date, in ink, in the licence. If caught without that date, he must cough up a fine of 200,000 lire (£60ish). When he takes a fish (he can take up to four trout over 22cm a day) he must record it with the time of day (morning or afternoon) in the licence before fishing again. For each unrecorded or undersized trout found about his person, he will have to find another 200,000 lire. I could see why Luciano measured that fish so carefully.

There are columns in the licence for other fish that swim these waters; the *temolo* (grayling) and the *marmolata*. This is the marbled trout, the large salmonid unique to these rivers of the eastern Adriatic coast. A few seasons back, Luciano caught a marmolata of 60cm. We could have done with one of those: it would have fed Lida and a fair part of Cavasso Nuovo as well.

We worked our way up the Silisia. On one corner, where the afternoon sun penetrated the gorge, a fish rose and I longed to throw a fly across its nose. Luciano uses spinner or bait until late June or July when the trout of the Silisia are well on the fly. Out of the sun it was cool and damp. The mossy boulders of the margins were slippery and wading in that clear water was deceptively dicey: it was hard to judge the depth you were sliding into. Luciano admitted that he rarely fished alone in the gorge these days – it was too remote and the wading too iffy. Others, it seems, felt the same way, because there were few signs of fishermen, and every damp and mossy corner held a huge and shiny snail, the large, brown, edible jobs. No self-respecting Friulan would have left such a delicacy lying around unmolested. I am rather partial to snails myself. As Luciano waded deep into a pool to fish the narrow neck, I rummaged around the rocks collecting snails. Luciano fished on. He had run out of bait fish and retrieved a box of worms from the rucksack. He fished these more slowly, letting them swing round each boulder. The trout seemed to like that. At every pool he tucked another little trout into the rucksack and wrote in his little book – or, at the very least, he pretended to. We were standing in the shadow of a dam that filled the gorge, holding back the waters of Lago di Selva when the storm began. That rain fell as only Alpine rain can, and it took a lot of the fun out of the proceedings. Our day of the Silisia was over. We changed out of waders to make the climb back out of the gorge. Luciano showed me his haul of fine little trout and I proudly produced my hatful of plump brown snails. Luciano looked around wildly: it turns out that the snails hereabouts are protected, too: if caught, I was liable for 40,000 lire per snail. That hatful would have set me back around £600. I hurriedly gave them their freedom. I have always been in favour of catch-and-release.

* * *

Look: the moral is that you can find trout fishing everywhere if you look. I will be going to Friuli next year, a little later perhaps, when the gorges of the Silisia and a thousand other streams in those mountains are full of fly. This is very cheap, adventuresome fishing. A day-ticket from the sports shop costs 30,000 lire (under £10): an annual licence is only three times this. Both cover all the waters of the region. Getting there is even cheaper. My return flight to Venice (Treviso) cost £60. I flew to the Shetland Isles the following week. That cost £505. There is a wheel off somewhere.

6

From the Ridiculous to the Sublime

I never know quite how these things happen.

The bloke from the computer shop said that, of course, I would want to be on the Internet. He got quite lyrical about the thing. On the Internet, he said, I could get anything I could ever want: I could get tickets to Broadway musicals, train timetables to branch lines in Tashkent and rare orchids from wherever rare orchids are to be got. What a boon. And so in the end I got myself wired up. I did not get any of these things. To date, the only thing I have got from the Internet is a Swede.

He was a very nice Swede and, incidentally, a very big Swede. His name was Christer and he came from Malmö. He arrived at our house on Thursday. That's how it is with e-mail: you get chatting in a general sort of a way about fishing and rivers and the heady air of the international-brotherhood-of-angling suffuses the ether and one thing leads to another and, wallop, Thursday morning you've got this Swede on your doorstep. And in the normal run of things that would be just fine and dandy, but my back had gone on the Monday and I was still in bed and unable to move.

He was very nice about it, of course, but there was a sort of something in the way he peered down at me, flat on my back: when he had flown over from Sweden, he had been banking on something a little more vertical in the way of a fishing companion. Something that moved.

But there it was. My back was slowly responding to pills and lying there watching the Embassy World Snooker Tournament, but there wasn't a chance of my fishing before the next week. So Christer went off to do London and Henley and Oxford and on Sunday evening he phoned. I was walking again after a fashion – albeit with a distinct list towards the south-west. So we arranged to go fishing on Tuesday, the day before his flight home.

On Monday it rained. In spades. The canal towpath was flooded for the second time in living memory and the small river Cherwell outside the back door was only just outside the back door and it was dirty brown. I would have given up then, but it was Christer's last chance, so we arranged to meet on the River Coln and hope for the best.

I had chosen the Coln for two reasons. First, it is a river of the Cotswold limestone. It is spring-fed and would be slow to flood and discolour with all that rain. The second reason I will tell you later.

I am not proud of what I did next. I took Christer to Bibury. Bibury is arguably one of the most famous and prettiest spots in the Cotswolds. William Morris thought it the prettiest village in England (but then William Morris, like other pre-Raphaelites, considered ladies with chins like Jimmy Hill were the last word in beauty). In Bibury the lovely River Coln sweeps serenely alongside the road before ancient cottages in honeyed Cotswold stone. There are trout in this stretch of the river. They are many and huge and obvious. The charabanc-loads of tourists that stop in Bibury sit on the stone wall beside the river and feed their sandwiches to the ducks. Only the ducks rarely get fed. As a bit of Mother's Pride hits the water a bulging bow-wave bobs the ducks aside and the morsel is gone in a swirl. These trout are not spooked by the crowds that line the wall along the river. They love them. They mean lunch. These trout will take anything. As a boy I used to feed blobs of ice-cream to their great-great-great-grandfathers and watch the stuff billow out through their gills. One way and another I thought we might have a chance of a fish in Bibury.

Tickets for this stretch are available from the ancient Swan Hotel beside the bridge. The water was a little murky that day: rain had washed down sediments from the trout farm above the bridge, but the trout were there and open for business. A foot from the wall a two-pound specimen shouldered a mallard away from a crust and then grabbed at a passing dead leaf just in case that might be edible as well. It is hard to choose a fly in these circumstances.

I was looking forward to this hugely. Although I had watched them many times, I had never fished for these greedy and indiscriminate trout of Bibury. It didn't seem quite the thing. They had always seemed a bit like a very friendly girl from Berkhamsted when I was a young lad: immense fun but not something you'd want your friends to find out about. So it was a bit of a blow when a huge guffaw rang out from behind me. I turned round to see Vaughan, an old friend, helpless with laughter. He had been driving through Bibury when he had recognized my car and stopped to investigate. A gentleman would have seen a friend preparing to fish between the tourists and passed on. He may have raised one quizzical eyebrow and the matter would be forgotten. But not Vaughan. Vaughan fell about. And then he fetched his friend to come and look and he fell about as well. A fair amount of hilarity followed us as we crossed the footbridge over the Coln to the meadow on Rack Isle and prepared to cast across to those trout waiting beneath the wall.

We knew where the trout were. A small crowd had gathered around Vaughan and Alan who were looking down at a fish that slid up from time to time to take a passing titbit. Vaughan snapped off a bit of Polo Mint and tossed it upstream. The fish shot up and ate it. I had on my absolute favourite dry fly, an Easy Rider Dun, and I cast the thing across to this fish.

Opinion on the wall was divided about what happened next. Some said the fish tilted, just slightly, towards the fly: others thought that was a trick of the light through the moving water. Everyone agreed that it made no attempt to grab the fly as it passed over its head that first time. Or any other time. I put on a large shaggy elk-hair sedge and the fish ignored that too. I put on a tiny black gnat: the same. I was beginning to get a very bad feeling about this fish. I had seen fish like this before: the trout by the bridge in Bakewell live on diet of tourist titbits and refused all flies until Philip White, then keeper of the water and a brilliant fly-dresser, devised the 'Mother's Pride', a fluffy concoction of palmered white hen hackle with a 'crust' of soft brown hackle. That works. Sometimes.

But I didn't have one. Or anything imitating a Polo Mint. The gallery was disappointed: other people, farther along the wall, wanted us to try for their fish, so we did, but the result was the same. Christer and I must have changed flies a dozen times each. We took to fishing the water beyond the sandwich zone. Here we could not see the fish in the murk but the result was exactly the same. Zero. Whatever we threw at these fish, they had seen it all before.

I cannot say these fish would not rise to a fly. I can only say that, for that hour or so, they didn't. I had looked on these monster fish as a soft touch and got exactly what I deserved for such arrogance. One day soon I will return with a little more humility and a credible imitation of a buttered scone and we shall see. But time was ticking away and Christer did not have his fish.

A few miles away through the lovely lanes of the Cotswolds lies the place I wanted Christer to remember as an English trout stream. And the second reason I had chosen the River Coln.

It is rare, in my experience of fishing hotels, for the owner of the fishing to greet you with a big hug and a smacky kiss. It is very nice but it is not usual. Perhaps I just don't get out often enough.

There may be, somewhere in the country, a lovelier hotel landlady than Judy Dudley of the Bull Hotel in Fairford. I rather doubt it – but if there is one such then I haven't met her and I'll bet she doesn't have one-and-a-bit sumptuous miles of the crystal Coln running down the side of the hotel garden. Which is something of a clincher in my book.

The little Cotswold market town of Fairford is six miles downstream of Bibury and the fish farm and the Coln here was a good deal more crystal. The river runs behind the back gardens of the village houses and out into the meadows that were beginning to warm as the day went on. Half a century ago the Bull at Fairford was a famous fishing hotel. Its waters were close-keepered, heavily stocked with large trout and ruthlessly culled of lowlier species. Fishing fashions change and so do hotel owners. By 1991 when Judy and Keith Dudley came to the Bull the fishing had been neglected and abused for years. What they did when they came to the river was remarkable, perhaps unique for a water of such quality and value: they did nothing.

They did not stock the river with large trout to flatter the fisherman. They did not cull the grayling that haunt the holes between the weeds. They just asked that all fish be returned and that fishermen use barbless hooks. The result is a growing reputation for that rarest of treasures, a natural limestone river with a natural population of fish.

There are a lot of small fish in the waters of the Bull Hotel. There are fewer medium-sized fish and there are a very few big fish. And perhaps a monster. That is how it is with a healthy population. But a fish from the Coln hereabouts is the right size for the Coln hereabouts: it is an honest fish.

Christer and I walked down through the meadows to the bottom of the water. The last of the spring's grannom were struggling from the surface and the first of the hawthorn flies were trailing about above the long grasses of the meadow. And the trout of the Coln did not seem to be fussed about imitations of either. So we did what fishermen usually do in these circumstances and we each put on our favourite flies. Christer's is a little nymph he is used to swimming between the rocks to winkle out the trout and grayling of his native waters. Mine was the Easy-rider Dun, a something-and-nothing of a general purpose fly with a mixed grizzle-and-red hackle and a tatty body of hare's ear fur.

And as we worked our way up the course of the crystal Coln, we both began to catch wild trout after wild trout.

7

The Doonesday Book

I find I have reached an interesting age. I might well be in my prime.

Of course, twenty-five years ago I believed I was in my prime – but then, twenty-five years ago, I was a very young man, and very young men can make foolish mistakes about things like that. I can see that now. I suppose that is the sort of clear-sighted wisdom that comes with age.

I have at last reached the age when my mind has fully matured, like some fine old Gruyere cheese. And, like a fine old Gruyere cheese, it has large holes in it. That is what makes it interesting. Years ago I would eke out the reading of the latest Maigret or Alistair Maclean, to make it last as long as possible. Once I had read it, I would know who-dunnit, with what and to whom, so I could never read the thing again. Not now though. Now I can re-read all my favourite books with only the vaguest déja-vu when it turns out that Johnny Vulcan was really Paul Louis Broum who had assumed the identity of the concentration camp guard in order to hide his past as a communist assassin. Came as a complete surprise – again.

You can see what a boon this could be. And there are other rewards. One of the pleasantest days I have spent on a river was the result of just such a happy lapse of the maturer mind.

I had been reading *Lorna Doone*. Don't ask me why, I couldn't tell you. Perhaps I thought I should. Lorna Doone herself is a rather droopy creature who has been held captive since an infant by a band of baddies, the Doones, who live in the stronghold of a secret valley, hidden in the tight folds of Exmoor, from whence they sally forth from time to time for a spot of murder and pillage. They are, no question, a rough bunch, and why they should wish to saddle themselves with an insipid item such as Lorna is a total mystery. The hero of the tale is one John Ridd, who lives in the neighbouring valley of Oare. He is fourteen years old when, on St Valentine's day 1676, he sets off to catch fish for his ailing mother. He fishes his way down the upper waters of the Lyn and then turns up a sizeable tributary, Bagworthy Water, a stream of ill-repute and chockfull of Doones at its headwaters. But the trout of Bagworthy are fatter than those of the Lyn – which may just be how it got the name – and each pool looks better than the last and he just has to keep fishing on upstream. Any trout fisherman will recognize that awful compulsion. Pretty soon he has a bagfull of fish. He comes to a large pool fed by a rushing spout of water like the log flume at Alton Towers. Forcing his way up this, he slips in the press of water, nearly drowns and crawls out, battered and bruised, into the daylight. He has discovered a back door into the Doone's lair. He passes out. When he comes to, this lovely young creature is kneeling over him wiping his forehead with a dock leaf, though why she thinks that is a remedy for drowning and concussion I cannot imagine. That's the soppy sort of creature she is. Anyway, being badly concussed, he promptly falls in love with her. He offers her the bag of fish (all thoughts of his ailing mother have gone, it seems). It is not the textbook Valentine's gift but, seemingly, it works. After another 580 pages of terrifyingly small print and several skirmishes and bloody battles with the Doones up and down Bagworthy Water, she is rescued and they stand together at the altar of Oare church for a Whitsun wedding – at which point, incidentally, she is shot, and not a moment too soon.

You will have spotted the bit that caught my attention. I have fished on the Lyn – the East Lyn – and it is as pleasant a spot as you could wish, a deep wooded gorge with its rumbustious little river tumbling between boulders and swelling into deep shaded pools. It is fished for its salmon and its sea trout but there is also a population of pugnacious little brown trout lurking in the shadows. When the sunlight pierces the canopy and lights up the pale bottom of a pool, you can see them holding station in the eddies of the current. And here was this account of a tributary carrying 'so far as I could guess by the sweep of it under my kneecaps, a larger power of clear water than the Lyn itself had; only it came more quietly down'. And holding fatter fish, too.

I could see it on the map. In the course of time it had gained a 'd' and become Badgworthy Water, but it was there right enough. The description was right enough too: Badgworthy water *is* bigger than the Lyn above Malmsmead where they meet. So Father and I went down to take a look.

When the polar ice-cap crept down across northern Europe it got to Weston-super-Mare and retreated – who could blame it? The result is startling. Where the valleys of the northern moors had been reamed by glacial ice into spacious glens, the valleys of Exmoor escaped, growing deeper and ever-steeper over the millennia. We dropped down the narrow lane from the A39 to the hamlet of Oare. It was a bright day in late spring and the air was full of the evocative smell of overheated brake-linings. We called in at Oare Mead farm for our tickets and threaded the van down between the tall hedges to Malmsmead. There are two ways to cross Badgworthy Water and you don't want to do either in a camper van. The ancient bridge is narrow and hump-backed and wears its trophies of automobile paintwork like an Apache's scalps. And below the bridge there is a ford. Fords are a bit iffy in a camper van. We watched a car go through the ford and followed that. We parked behind the gift shop that is Lorna Doone Farm and tackled up.

It was just one of those days: a bright river under a bright May sky. The beech trees were in extravagant full leaf and the twisted oaks of Badgworthy Woods were bursting to catch up; the grass of the small steep pastures was an outrageous colour. It was a good day if you liked green. We followed the river upstream, like John Ridd, dropping small flies into anywhere with depth and shade enough hold a feeding fish. The small brown trout of Badgworthy Water had caught the mood of the day. They were lightning fast and whether they stuck or not was more or less up to them: by the time I struck at any rise, the fish was either gone or tugging at the line.

The pastures disappeared as we worked our way further upstream and the steep moorland slopes of Cloud Hill began to crowd the stream. A well-worn path follows the river, trodden by the countless visitors that come to Doone Country, looking for the famous black pool with its lethal rock waterslide. It is there – sort of. There is a grand, deep pool, certainly, at the far end of Badgworthy Wood where the water slooshes in and a couple of trout were lurking in the bouncing current in the heart of the pool. A short distance above this pool there is a rocky cleft where a tributary tumbles down a smoothish channel from the side valley of Lanke Combe. It takes a powerful lot of imagination, and a lot more water, to see this as the fearsome back door to the Doone valley. But then, they do get a lot more water from time to time. It was the floodwater from a summer downpour that roared out of Badgworthy and the other moorland tributaries of the Lyn to kill thirty-four people in the Lynmouth flood disaster of 1952.

It was hot by this time. We had caught trout on a perfect day in a West Country stream. A trout of these moorland streams may not be not a big fish but it has one quality lacking in the larger trout of more favoured waters: a West Country trout is never very far from a cream tea. We fished our way downstream to Malmsmead. There, in the shady garden of The Buttery beside Badgworthy Water, we scoffed homemade scones and jam and yellow clotted cream.

This convoluted country of hidden valleys is made for tales of skulduggery and derring-do. The stories of the Doones had been told on Exmoor for two centuries before R.D. Blackmore wove them, and other local legends, into the story of Lorna Doone. While we had our tea, Graham Storey, who runs The Buttery, told us the story of another legendary fishermen of Badgworthy Water and the Lyn.

It had all the right stuff: a young man back from the wars to find a river plagued by poaching gangs snagging and netting the salmon in the deep pools; the leader of the local poachers warning the young stranger off the river and getting a ducking for his pains; the young man's uncanny skill at taking salmon arouses the suspicion of the bailiffs who set out to tail him; a perilous chase across the boulders, a prodigious leap that leaves our hero safe across the water and the misguided agent of authority carried off downstream. It was all rather Robin Hoodsy. Even his name – Tom Farthing – was the stuff of a local legend. All the more surprising, then, to find it was all true. And, fifty years on, Tom Farthing is still fishing the rocky pools and wooded banks of the Lyn gorge. That afternoon we called in to see him at his house perched beside the wooded gorge above Watersmeet. It was like dropping in on the Sundance Kid for tea.

Later that evening we climbed down the path through the trees into the cool of the Lyn gorge and fished the last hours amongst the mosses and ferns, the tumbled boulders and long, still pools. It had been a perfect day.

Did you wonder why this day came about through a lapse of memory? Or had you forgotten that? I will tell you. I only found out myself yesterday when I went back to the pages of the dreaded *Lorna Doone* to look up John Ridd's description of his fishing of Bagworthy Water. The story is set at the time of Izaak Walton and *The Compleat Angler,* but there is precious little of the pastoral idyll about this fishing trip. He is wading, barelegged in an icy stream with snow on the ground; also he is fishing with 'a three-pronged fork firmly bound to a rod with cord'. Fair enough, trout don't feed much in February and he was after some fish for his poor old mum. But what I had completely forgotten, what had dropped through one of the larger holes in my memory, was that he was not catching trout at all. *He was fishing for loaches.*

If I'd remembered that, I'm not sure I would have bothered to come.

The Mouse Diet

What am I doing here? Over in New Zealand fishermen are having their best season in years: records are tumbling with huge trout being caught right and left. The record for Lake Rotoruoa had just fallen to a monster of 12 pounds when a brown trout of over 20 pounds was pulled from Lake Ruataniwha. And these things are not just in the lakes: great lumps of fish are being reported from the rivers of the South Island. The reason for this fishy bonanza is simple, if bizarre.

Mice. A mild winter combined with a bumper blossoming of beech trees has resulted in an explosion of the mouse population. This population pressure seems to have triggered an urge to migrate, like the legendary lemmings of the arctic, because the mice have taken to swimming the lakes and rivers – and the trout have taken to eating them when they do. Trout can put on a lot of weight on a mouse-rich diet.

Before you start muzzling the family moggy and tossing mouse-imitations into the local reservoir, there are many other instances of fish that have grown oversize on strange diets. Several rivers have lamented the loss of large trout when the local abattoir stopped discharging its cleanings into the river. One of the finest wild trout I ever saw was hooked in an unlovely concrete tank, part of a hydro-electric plant in northern Spain. Water barrelled into the tank from a covered culvert that wound for many kilometres around the contours of the mountain. Frogs, newts and lizards crawling into the cracks of the culvert lid would tumble into the racing water and be swept into the tank and the jaws of the trout that had found their way along the culvert. When Ruben, the local fisherman who had discovered the place, held up the superb 5-pound trout he had just landed, the fish promptly regurgitated a somewhat second-hand salamander.

The most dramatic smashing of an angling record, eclipsing any mouse-enhanced performance of antipodean trout, happened in Britain in the 1980s.

If it was largely unnoticed at the time, it was because the fish, the arctic char, is largely unknown to most British anglers. The char is a cold-loving species, a remnant of the last ice age and a constant reminder that we are living within a warm, but probably brief, interlude in a chilly world. They have survived in the depths of the deep glacial lakes where the water temperature rarely rises above 4°C, beyond the reach of the rod fisherman and largely forgotten as a sporting species. It is not a big fish: in the spring of 1982 the British record stood at 1 pound 12 ounces.

And then, in October of that year, the record was broken, shattered by a fish of almost double the weight. Imagine a mile being run in two minutes. Something remarkable was happening. Loch Garry produced a fish of 4 pounds 13 ounces in 1987. The record was held briefly at 5 pounds 10 ounces – three times the record at the beginning of the decade. In 1990 the record went to a massive fish of 7 pounds 7 ounces – four times the record a decade before – but it lasted less than a year. In 1991 a locksmith from Barnsley, trolling the depths of Loch Arkaig, took three fish over six pounds, the largest of 7 pounds 14½ ounces, and a few months later a char of half-an-ounce over 8 pounds was taken on a worm ledgered at 300 feet by Finlay Nicholson.

If the mile had been run in something under a minute, we would suspect illicit substances. We would be right. During this decade the surface of these deep lochs had become infested with cages of salmon farms. Three hundred feet below the cages, the arctic char were gorging in a steady drizzle of crumbs from the salmon's table.

What might be overlooked in these tales of fishy overindulgence is the remarkable variety of sizes that trout can come in. A rabbit with unlimited grass may become a fat rabbit but it is still more or less rabbit-sized. Adult humans, with their vastly different diets, show more variation than most species but the very largest is only four times the weight of the smallest – and neither are apt to be fighting fit. That 20-pound brown trout of Lake Ruataniwha, not even close to the European record for the species, is 160 times the weight of a feisty, fully-grown brown trout of Dartmoor – and both are in perfect condition.

Creatures of the land and air must deal with gravity. The design limits of each species are restricted by the forces on joints and limbs. That is why the 10-foot killer ants of science fiction are just that: science fiction. Fish, supported by water, have no such problem, and given unlimited supplies of, say, mice, can grow very large indeed.

And the time to visit New Zealand will be *next* year – when a lot of very large, very hungry trout will be wondering where the next mouse is coming from.

Fish Finder

The contents of this article carry a Government Health Warning: if you read on, you could seriously reduce the number of fish you catch. How so?

The way to catch lots of fish is to fish one piece of water in all its moods, in all seasons and for a long time. Over the years you will learn the spots that always hold good fish, the best approach to a tricky lie, the slack spot where a dry fly can sit without drag for a vital extra second, and so on. You will be able to see the fish in the water: things are much easier to see when you know where they are. In time you will know the best fly for the conditions and the best place to put it. And it would bore me spitless.

As I have said before, I love to explore. It's the beginning of the trout season and I have the whole country at my disposal. This year I will find a dozen or so rivers I have never fished before, some of them I will not have heard of before. And when I get there (often *before* I get there, because I can usually contrive to cross the river by several bridges before I arrive at the fishing), I will get out of the car and peer down on some shady little run or a dark pool or a sparkling riffle. And that whole delightful conundrum of fly fishing – where are the fish? what are they eating? what fly to use and how? – starts all over again.

Finding this fishing is fun. It is a thing to do in the dark days of February and March. Where to start?

I do like a story: I enjoy fishing somewhere with a background, the sort of story that crops up in the *Fireside Book of Fishing* or some such. Here, there lurk passages of purple piscatorial prose under titles along the lines of 'The Muckle Troot O' The Dulnain'. I did not make that up. I have just found it in *The Fisherman's Bedside Book* of 1945 by 'BB'. I bought this book on a second-hand book stall last Saturday; I have not yet read it. I have just flicked through the contents page for an example of a title and lo! the magic has started to work. I have just idly turned to the story beneath that title and read, amongst a description of the weather and why the writer happened to be there in the first place, '. . . the Dulnain is roughly thirty miles long and *is famed for the size of its trout'*. Thereafter the writer unfolds a tale of derring-do, but I am already hooked. I have a new river to explore – the Dulnain!

There are more prosaic ways. Start with a road atlas. Some road atlases are good about rivers and name even the smallest tributaries, others do not. Don't buy the second sort. Find a river that is famous for your sort of fishing and then look around. The tributaries are obvious places to look. Not so obvious are rivers that share the same origin: they probably share similar water chemistry and maybe the same quality of fish. Some years ago I had a splendid couple of days on the River Clough. The where? The River Clough is a tributary of the Lune but its pedigree is impeccable for it runs from the same hill as the River Ure and a mile or so from the source of the River Eden. There were small hill trout in every pool as it dropped down the hillside in slabbed steps, and beneath a trailing bramble in a pool beside the chapel I had a fat fish of one pound. In Garsdale the ticket to fish this upper Clough cost £1 per week. The lower Clough and the Lune can be fished hereabouts for £50 a week. The difference is a waterfall, impassable to the Lune salmon, at the bottom of the Garsdale water. If you are after trout, it is worth taking a close look upstream of a waterfall. The Caldew is an overlooked Eden tributary with some fine trout fishing – but hurry, a fish pass has been constructed in Carlisle and migratory fish are on their way back.

You have found a stream, a thin blue line on a map, a golden scene in an anecdote. Can you fish the thing? The first recourse is to that invaluable publication *Where to Fish* (ed. Dick Orton, published by Harmsworth).

Where to Fish is updated every two years. A new one is due early in 1992. There is no real need to wait. It will be out of date. It is out of date for two reasons. The first reason is that things change in the time it takes a book to get into print. With every game angling club holding its AGM between Christmas and the new season, it could hardly fail to have last year's club secretaries listed. The second reason it is out of date is that people like myself, and maybe you, look through and think, 'Oooh, they got that wrong' and then wonder why it is still wrong in the next issue. Write to the publisher and tell him.

Read *Where to Fish* as 'Once upon a time'. Once upon a time a stretch of the River Dulnain (I have got the bit fairly between my teeth about this one) was leased by the Strathspey Angling Improvement Association. 'Inquiries to the Hon. Sec.', it says in *W to F*.

This is a bit daunting. Sometimes Hon. Secs are the only place to get tickets and information. Look up the club in one of the sections on Clubs and Associations in the book and you will have a name and address. You can write to this man. This is a last resort. You can try the phone first. You may be lucky: the chap may not have moved, directory enquiries may have his number, he may still be Hon Sec. He probably isn't. They usually aren't. I consider myself ahead of the game if they are still alive when I ask their wives if I can have a word with them. If they are not Hon. Sec., they will usually know who is – or was – and on you go. Since BT got greedy and began charging for directory enquiries, you will find this search a lot cheaper on a public payphone where such enquiries are still free.

I look up the Strathspey A.I.A and find that the Hon. Sec. is one G.G. Mortimer, 61 High Street, Grantown-on-Spey. This is an enormous piece of luck: Mr Mortimer is a well-known and most knowledgeable angler on the Spey. He has a tackle shop in Grantown. And I have the number. Tackle shops are probably the best places to get information: the tackle dealer has no direct vested interest in enticing you onto the water and he is in touch with how the water is fishing. He may also have tickets on other, similar waters. Hotel waters can be great, but their proprietors are inclined to be a trifle gung-ho about the prospects of good sport – particularly if they are not themselves fishermen.

You have found a bit of water you fancy fishing. It is available. Now we are getting serious. My next step is to get hold of a good map. Sometimes you will be given a map with your ticket. Often you aren't: what you are given is directions or just the beat boundaries on the ticket. These are often meaningless to anyone who doesn't live there and frequently just as opaque to someone who does. Recently I have been looking into fishing on the Deveron. Let me give you the limits of the Huntly Fishing on that river: 'THE DEVERON – From the boundary with CAIRNBORROW, GLASS, downstream, to a point on the right bank at the outlet from the Duchess Well near Huntley Castle' . . . (OK so far?) . . . 'and on the left bank to the boundary between WESTERTON and GIBSTON, and the part of the said left bank from the western boundary of what was previously the Huntly Lodge Policies, to a point on the said left bank opposite the said outlet of the Duchess Well'. Fair amount of spin on the ball there, I should say. I know it's in English because I recognize the words, but I have only the vaguest notion of what it means.

I furnish myself with an Ordnance Survey map, preferably the 1:25,000 scale series, which is the smallest scale to show fields – which is how most beats are divided. Did you know most road atlases are based on the OS and the square grid they use to divide up the pages is usually the grid of these maps. Stamfords, 12–14 Long Acre, London WC2E 9LP (tel: 020 7836 1321) has the lot: they take credit cards and post the maps to you. With such a map in front of you as you phone or pick up your tickets, you can get the exact beat limits, parking places, access points and pools. You may also find that the '2 miles' of fishing in the hotel brochure is something of a moveable feast. I have seen this claimed for something under a mile 'because it has both banks'.

If the Hon. Sec. or tackle dealer or hotel manager appears genial, you might try to glean a little more about the fishing while you are at it. Perhaps the first thing to check is the time of the trip. It is no good reading about Bustard fishing in the small hours of the night on the Cumbrian Eden if you aren't going to be there in July or August. If your imagination has been fired by someone's account of the fishing, find out when he was there. Failing that, ask the Hon. Sec. etc. for the likely seasons. And read the fishing reports in *Trout and Salmon*. By a happy chance I see that the opening six words of 'The Muckle Troot O' the Dulnain' are 'It was the 27th of July'. Hardly the best time for a spate tributary of the Spey, one might think.

Ask about the wading – necessary? forbidden? – and favoured local methods – upstream wet fly? Cymag? – and suitable tackle. This may all sound obvious but, in truth, I have no notion of the size of this Dulnain.

It is a matter of temperament. Some prefer to bowl up and take the river as it comes: for me, in the dark days of February and March, there is much pleasure in the anticipation and preparation. I scour the bookshelves for references to the Dulnain and its fishing. Perhaps the hardest thing to get a handle on is the character of the place; dour or cosy, a cold glint across a treeless and boggy moorland or an intimate gurgling in a bosky tunnel. *Where to Fish*, or some such useful publication put out by an NRA or tourist board, is quite useless for this sort of stuff. It is like trying to catch the splendour that was steam from the railway timetable. Two little gems there are (or were) for the travelling fisherman, both edited by David Barr, both Haig Guides: *Salmon Fishing in Scotland* and *Trout Fishing in Britain*. In here you will find descriptions of the rivers and lakes as they live and breathe. It is heady stuff for February and March.

And dangerous stuff. There is a reference to the Dulnain. I have just turned to the page and found the river in a piece on the Spey. It says nothing much: it is there, no more. And then I start to read about the Spey, and not of its salmon, but of a section between Kingussie and Loch Insch. 'This part of the Spey,' I read, 'is unique in Scotland as it has the only known population of migratory arctic char, *Salvelinus alpinus*, which come up from Loch Insch to spawn in the tributaries of the Spey at certain times of the year.'

Golly! Migratory char, eh? But which tributaries? And which times of year? And, oh dear, here we go again . . .

10 ℒ

A Fish on the Line

He was that tall sort of Englishman. She was that droopy sort of English girl. He had looked around the dining lounge and then asked her if anyone was sitting at her table. We all heard him. He sat down. We must have been somewhere in the Chilterns but it was getting dark outside and I didn't recognize any of the scenery whipping past the window.

We were on the West Highlander, the sleeper from London to Fort William. My first time on a sleeper, although I had seen *The Lady Vanishes* and *Murder on the Orient Express* several times, so I knew what to expect. I was feeling pretty damn debonair: the small man at the next table could easily have been a mittel-European arms dealer if you ignored his walking boots. The steward brought drinks as we sped north into the night. A few conversations eddied around the dining car but I think most of us by now were listening to the tall Englishman as he commenced to chat up the droopy English girl. He was giving her some amazing tosh: whopping great fibs, breath-taking braggadocio, mountain-climbing stuff mostly, all delivered in a firm and fruity baritone rarely heard outside the offices of the posher estate agents. I had never really appreciated just what girls have to put up with. After one particularly eye-stretching porkie, I looked up to find my gaze held by the other man at my table. His face was studiously expressionless: in a crisp and audible aside, for which a Scottish accent is essential, he summed up the case for the prosecution in a single word. Quite unprintable.

We got to talking. My companion was a fisherman with a beat on the Dee. By taking the sleeper from Euston he can work until 9 p.m., have a leisurely meal on the train and be on the river, refreshed, first thing in the morning. And the reverse three days later. At some time past 11 p.m. we set about the leisurely meal. Iain ordered a bottle of wine and I can tell you that there is much simple pleasure to be had in speeding north through the night, sipping champagne, talking of fish and fishing and listening to a tallish Englishman getting absolutely nowhere with a girl.

I woke with breakfast in bed and Loch Lomond on my right. At some time in the night the carriages of the night sleeper had been disentangled. Those bound for Inverness and beyond had taken most of the fishermen on their way to the Tay, the Spey and Helmsdale, whilst we were heading north and west for Fort William and on to the Western Isles. We were mostly walkers on board now, and at each tiny highland station we lost another one or two, stepping down onto the platform and shouldering backpacks before striding manfully off into the middle distance. The tall Englishman was having a row with the steward who was explaining that there was no cooked breakfast available as he hadn't ordered one the previous evening. We all enjoyed that.

Ardlui, Crianlarich, Tyndrum: I had travelled this route before but always as a car driver. Now I was free just to gaze as the train chuntered north past the Bridge of Orchy where the road is left behind and the train climbs alone across the haunting wilderness of Rannoch Moor. The moor was bright with June sunshine that morning, its sweeping wastes and barren heights looking almost benign. Almost.

I was the only one to get off the train at Rannoch Station. I had bought a big new rucksack for this trip and it bulged and tottered above me as I heaved it up from the platform. I had waders in there, and waterproofs and spare socks and pants and nets and reels and tackle and cameras: a rod tube was strapped to the outside. I bet I looked the part – some sort of part, anyway. I climbed the metal bridge over the line and that took a fair amount out of me. I began to wonder just how far it was to the Moor of Rannoch Hotel. Rannoch Moor is a big place.

I was fair tuckered out by the time I got to the hotel. If it had been more than 40 yards from the station, I doubt if I would have made it. It was 9.15 in the morning. I dumped the bulk of my stuff in the hall. I was ready to go fishing.

Loch Laidon is a long finger of stony water pointing deep into the heart of Rannoch Moor. There are rocky shallows and sudden drop offs that make for fine fishing and frightening boating, so I went up the loch with Jimmy Adams. He first came, like I did, by train. Jimmy is a Glaswegian railwayman who has fished a lifetime on Laidon – which is a long way from Glasgow – but if I had a railworker's free pass, I think I would do much the same. Later he moved to Rannoch and, long retired from the railways, he is still here and still fishing.

The sinister mountains that guard Glencoe emerged over the bright horizon as we headed down the loch, past small beaches of white sand and low, rocky headlands. I do not know the name of the bay and I probably wouldn't tell you if I did, but it is some way up on the northern shore, hidden behind a string of rocky islets. Jimmy cut the motor and we edged through the shallows, the sunlight dappling on the rocks beneath the boat. The wind was strong from the west and each drift between the shore and the islets took just a few minutes. But, for me, they were a remarkable few minutes.

I am not by nature a stillwater fisherman. It always seems like hard work. While Jimmy shipped the oars, I began working out one of those great lengths of line I always associate with stillwater fishing. He didn't exactly say anything. He just unhitched his fly from its keeper ring and flipped it ahead of the boat. I thought he was straightening the thing out. He didn't have to: a fish was doing that for him. I was retrieving now. My line was a satisfying distance from the boat and when I felt a tug I damn nearly connected. Not quite though. Jimmy gently suggested I didn't really need all that line out: we would be drifting over that spot soon enough. I shortened my line and put on the Blue Zulu Jimmy offered me and flipped it ahead of the boat in the prescribed manner. And lo! trout.

I had not had so much fun fishing in a long, long time. It all seemed, it still seems, as if the normal laws of life had been suspended. In most things, we are led to believe, the harder you work, the more you achieve; no pain, no gain; you only get out what you put in; never take the easy way out; *per ardua ad astra* – all a bit depressing but only what we have come to expect from Life. A long cast of a leaded nymph into the teeth of the wind is much harder; it ought to be more effective. It isn't. A short cast flipped down wind was dead easy and worked a treat. That sort of thing takes a bit of getting used to.

They were not big, these obliging fish of Loch Laidon. Three to the pound is the general consensus. There are certainly bigger fish in the loch: I was shown photos of some that had been caught that year, trout up to 7 pounds, but these were not the sort of fish you would like to catch if there were women and children present. And you do not catch them with a Blue Zulu in the sun-dappled shallows. So we fished on through the bright June day, flipping short, easy lines amongst the rocky islands of yellow broom and caught lots of beautiful fighting fish at three to the pound.

I will pass on Jimmy's method of cooking trout. It was new to me. Wrap the trout loosely in muslin. In a pan with a lid, heat some water with one cup of vinegar for each pound of fish. Bring to the boil. Remove the pan from the heat. Place the trout in the water and put on the lid. Leave until cold. The trout is cooked.

In the late afternoon the fishermen gathered in the cosy bar of the hotel. Three had had a field day like ourselves further up the loch. The other two had been catching trout on the Gaur, the river that flows out of Laidon on its way to the Tummel and on to the waters of the Tay. I thought I might have an hour on that before dinner. A surreptitious fisherman's track to the river winds alongside the railway line. It is, of course, terribly illegal to walk on the roadbed itself, so I didn't. Hugh Falkus, beside his famous books on salmon and sea trout, wrote *Nature Detective*, a handbook of sign reading. A nibbled sapling here, a bloodied feather and a flurry of paw-prints there, speak volumes to those of us who follow the master's methods. On the embankment of granite chippings that carries the track above the boggy wastes of Rannoch, I came upon a long-discarded pair of gent's corduroy trousers; 20 yards further along the line lay the sorry remains of a long-deceased sheep. Falkus does not cover this combination.

A few Gaur fish were fooled by my dry fly that evening. Three of them would have weighed a pound.

I was on the station at 9 the next morning after a huge and satisfying plate of fried stuff. Two chaps with rucksacks were waiting for the train as I tottered down to the platform. I tried to look like someone who had bagged a couple of Munros before breakfast. The West Highland Line wanders north from Rannoch past stations even more remote, places with no road access at all – just a lonely hostel for walkers and wandering fishermen. At Tulloch the line swings west past the spectacular Monessie gorge of the River Spean. Some of these tiny stations are request stops and so, just for the hell of it, I requested a stop at Roy Bridge where the River Roy tumbles out of the mountains to the north. The Roy is a fine salmon river but you can fish free for trout provided you use a leader of three pounds or less. Please check this before you do: I could hardly believe it. I left my luggage with the obliging barman who had assured me this was true, and went off to try my luck. I fished for a warm hour in the deep gorge of the Roy without seeing a rise or feeling a tug, so I collected by rucksack and hurried on to the platform to stick my hand out and stop the next train west.

The journey from Fort William to Mallaig is simply stunning. The track winds between mountains and sea, along jewelled lochs strung with wooded islands, through cuttings that are a riot of rhododendron. I'm sorry if that seems a bit overblown: it is how it is. I got off the train at Morar, shouldered my pack and trekked clear across the road to the Morar Hotel. It was 3 p.m. on Saturday, 15 June.

Morar is a place of quiet extremes. Loch Morar is the deepest freshwater loch in Europe, at something over a thousand feet. The River Morar, which drains this little lot to the sea, is the shortest in Britain, a few hundred yards. Oh yes, the loch also has a monster, less persecuted perhaps than the one in Loch Ness, but regularly witnessed by the fishermen who troll, fly and dap for the fine trout of Morar. I had come to do a bit of that myself, but it was the afternoon of Saturday, 15 June and no one was about to hire me a boat. So I sat in the bar of the Morar Hotel and watched television. Along with the rest of Morar. I don't know if you remember Saturday, 15 June: England were playing Scotland at Wembley in the finals of Euro 96. It was just fine in the bar of the Morar Hotel until that couple of minutes when Seaman saved the penalty at one end and Gascoigne scored at the other. After that it seemed like a splendid time for an Englishman to take a walk down to the loch and watch the boats come in. The few Morarians who had not been watching England beat Scotland had been out on the loch for an all-day fishing competition. I saw some fine fish landed that evening, the biggest a whisker under two pounds, and some fine bags. The lion's share were trolled but not a few were taken on wet fly. We all went back to the hotel bar for the weighing and the counting and the kisses from the bar-maid and all the ritual of a local angling competition. A twenty-first birthday was occurring in the hotel dining room where a man in a crimson shirt and tartan trousers was committing grievous bodily accordion playing, and what with that and the fish and football, it was some night in the Morar Hotel.

So no one really wanted to go out on the loch in the morning either. No matter. North of Loch Morar the hills are studded with a pattern of splendid hill lochs. It was a fine morning when Alistair MacLeod, the obliging owner of the hotel, dropped me off on the shore of the loch and I began to climb.

A faint path crunched into the granite leads east and up from Bracorina. The western end of Morar, dotted with wooded islands, spread out beneath me, with the isle of Eigg floating above the morning mist beyond. A stiff climb across springy turf is quite the best thing after a night of accordion music.

There are a dozen or so lochs and lochans in the hills north of Morar. I had had my first brush with hill lochs a couple of weeks before, in Argyll. What had struck me then was how idiosyncratic these little waters could be: one would be fishing its head off while another a few hundred yards away would be in a terminal sulk. No rhyme or reason to the thing but great fun finding out. And so it was above Morar. I had fished steadily around two-and-a-half lochs with just a single rise – which I had missed. Then, on the southern end of the third lochan, on the fringe of a sparse reed bed, a small fish stuck. It was a nice surprise. I cast again and got a second fish from the same spot. Not big fish, 9 or 10 inches, but two in a couple of casts looked like a trend. I took four more from that corner before I dared move on up the western shore away from the reeds, but I need not have worried: now I was getting a fish, or at least a pull, on every other cast. I had been fishing all morning on banks identical to this without a sign of fish. Perhaps the water had warmed or a hatch had happened or they had just got hungry. I had. It was way past noon and I had arranged to meet two of the fishermen I had met in the bar last night. I kept fishing until I was thoroughly late, then cut across the hill-side to join the path at the first lochan I had fished. Someone was fishing just where I had started the morning. I stopped and watched a while to see if this little loch had switched on. Not a thing. I still have no idea why half a hill loch fishes like a mad thing while nothing moves in the other two-and-a-half.

Nor why Donny MacLennan, who had caught the most fish in yesterday's competition, and Ewen MacDonald, who had caught the biggest fish in yesterday's competition, and I could not catch a single fish on a perfect evening amongst the islands on Loch Morar.

*   *   *

Do you remember Uncle Mac?

Every Saturday morning on *Children's Favourites* he would broadcast songs requested by eager little listeners: songs of towering majesty – 'You're a Pink Toothbrush, I'm a Blue Toothbrush' – or the plaintive *cri de coeur* of 'The Railroad Runs through the Middle of the House' and the stirring melodrama of 'Sparky's Magic Piano'. But these were just the high spots, the plums in a suet of worthier items of an improving nature requested, we imagined, by pale, bookish children with lank hair and owlish spectacles and name-tags sewn onto every item of the school uniform they were wearing on Saturday morning. Who else would write in every week asking for 'The Trish-trash Polka' or 'The Skaters' Waltz'? Or those songs sung in a cultured and fruity baritone about the life of a vagabond sleeping under the stars. One of these uplifting numbers had always been something of a puzzle for me. It went:

> Speed bonny boat, like a bird on the wing,
> Hark to the sailor's cry
> Larry the Lamb who is born to be king
> Over the sea to Skye.

A strange sort of succession, it seemed to me then. Forty years on I was humming the tune on a bright Monday morning as the Skye ferry pulled away from the lively little port of Mallaig.

I was fishing my way through Scotland by train but on that Monday I needed to catch a boat and a bus to bridge an awkward little gap in the system. The West Highland Line meanders north from Glasgow, along Lochs Long and Lomond, across the wilds of Rannoch Moor and then swings west to Fort William and the Road to the Isles. Mallaig is the end of the line. Literally. So at 9 that morning I was on the boat speeding like a bird on the wing over the sea to Skye.

A bus was waiting for the ferry and soon I was speeding like a bloke on a bus over the island of Skye to Kyleakin and the infamous Skye Bridge. Until last year you could take a bonny boat from Skye over to Kyle of Lochalsh on the mainland, but then The Bridge opened and the car ferry stopped and I really don't want to get into all this because feelings run high in these parts and if all the people I have met who claim to have been on that last, tearful trip of the old ferry were actually on the ferry, then it would have sunk like a bird in a cage, no question. But the bus driver paid the bridge toll and I was dropped at the station ready to ride the early train on the North Highland Line to Inverness, the east coast and on up to Caithness and as far as Scotland goes.

The trouble with Scotland is the rivers: like as not, they have got salmon in them. And because they have salmon in them, they don't have trout in them. I don't mean that salmon parr eat the food that the trout might eat (they might, but that's not my point) and I don't mean that trout don't thrive in rivers that are good for salmon (arguable, but that's not my point either). What I mean is that if the river has salmon in catchable numbers, then people will pay to catch them and they will pay far more than they would for catching trout and so they won't fish for the trout. And so, with some notable exceptions, quality river fishing is for salmon. Quality trout are caught, of course, but usually by folk fishing for salmon. Contrariwise, there are many fine lochs where salmon swim but are rarely caught and so these are left to the trout fishers and some of these lochs are very fine trout fisheries. Salmon are caught, of course, but usually by folk fishing for trout.

So I wasn't expecting much of the River Blackwater that runs along the lawn of a small hotel on the road from Ullapool to Inverness, not far from the railway station of Garve. I will tell you now that the Inchbae Lodge would have been worth a visit if it had nothing more than the ornamental pond in its garden, even if you had to travel there from Ullapool or Inverness. It was

one of the cosiest little corners I had ever encountered. It was run by Patrick
and Judy Price, and Patrick was meeting me at the station in Garve. He was
there with his friend and gillie Rob Jones. Patrick and Rob are fishermen.
That's what they do. Together they have fished most of the loch systems in
the north of Scotland – and that is an awful lot of fishing – and from Inchbae
you can fish it all. And yet at the bottom of the garden there is the River
Blackwater.

It looks a bit like the Dart, only more so. A river studded with large rocks
and laced with channels between them. Then the valley squeezes the
Blackwater between the rocky sides and it slips over rocky ledges into rocky
pools. Rocks are a constant motif of the Blackwater at Inchbae. It was getting
on in the day. There were several small rises in the channels, splashy blips of
salmon parr and one or two drowned my fly without hanging on. It is hard to
describe how a rise can look purposeful, but something slower, hard against
an undercut bank, had more business about it. A fish rose without making
contact to my favourite Easy Rider Dun, so I changed to my second favourite,
a parachute Black Gnat with a white wing. And then there was a fish on the
end. On this rocky river I was expecting a six-inch Dart trout, all dash and
verve, but this was something twice that length and several times the oomph.
I was chuffed to little mint balls.

The Blackwater was once a fine salmon river, but then came the hydro and
two of its three spawning headwaters were lost and, though salmon could
make their way up through the fish ladders below, it was decided to trap all
the returning fish at the head of Loch Garve way below Inchbae and stock the
upper river annually with fry and parr. The result is that the Blackwater has
no returning salmon, no salmon fishing, a fairly constant flow of compensa-
tion water from the hydro dams and simply splendid brown trout fishing.

Rob and I worked our way downstream, moving a pair of deer through the
trees before us. A series of rocky falls empties into a large pool beneath a
makeshift bridge and in the middle, where the current rounded a large rock,
a fish was rising boldly. No one but its mother could call this second fish
'pretty'. I suspect it had never been beautiful: the state of its fins suggested
that it had been reared in a stew pond but that had been long, long ago, and
now it was dark, with the beginnings of a hook on its big old head. The third
fish, on the other hand, was a honey. Not huge, about 12 inches, but just perfect and, plucked with a passing Endrick Spider from an unseen pocket in a
riffle, all the better for being unexpected. And so it went on. A late afternoon
on a lovely wild river in the Highlands. What could be better than that? I'll
tell you what: the meal that followed it and on into the early hours with Rob,

Patrick and Judy in a sitting room cosy with log fire and chat of food and fishing. Fragments of that evening come back to me: Patrick and Judy were considering naming the rooms after famous fishing flies ('a full breakfast for the two gentlemen in Hairy Mary'). We had lots of fun with that idea. At one point in the early hours I recall stretching and putting my hand straight into the mouth of a stuffed deer head mounted on the wall above me: it frightened the life out of me. And then I was in bed.

And up again at 6 a.m. Patrick was driving me heroically to Dingwall to catch the early train north to Caithness.

Kinbrace is on the map but only because there is nothing else to put on the map hereabouts. There is a platform at Kinbrace and there is a shop. And a couple of houses. And all around are the vast sweeping moorlands of Caithness. This is not a cosy countryside: it is not so much countryside as terrain. At Kinbrace you are a long, long way from anywhere, and the Garvault Hotel is a long way from Kinbrace. This makes the Garvault Hotel about as remote as you can get – which is just what the *Guinness Book of Records* says it is. I rode on the postbus from Kinbrace and arrived at Garvault along with the letters, newspapers, milk and groceries from the outside world.

I have an old tweed jacket I keep for gardening. Over the years it has stretched where I have stretched, frayed where I have frayed and we have grown disreputable together. It is far and away the most comfortable thing I own. The Garvault Hotel is a bit like that. It has been home to Catherine and Tony Henderson, their children and a large and devoted band of fishermen for twenty-three years. I came in, out of a wind full of rain, and was presented with a tray of tea and biscuits by Cath. I felt right at home.

The place was deserted. All the guests were out fishing. At 6 p.m. folk started to appear in the bar: the talk was of the day's fishing. The fishing talk at Garvault is enough to turn an impressionable lad's head: they talk in forties and fifties and, by golly, they are not joking. Over a huge and warming dinner I sat with Bob and Dave. That day they had been dapping on Loch Rimsdale. They had caught in the region of 100 trout. I love it when fishermen talk dirty like that to me.

Listen: I had always wanted to dap. Somehow I had got to the age of forty-six without ever having dapped and this was my chance. Well, now I have dapped and now I regard those previous forty-six years as years wasted. The next morning I was to dap with Bob and Dave.

I could not have had better tutors. Bob Beech and Dave Downs have dapped all over. They have been coming to Garvault, June and September, since 1990. They have got the thing down to an art form. I sat between them in the boat at the northern end of Loch Rimsdale, a long finger of water pointing nearly three miles southwards. Bob scooped a glob of Mucilin from its tub and wiped it onto the side of the boat in front of his seat.

'Saves time regreasing after you hook a fish'.

I had never caught fish quick enough for that sort of thing to matter. This was going to be good.

The dapping rods were telescopic, collapsed with the lines and leaders through the rings. Bob detached the fly from the rod and hooked it into the zipper of his jacket. Then he pulled out the rod, starting with the top section, and the line was pulled off the reel as the rod is lengthened to its full 15 feet. There is nothing fancy about dapping tackle. As the fly is the only thing to touch the water, there is no need for delicacy in the leader and every need for strength. Three years ago Bob took a brown trout of 9 pounds 6 ounces on this loch and salmon are taken on the dap here every year. Bob and Dave use 8-pound leaders. Next comes the blow line or dapping floss, which is strange, unravelled stuff, like something you might come across in the bottom of a lady's handbag. Eight feet or so of this stuff catches the breeze and wafts the fly down the wind. Behind the dapping floss is another couple of rod lengths of strong monofil before the main reel line of backing or flyline.

The fly was a huge daddy-long-legs. Bob and Dave carry other dapping flies and from time to time, when the current daddy-long-legs became soggy and mangled under the onslaught of trout, they would produce boxes of these flies and scan them, for all the world as if they were deciding what fly to use. Then they would put on a new daddy-long-legs. It is all rather masonic: a ritual cloth for drying a soggy fly is laid on the left knee, the fly is rubbed with Mucilin unguents, the rod is raised and the sacred daddy-long-legs is set flying down the breeze. I loved it.

The line is let out until the all the floss is beyond the rod tip. Now, by raising or lowering the rod tip the heavy fly can be made to trip onto the water, dancing amongst the small wave crests as the boat drifts down the rocky eastern shore of Rimsdale.

A dapped fly disappears in more interesting ways than in any other fly fishing I have found. Sometimes it is simply sucked under the surface or it goes in a swirl or the trout porpoises over the thing or chases on the surface. Sometimes, as the fly dances away in the breeze, a fish will fling himself a foot out of water to grab the fly. Often he misses but only to have another crack at the thing as the fly settles onto the next wave. When we drifted too close to the rocks, Bob would start the engine and drive us out a bit with the flies skating across the surface. Often this extra movement would bring a rise to Dave's fly, but the zipping fly would elude the game little trout, who would have a second stab at mine in the middle. And then a third at Bob's – who, having the engine at his end, would have slowed down enough to hook the thing.

I had been told about dapping and striking. Many times I have been taken aside and told the secret and made to repeat it to check that I had it right. The trick, I was told, is counting to three – or counting to five – or reciting 'God save the Queen' – or reciting the Gettysburg Address – before striking.

'Just tighten when you see a rise,' Bob told me. So I did. That works pretty well.

The wind blew steadily out of the north and we could drift the length of the loch, easing in and out of the shallow bays with a flurry of action around each rocky headland.

That day on Loch Rimsdale was the most fun I have had with a fishing rod for many a long year. And for the record we caught well over a hundred fine Rimsdale fish (although I was continually haunted by the fear of lowering the average by not Mucilining fast enough). The largest that day fell to Dave Downs, a fine trout of 1 pound 14 ounces.

He caught it on a daddy-long-legs.

Boys from the Grey Stuff

I did Durham once. It was in fourth form geography under the gimlet eye of the geography master, Ted Eames. He had been a wicket keeper in his time and had hands like battered bunches of bananas. We had to do sketch maps. We drew the outline of the Durham county with scribbly blue along the coastline. We drew the rivers in blue crayon, the Tees at the bottom, a bit of the Tyne at the top and the Wear across the middle. And then we outlined a large lozenge in black crayon, with black diagonal hatching, and wrote 'COAL' and 'STEEL' and 'CHEMICALS' and things like that across it. Down the left hand side we wrote 'PENNINES', on its side, and somewhere between the two, 'MILLSTONE GRIT'.

It was this last thing that stuck. I had no idea what millstone grit was, but it sounded a hard, uncompromising sort of rock, a bit like my father's carborundum sharpening stone. I dimly pictured the Tees and the Wear trickling through vast grey wastelands of the scratchy stuff.

I went to Teesdale last month: it's not like that at all.

Middleton-in-Teesdale is a charming little place, bustling that morning in the September sun. On the corner of the main street there is a hardware store. J. Raines & Sons is a proper hardware store with a door that tings as you go in and bits and bobs hanging from the fitments and a labyrinth into other parts of the shop and balls of string and pan scourers and clothes pegs – and fishing tackle. And in amongst all this you will find Christine Mitchell, who will sell you a ticket to fish the Tees. You have a choice. On the south bank you can fish the waters of the Earl of Strathmore. On the north bank you will be fishing Lord Barnard's water. Dress is optional.

A few miles upstream of Middleton, the Tees plunges over two spectacular waterfalls, prosaically named Low Force and High Force. High Force is the highest single fall of water in England and our tickets on Lord Barnard's Raby Estates Water seemingly entitled us to fish it. I fancied this. I was hoping, at the very least, to use a lot of adjectives I don't get to use much in describing the towering majesty of it all, but when we arrived at the path to the falls there was a large notice to the effect that High Force was closed. How can a waterfall be closed? But it was.

Above High Force the Tees crosses the high fells from its headwaters on the Pennine ridge, and the Pennine Way follows the river for several miles. A multitude of walkers pass this way each summer and the signs are everywhere – small, hand-written signs on every gate saying 'Beware of the dangerous bull', 'Trespassers will be gored' and so forth. We ignored these, almost, and followed a winding path over a shoulder of fell and there was the Tees.

It was something of a shock. I was expecting the upper Tees to be a moorland beck, shrunken by another dry summer into the stones of its bed. What we had here was a broad and brawling river, sporting a tinge of colour and barrelling along in one mighty rocky riffle. It was a magnificent sight. And slightly daunting. I am at home on small rivers where a single main current swings in an orderly fashion through run and pool, first this side, now that side, and the fisherman knows where the fish are to be found. The upper Tees looked more like a stampede.

But as you look again there is order to be found. The tumult is caused by a broad boulder-strewn bed, and each pair of boulders produces its own small pool with a head and tail and a lip down to the next pool and so on, the whole thing a complex braid of small becks.

Occasionally it is more obvious. The Pennine Way crosses the river here by Cronkley Bridge. Downstream the bridge has created a larger pool. I left Father to finish tackling up beside the bridge and slid down the bank to begin.

My father firmly believes that the devil looks after his own, but I prefer to think of it as a reward for clean living and pure thoughts. It was the third or fourth cast, I was gradually lengthening the line down the pool and, lo, there was a fish on. And not a tiddler. I called to Father who stopped his knot-tying and came down the bank muttering something rather unpaternal. I asked if he would mind landing the fish for me: it was the first of the day and I wanted a photograph. He took the rod and began to reel in the line while I peered into the viewfinder.

'It's a bit small', he said – rather ungenerously, I felt.

Now, I had seen this fish before I handed the rod over. I wouldn't claim it was huge but it certainly wasn't small. He was probably a bit miffed that I had got down to the pool while he was still tackling up. I suggested this.

'And anyway, if it's so small why are you making such a meal of landing it?'

He was, too. The line was cutting this way and that and the fish refused to slide into the net.

'I think you've foul-hooked it,' he said by way of an explanation for the difficulty. This was a downright slur. I had seen the fish, the dropper fly fairly hooked at the front of its mouth. The line sliced away yet again. I took my eye away from the viewfinder: he was doing this on purpose. And then the fish broke the surface between us. It was rather small. Smaller than when I had hooked it anyway, although the thing still refused to come in. They build Tees trout tough but surely not that tough. As the rod bent, another, larger trout on the dropper broke the surface and everything was explained. It was the first time I had hooked two fish at the same time in a river. And the first time Father had landed two.

We struck out to follow the Tees upstream. Harwood Beck joins the Tees on the north bank. The beck barely trickled through the stones of its bed, which made the furious progress of the Tees itself all the more bizarre. The headwaters were impounded a quarter of a century ago, forming Cow Green Reservoir in order to supply the industrial needs of Teesside – remember the black-hatched lozenge – but how much COAL and STEEL and CHEMICALS are left to need water these days is anyone's guess. Besides, a fair amount of that water was pounding past us as we made our way upstream. Thirty years ago when the reservoir was being planned, there was vigorous opposition from conservationists and today much of the area is a national nature reserve, rich in flora, 'with rare species of violets, primroses, pansies and saxifrages, and the rare blue gentian'. I had read all this before we came to Teesdale and now I rather wished I hadn't. If you have no wish to trample a rare saxifrage but haven't the slightest idea what a rare saxifrage looks like, it takes a lot of the carefree fun out of a riverside walk. We picked our way upstream, ever mindful of the rare blue gentian.

In Middleton we had asked Christine Mitchell what sort of flies to use on the upper Tees. She told us the locals favoured slim spider patterns with a touch of orange at this time of year: Partridge & Orange, Woodcock & Orange. I fancied something with a touch more weight about it in the heavy water and was fishing an Endrick Spider on the point. This fly is a favourite of mine. It is virtually a pheasant-tail nymph with a spider hackle of partridge to give it that pulsation of life. A winged hare's ear was on the dropper because I am only really happy if I have hare's ear fur somewhere in the water. Fished across the brawling current, swinging into the eddies and runs, they were picking up fine little Tees trout the length of my handspan but never from the places I expected to find them. This is an unsettling sign. I take it to mean that I am not interesting the better fish in the better lies and only getting the random idiot who would have grabbed at anything anyway. I began to ring the changes of flies but without interesting anything over 9^1/$_2$ inches.

Now, 9^1/$_2$ inches is my handspan and on most of the small upland rivers I visit I would be quite happy to catch such fine fat fellows all day long. But here's the rub: on Lord Barnard's water on the upper Tees the size limit is 10 inches. Look, I did not want to take a fish but the implication of a 10-inch limit was that I was only catching the babies and that there were much bigger fish to be caught if I only I would pull my finger out.

My finger, it seems, remained fully inserted. However I laid the bright little trout across my hand, I could still see bits of thumb or pinky at either end. We retired defeated: unbloody but bowed.

*   *   *

A mile up the road from Cronkley Bridge a small lane climbs up the side of the fell over Langdon Common and carries right on climbing above 2000 feet. This lonely little road is lined with wind breaks and marker poles to guide the snow ploughs. You get the feeling it could get a bit nippy hereabouts.

Beyond the summit the road over the fells drops steeply down to the next valley, Weardale. The Wear had been another line of blue crayon on my sketch map of county Durham. I thought I had learnt what to expect from the Tees. I had to think again. We got our first glimpse of the Wear at Wearhead where the road crosses the river. As with most British bridges over most British rivers, a glimpse is all you get. To see anything at all we had to park the van at the far side, walk back and peer over.

We were just 7 miles from the river Tees. We could have been in a different country. Where the Tees was a maelstrom of broken water, the infant Wear is a brook slipping over smooth bedrock as sweetly as swallowing an oyster and with just as little fuss. Where the upper Tees had rampaged across open moorland, the Wear below the bridge was dappled with shade, and in the first of those shady little pools a trout broke the surface. We had not intended to fish, we had other places to be that day, but after all that white water, the sight of a small rise on a shaded pool was too tempting. A post office and general store stands beside the bridge at Wearhead and there you can get ice creams and a ticket to fish the waters of the Upper Weardale Angling Association. We got both. And while we ate our ice creams we strolled up the road and knocked on the door of Mr Lee, the club secretary.

He was not hopeful. Later on there might be salmon and sea trout, but they would need rain to bring them up the river. But we had seen fish rising. We might find a few small trout, he said, but the trout fishing had declined in recent times. It was hard to say why.

It was still a sunny day near the end of the season. It might be fun to cast to a rising fish. Below the bridge a path follows the little river through the trees and down into a meadow where the river slides over a series of smooth slabs of bedrock. In places you could cross the upper Wear in galoshes – provided you could keep your footing on those polished rocks. And in between these sluices, wherever the bedding planes provided a cleft or channel, we could see grey shapes hovering over the bed, tilting up to grab at something unseen in the surface before darting back. Unless, of course, that something on the surface was a dry fly. Then there was a flurry of sparkling splash in the shallow water and a bright little trout would dash around the pool or slip down to the next. There were fish in every pool down the river and sometimes we caught one and often we didn't. It didn't matter much because beyond each pool there was another much the same. From time to time there was a deeper pool and deeper shade and a trout hooked here pulled harder and the first glimpse of a golden flank in the depths looked bigger than the fish of the bright shallows. But it wasn't: it just felt that way.

The upper Wear that day was full of trout. They were fine little fish that stretched to about a handspan. And if that is the size they are, what more can you ask of a river?

*   *   *

P.S.
In 1960, before Cow Green Reservoir was empounded, a survey of the natural brown trout of the high altitude becks of the upper Tees was made by D.T. Crisp of the Nature Conservancy. The 1960 survey had found 183 trout. The average size was *6 inches.* Only two fish over 10 inches were found. Only two fish over seven years old were found. The average size of a five-year-old trout was 8¹/₂ inches. Slice it how you like, these are not big fish. The Tees at Cronkley Bridge and the Wear at Wearhead are some 190 metres lower than these surveyed becks. Looking back, I am rather pleased with our fish that day.

The Lost Weekend

What did Alistair Gowans look like? I didn't know.

I knew him to be the originator of Ally's Shrimp but I had no clear idea how one might recognize a creator of shrimps.

We were supposed to be travelling on the same plane to Bilbao. I looked around. None of the blokes on flight SN867 from Brussels gave any indication of shrimp-inventing. They were mostly wearing suits and they looked quite comfortable in them. Fishermen usually find that hard.

It was mid-afternoon in Bilbao. A very attractive girl stood amongst the thin crowd waiting at the barrier. She held a cardboard sign bearing the words 'LA RIOJA'. On the few previous occasions I have been met at airports, it has always been by some seedy bloke with a crumpled jacket and moustache. But I *was* going to La Rioja. Perhaps she was waiting for Alistair Gowans.

She was. So we both stood at the barrier and scrutinized the other passengers for designers of artificial crustacea. He was not there. The attractive girl was called Pilar and she was a little put-out to have lost Mr Gowans so early in the proceedings. But he was just the first thing to get lost that weekend.

Pilar and I headed south from Bilbao, driven by a seedy bloke in a crumpled suit and moustache (he had probable been there to meet me). We climbed through the Basque hills behind the coast and dropped down into the valley of the River Ebro and into La Rioja. La Rioja is the smallest and one of the troutiest of Spain's autonomous regions. To the rest of the world it is the finest of Spanish red wines, and its vineyards crowded the road as we crossed the Ebro at the town of Haro, wine centre of the region. Across the dusty red plane of vineyards, a line of mountains climbs beyond 7000 feet. We turned south and headed for those hills. Somewhere in the heart of those mountains, tucked down in the tight, twisting gorges of the Najerilla river, the Fifth International Meeting of Fly-fishers was gathering.

I don't know about you, but these sorts of things intimidate me more than somewhat. I imagine they will be full of ardent types who Know What They Are Doing. Not really my sort. The bloke in the water certainly knew what he was doing. Venta de Goyo consists of a filling station, a bar and a hotel squeezed between the cliffs and the river. As we arrived, a figure in immaculate chest waders was descending the steep path behind the petrol pumps, watched by a knot of interested fishermen. Down in the gorge the splendid Najerilla river swelled into a pool. The fisherman edged into the water and began to throw an immaculate line upstream. One of the spectators called down to him and, as he looked up to reply, a fish rose, took his fly and promptly spat it out again. So that sort of thing happens to everyone. Quite reassuring, really. A dozen casts later he made contact and a trout of 10 ounces or so came skittering across the surface. As he took the hook from the fish, we could see the curious markings on its flank, the spots clustered into three prominent bars, the hallmark of a wild trout from limestone country. In France these are the *zebrée* trout of the Jura and Lozère – wherever rivers spring fresh from the limestone. I have never discovered whether this is a reaction to water chemistry or an ancient genetic strain of trout, but here they were in the high sierras of Spain.

We were a mixed bunch that evening – and getting more mixed with every bottle of fine Rioja that magically appeared in our midst. Rod-makers, fly-dressers, tackle-dealers, magazine editors, fishing guides and some blokes who just like fishing had come from most parts of Europe to fish, chat, eat and drink in whichever order they chose. And at some point in the proceeding we were joined by a belated shrimp-architect whose connections had become unravelled in Brussels. We were complete.

The morning was painfully bright. We sorted ourselves out in whatever languages we could muster and set off along the 20 miles of hairpin gorges downstream. There are no private rivers in Spain. They belong to the people. But to prevent the people from thrashing the best bits to pieces, the best sections of water are preserved as *cotos,* where fishing pressure is strictly controlled. We had been allocated a day on the Anguiano *cotos* of the lower Najerilla.

We emerged from the gorge and arrived at the village of Bobadilla. Half a dozen cars pulled into the shade beside the bridge. Two dozen burly blokes got out and spread out amongst the trees, stabbing frantically at mobile phones, walking in circles and talking to themselves – these were hi-tech fishermen – but the steep sides of the Najerilla gorge had rendered them *incommunicado* for some eighteen hours. By now some of them were desperate.

A few fish were rising beneath the bridge, in the channel beside the wall. They were not big fish – a couple of small rainbows, escaped from the fish farm upstream – but it got us in the mood. Andrew and I wandered off downstream looking for something better. Andrew Ryan is a professional: he runs the Clonanav Fly Fishing Centre on the magnificent dry-fly waters of the Suir and Nire in Co. Waterford. He had spent the winter guiding on the pro-lific trout waters of Argentina. This was one of the chaps who Know What They Are Doing. It was just a shame the fish didn't.

It was a warm day at the end of June. The river was a picture, a sparkling limestone stream rattling over pebbles, between bright beds of ranunculus in full bloom. And there was not a trout to be seen. We searched in the shady bits, in the deep holes, in the quiet runs, in the weedy channels. We searched with dry flies and nymphs of every weight. Nothing. The trout of the Najerilla were off duty. We met others equally baffled and as the morning passed into lunchtime we worked our way back to the bridge.

The small rainbows were still rising under that bridge. But by now they were not alone. A dozen of fly-fishing's finest were besieging the bridge from both sides, hurling flies at the only rising fish any of us had seen. It was not an edifying sight. Andrew and I were watching from the pool below when he spotted a quiet movement beside a bush trailing in the current across the way. He flicked the fly, a Sparkle Klinkhamen Special, into its path and the trout took at the first pass. After three more we adjourned for lunch.

They had set out long trestle tables in the shade beside the river. Three huge barbecues grills were blazing, salads were being sprinkled with nice stuff and bottles of Rioja uncorked. The wine was passed back and forth, the grills died to cooking heat and whole ribcages of pork set sizzling. You know the last scene in any Asterix comic book? The villagers are all feasting off wild boar roasting over fires. It looked a bit like that. Chops followed the ribs and then large knobbles of something that looked like giant pork scratchings. It tasted wonderful. Until I turned it over and found that I was gnawing on a grilled nostril.

It was 3 p.m. We all fancied a quick coffee before the afternoon's fishing, so we straggled across the bridge and up the path to the village of Bobadilla and into the bar.

It may have been the heat – we northern Europeans are not used to the heat – or I may have eaten a dodgy nostril. Or jetlag. Something, anyway, because when we came out of that bar six hours later, I was feeling distinctly wobbly. Some of the others looked a bit wobbly too. Andrew, like me, was doing a lot of leaning. Ally Gowans was wandering vaguely down the main street. Pilar and Anna, our gorgeous guides and translators, were giggling. Gerardo, distinguished editor of Spain's top fishing magazine, was sitting on the pavement, looking like he had lost something if only he could remember what it was. I knew how he felt. I was wondering how I came to lose six hours on one of the best trout streams in Spain. Also two camera lenses. And my favourite hat.

I think I found the answer next morning. I carry a notebook and at breakfast I turned to the last entry. On the left hand page it mentions lunch under the trees – up to where we went for coffee. Then there is a Spanish word in someone else's handwriting. It says 'PACHARAN'. Beside it, in my handwriting, there is a note: it says 'Red stuff sloe berries'. After that the right hand page becomes rather hard to read. I can make out one or two words and a time, 8.30 p.m. The last word is underlined. It says 'fubar'. That's Spanish, I fancy, for sloe berries.

And I wasn't the only one to lose things. José lost a pocket. It was quite a big pocket, too, the one on the front of his neoprene chest waders. He had decided to go fishing after the bar. He was about to step into the water when he noticed this pocket had disappeared. It had been there before lunch. We told him not to worry: it would turn up. And so it did. When he turned round someone noticed the pocket on his back: José had managed to get chest waders on back to front. Perhaps he was allergic to sloe berries like me.

Fishing did not start early the next morning. The day was even warmer and the sun had a curious jangling quality that bounced off the shimmering water and reverberated around the skull. Not nice. We were fishing in the gorge of the Najerilla on the Viniegras *cotos* beside the hotel. Here the water rattled between the walls of the gorge. It was mercifully shaded down here and the water was cold, flowing from a mountain reservoir a few miles upstream. A few small sedges fluttered but only small fish moved in midstream, well away from the tasty pockets and shaded runs where the larger fish must lie. Occasionally a larger insect, much larger, fluttered into the sunlight between the trees and rattled into the leaves. It was a stonefly, a huge stonefly. The rocky margins of the river told the tale. Every other stone carried the empty case of a stonefly nymph that had hatched in the hours of darkness. I turned over a pebble on the river bed and a knot of these creatures, waiting their turn to emerge, scuttled away from the sunlight. I had seen hatches of these beasts in the limestone rivers of the Jura, the winged females flapping and gliding high above the water I had at first taken for a flock of birds. Before hatching, the large nymphs must migrate across the river bed to the shore. It is a dangerous journey for anything as conspicuous and tasty as a stonefly nymph: the trout feast on the migrating nymphs. They must have been stuffed.

Just how big a Rioja trout can get on a diet of such things we would see later that afternoon. For now we retired to the cool of the hotel for lunch. A local newspaper, *La Rioja*, lay on the reception desk. On an inside page there was a report on this 'Fifth International Meeting of Fly-fishers' on the waters of Rioja. The photograph was of Ally Gowans. The caption read: 'Alistair Douglas, fishing instructor to the Prince of Wales, yesterday on the Najerilla.' Local newspapers are the same the world over.

When the worst of the heat had gone from the day we made our way up the mountain to the Embalse de Mansilla where the Najerilla begins in the cold waters of the reservoir. The lake is not *acotado* and anyone with a rod licence can fish freely by most methods. It is a beautiful, haunting spot, a large sheet of water, much of it inaccessible beneath towering cliffs of limestone. A man with a float tube could fill his boots (but he would also be shot: boats of any sort are not allowed). As it is, people come here to cast at the huge fish that occasionally cruise into range and, by and large, the fish ignore them – as is the habit of huge fish. The road flies over a shallow arm of the lake. We were standing on the bridge, idly staring over the waters of the lake. I looked down and saw a pale shape gliding out of the shadow of the bridge. All wild trout over 5 pounds are giants. It doesn't much matter if they are double that. This was probably somewhere in between.

We ate late that evening but it was still pleasantly warm when we stepped outside just after midnight. Ally asked if I fancied going with some of the others to the bar in Bobadilla: apparently he fancied a coffee after dinner.

I did not go for that coffee. The Fifth International Meeting of Fly-fishers would fish the River Iregua the next morning but I had to fly home – I needed all the brain cells I could muster. Besides, I kept losing things in Bobadilla. They got back at 6 a.m. the next day: six hours is about par for a coffee at the bar in Bobadilla. On the way back they had lost the door to Javier's car.

Don't ask. I don't know.

Things that Go Clonk in the Day

I met a man the other day. His name is Joe Taylor and he is a clonker. I had never met a clonker and, in truth, he was not clonking when I met him. We met in the Oxfordshire town of Bicester and he told me that he never clonks in Britain. Well, you wouldn't.

Joe has clonked all over: he has clonked in France, he has even clonked in Kazakhstan. Kazakhstan, it seems, is a clonker's paradise. Not a lot of people know that.

Clonking is much more than a rather unconvincing item in *Call My Bluff*. Clonking is a bizarre method of catching a fish – but then, the fish it catches is every bit as bizarre.

The Wels, the European or Danubian catfish, they are all the same beast, *Siluris glanis*, a monstrous creature growing up to *200 kilos* and measuring several metres from its insignificant tail to an extremely significant mouth. A 300-kilo record specimen from the River Dnieper was *5 metres* long. That is a fair-sized fish to find in your pond. And you might: we have wels here in Britain, introduced into a few ponds and lakes in southern England earlier this century. On the continent they are found in many of the larger, slower rivers, in marshes and deltas from Spain to the Chinese border with Kazakhstan.

You have to eat a fair amount to put on weight like a wels, and they will eat anything – and everything – from small larvae, fish large and small, frogs, ducks and water voles. And by repute, even dogs. The wels is a voracious predator, hunting mostly at night, which – considering its nightmarish appearance, a huge mouth, well-stocked with teeth and topped by a pair of long, mobile feelers – is something of a blessing for those of a nervous disposition. But these nocturnal habits are a nuisance to the fisherman. Catfish are most active in the summer when the water is warm but the nights are short. A fisherman who has made his way to catfish heaven among the limitless, unfished marshes of the Ily delta in eastern Kazakhstan will catch nothing during the long hours of daylight.

Unless, of course, he has a clonk.

It is little more than a slim, curved stick, about 15 inches long, swelling into a handle at one end. At the other end is a flat-bottomed foot an inch or so in diameter. It can be round or oval. The shape, size and angle of this little foot is terribly important – to the man who clonks.

Clonking is done in a boat, drifting slowly between the reeds and mud banks of the marshes. We did not have a boat that day in Bicester. Or a marsh. So Joe took me through his tackle shop to a water tank outside the back door. He gripped the clonk by the handle, with the foot just above the water. By swinging his forearm down and snapping his wrist over, Joe thrust the foot of the clonk into the water and immediately out again behind him. When done by an expert, this produces an extraordinary, hollow, resounding 'CLONK' reverberating from the tank. When done by a bloke having his first go at clonking, it produces a sloshing sort of sound and a trouser-leg full of water. I persevered and got a 'CLONK' of sorts about one swing in four and a trouser-leg full of water on the other three. Joe gets a 'CLONK' every time.

It is what happens next that is bizarre. Any fisherman will tell you what happens if you start smacking the water with a wooden stick: the fish depart the scene. And so they do – all except the catfish. The catfish that was dozing the daylight hours away on the muddy bed of the river wakes up. It swims towards the eerie, rhythmic clonking echoing for miles through the muddy water. It is agitated. Catfish have been known to grab the clonk from the fisherman's hand: a good clonk can boast honourable tooth scars on its business end. But the clonk is only used to stir up the catfish and bring them to the boat. Once there, the fish will find the fisherman's baited hook and normal service is resumed. But if the catfish is unsure, if it can be felt nuzzling the bait, a single 'CLONK' from the clonker will usually make the fish grab the bait.

Why? No one seems to know. Suggestions abound: the clonk imitates a mating catfish, it imitates a feeding catfish, it stimulates aggression or it is simple curiosity that kills the catfish. What is certain is that it works. On his last trip to the Ily marshes, Joe took twenty-four giant catfish – all in daylight: all on the clonk.

*   *   *

There is a sequel to this story. After it had appeared in the *Telegraph*, I went back to Joe's shop to record an interview for a fishing programme on Radio

Five Live. I poled up first thing in the morning and Joe and I got to chatting about clonking. I wanted to record the sound of the clonk in the tank of water at the back of the shop. I wanted to hear what a catfish would hear. This meant sticking the microphone underwater. There is really only one way to do this.

I am still remembered in the Bicester branch of 'Superdrug' as the bloke who ran breathlessly into the shop, demanding, 'Quick, do you have any condoms?' – at 9.15 in the morning.

My tax return for that year contains a claim for one packet of condoms.

14

Boys' Toys

Do you remember General Jumbo?

He was in the *Beano* comic. Every week through the 1950s and 60s he would thwart villains, trap spies and save people in peril – all this at only nine years old. He accomplished such thwarting, trapping and saving by deploying an army of tiny mechanical soldiers in miniature tanks, helicopters and jeeps, the whole lot controlled by a sort of radio thingummy on his left wrist.

It was all a long time ago: General Jumbo must be fifty years old by now and I think I might have met him last week at a lake in Wiltshire. Phil Fry is the inventor of the Microcat, the latest escalation in Man's eternal contest with the carp.

In the beginning there was the rod. The rod allowed Man to cast further than he could throw a baited hook – which isn't very far. But the fish moved out from the bank. Then came the reel with its store of line, allowing a longer cast and the fish just moved a little further. Powerful rods in plastics and fixed-spool reels made prodigious casts possible – and the fish kept moving a little further away. And so on.

There is a limit to the distance a bait can be cast. Long casts need weight and speed. The force of casting the thing will tear a soft bait from the hook: a bait tough enough to stay on the hook can be too tough for the fish to eat. There is another problem. All that weight and terminal tackle cartwheeling across the sky can create some impressive tangles; it certainly creates an impressive *kersploosh* when it lands, hopefully in the vicinity of the carp and bream. You can hardly blame them for wanting to move. To encourage them back, the fisherman then peppers the area round the hook with quantities of ground-bait launched from a powerful catapult – provided, of course, that he can fix the spot where the baited hook had landed, far out across the water. No one said long-distance fishing was easy.

Until now.

The Microcat comes straight from General Jumbo's pages in the *Beano*. The ultimate in fishy Toys for Boys is a sleek black catamaran powered by four silent jet pumps. There was something of the Stealth Bomber about the thing as Phil lowered it onto the water, an impression helped by a couple of bomb-bays in the centre of the boat. These were full of ground-bait but also carried the baited hook and weights, pulling the line from the reel as Phil sent the Microcat out across the lake like a sheepdog on its outrun. It was 200 yards away, twice the range of a very good cast, when Phil announced that we were there. Where? A steep drop-off on the lake bed, a favourite haunt of carp here-abouts: the Microcat is armed with an echo-sounder which transmits information on the depth – even the fish – back to the operator ('fisherman' doesn't sound quite right). The deluxe version has a radio-linked TV camera that can peer down into the water, looking for fish. Phil twiddled something on the controls and the navigation lights flashed, confirming that one of the bomb-bays had opened, releasing the hook and line and a generous sprin-kling of ground-bait. Which was all fine and dandy but how would we find the place again when it was time to deliver more ground-bait? Phil sent the cat forward with a dab on the controls. The lights flashed once more and then the cat swung round and headed back to shore – leaving a bright marker buoy, the payload of the second bomb-bay, to mark where the bait had been dropped.

I wanted to play General Jumbo. I took the controls and spent some time whizzing hither and yon dropping bait and marker buoys and even more time retrieving them again with the cunning little gizmo on the back of the boat.

What fun! Much better than fishing. All it needs is one of General J's little mechanical soldiers to catch the carp, weigh it, kiss the thing and return it to the water and I could really take to this carp fishing lark.

15 &

Monnowphil

Where I live I am surrounded by countryside. It is not outstanding country-side. There are no soaring cliffs, no sweeping plains or hidden, ootsy valleys. There are no distant purple views of majestic mountains and no breathtaking vistas: you cannot, as far as I am aware, see five counties from anywhere round our way. There is not much thatch and we are not quite in the Cotswolds. It goes up and down a bit, particularly if you are on a bicycle, and it is very green. It is quietly pleasant. It is just bog-standard, off-the-shelf English countryside. It is gorgeous.

And so it is with the River Monnow. The Monnow slips gently through deep countryside, hidden below high banks of red sand eroded from the old sandstones of the Welsh Borders. It has been doing this for a long time, long enough to remove any serious obstruction to its path. There are no waterfalls, no gorges, no majestic sweeps: the Monnow moves on about its business, slipping over a gravel bar into a broad gravel pool, the tongue of faster water bouncing along before settling into a broad streamy run with a slower sandy tail before the next gravel bar. And so on. Mile after unobtrusive mile the water slips quietly under the dappled shading of wooded banks. The River Monnow must have been a big disappointment to King Offa.

For most of its length the Monnow forms the border between England and Wales. It is hard to imagine a less convincing obstacle to marauding: it must be one of the most diffident natural frontiers in the world. To the north, below Hay-on-Wye, Offa's Dyke follows a forbidding ridge, much of it above 2000 feet, plunging 1400 feet on either side to the valleys of the Afon Honddu in Wales and Olchon Brook in England. You know where you are with a border like that. Both these streams are headwaters of the Monnow, one fair-haired with a receding chin, ineffably English, the other small and dark and implacably Welsh. They tramp down either side of the Hatterrall Ridge like two unsighted and unwitting gunfighters – Bob Hope and the baddie in

Paleface, say. The ridge ends abruptly, like the clapboard buildings on Main Street, at Llanfihangel Crucorney where the Welsh Afon Honddu swings round the corner to encounter the English Monnow at Pandy. They meet and wander off tamely to raise trout and grayling together in the rich meadows towards Monmouth and the Wye.

Time was when the Monnow was a famous trout stream with enormous trout in its prime reaches, the middle section from Pontrilas to Skenfrith. Come the cayfly (and the Monnow still has a cracking hatch of mayfly), these large fish would be taken under the bosky banks and a good time was had by all. In recent years the river has been a shadow of this former glory. Quite why or how is hard to say: farming methods perhaps, they usually get the blame, but I do wonder just how much our present inclination to stock and stock again with what would have been whoppers on these rainfed streams has warped our perceptions of the fishing in the past. I don't know. At all events the reputation of the Monnow has declined of late and that may be no bad thing for those fortunate enough to fish this delightful, unassuming river.

I first found the Monnow many years ago. We had rented a cottage for a summer holiday. A mile of the Monnow, the Home Beat of Kentchurch Court, for two rods came with the cottage. It was the first time I had every rented more than a day ticket on a river, and it seemed the most sybaritic luxury to have two banks of a whole river to wallow in whenever I felt like it. It still does. Throughout that week I would get up at first light and totter down through the dew-soaked grasses to the footbridge at the bottom of the beat. Over that week I got to know every rock and eddy on our stretch of river. It was a boiling week in August and the country had been drought-ridden for months, with the worst affected region being east Wales. Still the Monnow bobbled along carrying my flies in the morning, the children on an inflatable dingy in the afternoon and my flies again in the evening. We did not, as I recall, trouble many of the trout of the Monnow. Memory is a curious thing. I have difficulty nowadays holding more than one task in my head for more than a minute or so. I have taken to writing lists, but then I forget to take the lists with me. This is normal enough. But I can recall every lie on every river I have fished and most of the fish I have caught there. The one decent trout I caught that week on the Monnow lurked at the top of the beat below a slight riffle and it grabbed at a Mallard & Claret I was swinging diffidently across the drought-weakened current in the tag-end of a hot afternoon.

I had not thought of that trout for many years – until last Friday, when we arrived at the river and pulled up at the same footbridge at the bottom of the

Home Beat. We were lucky to be there: fishing on the Monnow does not come along every day of the week. For years I had tried to book that cottage again for the Whitsun holiday when the fishing would be at its glorious best; each year it had been taken. Not just for that year but for the next and the one after that. Curiously enough, a few years ago I was invited to a fishing club dinner somewhere in Gloucestershire. The chairman was like fishing club chairmen the world over: nuff said. He had instigated a competition for humorous essays on the subject of fishing, the winners to be announced at the dinner. The chairman's wife, a luminary of the local amateur dramatic society, agreed after hardly any pleading at all to read the winning essays for our delight and entertainment. To claim, as the minutes of the meeting undoubtedly did, that a good time was enjoyed by one and all would be to tamper with the truth. The chairman looked as if he was having a good time. So did his wife. That was about it. Such things leave scars. Later on, when the speeches had come and gone, we were talking, as people will when they are several gin and tonics downwind, of favourite rivers. It was maudlin stuff, thinking back to golden days and bright waters and so on. I mentioned the Monnow. The chairman perked up. He knew the Monnow. Fished it every year as a matter of fact. Seems he rented a cottage with the Home Beat at Kentchurch for the week of Whitsun each year. What this man deserved was to be chairman of a fishing club and to be married to an amateur dramatist. He did not deserve to fish the River Monnow on the best week of the year. Every year.

Time has passed. The scars have healed. The Home Beat is no longer let with the cottage that nestled at the edge of the deer park of Kentchurch Court. The Home Beat, together with the beats upstream and down have been leased, as so much of this delightful river is leased, to a private club. But it is an enlightened private club: in addition to the twenty members who fish the 2½ miles of double bank fishing, three rods are retained for bookable day tickets. And last Friday, Father and I had two of them.

Nothing had changed. The little wooden hut at the end of the bridge had been painted and now serves as a fishing hut for the club. It was the warmest morning of the year so far and a couple of fishermen were standing on the footbridge peering down on the current between the rocks. When I had fished here years before, a pod of huge grayling would hang in the shadows of the bridge to tantalize and excite the angler as he tackled up. They are still there. The water held a comforting tinge of colour from the last rains at the beginning of the week. The water in the beat below often has this ochre tinge: tractors crossing the river by the ford upstream of the footbridge help the fisherman with a little colour. Although it was warm, the water was still freezing at the end of April and few fish were rising and none with the steady rhythm of a feeding fish. Through the Kentchurch Estate the Monnow has cut a deep meander through the sandy soil and the wading angler is rarely troubled by any wind. Father had taken a fish on the dry fly by the time I had wandered downstream with Bertie, one of the local members we had met on the bridge. I was fishing a weighted nymph upstream, mainly because on our walk downstream from the bridge Bertie had been telling me about a visitor they had had last summer who astounded every one with his ready way with a nymph, vacuuming fish out of the river like shelling peas. That is fighting talk. No one was more surprised than me when my leader shifted violently across the current and a bright brown trout smashed through the surface. (Actually, the trout looked more surprised than me.) Other fish followed slowly. Some were fish that the club had stocked before the season. In truth, these were sorry fish: all the stockies had battered fins where they had been crowded in their stew ponds. There is no need for this. Many trout hatcheries produce brown trout that are indistinguishable from wild fish, and any with tatty bits should be rejected.

It was time for lunch. The top beat of the club water is called the Bridge Inn beat. This is a good sign. The Bridge Inn nestles above the Monnow like a fussy hen. It is my sort of pub. It is outstanding in no way. Queen Elizabeth did not sleep here. It is not thatched. It has wooden beams, to be sure, but they are to keep the ceiling up. It could arguably be the last pub in England, as the border flows underneath its dining room window but it keeps very quiet about this. The food is good and fresh and home-made. On the wall are a selection of cards from farms and cottages that do bed and breakfast in the vicinity if you are tempted to stay for a while. The Scudamores were. They came to the valley of the Monnow in 1086 and they liked it well enough: they are still here 900 years later. They live just round the back of the church at Kentchurch Court. Kentchurch Court is *definitely* my sort of house: not many more windows than you could shake a stick at, not all the turrets are crenellated and the deer park only surrounds it on three sides. And it has only mile upon unassuming mile of the River Monnow to fish.

16

The Peach to Moscow

I'm thinking of giving up this fishing lark. I'm thinking of going into snail breeding.

Fascinating little beggars, snails. Did you know that your average *gros-gris* snail will produce 100 little snails every couple of months and that these are fully grown within three or four months? And they don't need much space: you can stock 150 to the square metre. This explains quite a lot about the state of the plants in my allotment. I'm thinking of turning the thing over to snail production. A bloke could start off with a couple of dozen and be pretty much self-sufficient in snails within a year. And if the Red Lion up the road introduced snails as a tasty bar snack, a bloke could make a very nice living.

That's the trouble with the Internet: there's so much fascinating stuff that I get side-tracked. I start off on a pleasant, out-of-the-trout-season look at what there is on fly-fishing and before I know what's happening I've made a career change.

The Internet may be a boon for the strong-minded, firm-jawed, gimlet-eyed sort of chap who can dive in, eyes firmly on the prize, pluck what he wants and step out again. It is a different story for blokes like me. We click on something interesting and that leads us off to something else, and so it goes on until we find ourselves snail farming and no idea how we got there.

If you just fancy a ramble, you can start with Fish & Fly (www.fishand-fly.co.uk). There are several internet magazines with similar names and addresses – you will find them if you ask your searching gizmo to look for things like 'fishing' and 'fly' or 'flyfishing' or some such. It will also find a lot of shops in Montana wanting to sell you stuff. Fish & Fly is the best British fly-fishing site I have found. It has monthly features, much like a magazine, and I may be a little biased because I write one for them each month. But then, so can you: anyone who has something to say about fishing is welcome to submit an article and tell a waiting world. If you want to say a little something to the waiting world – or if you want to ask it a question – most of these Internet fishing magazines have a readers' forum or noticeboard where you can pin up your question and wait for someone to answer it. Or you can browse through recent questions and see if anything grabs you.

I was grabbed the other day – by a question on amadou. The chap had got some of the fungus but didn't know how you made it into the stuff that dries flies. I remembered an article on just that in *Trout and Salmon*. I looked it up. There wasn't a lot on the preparation, so I got to wondering if there might be something better out there. I set my gizmo to search for 'amadou' and 'fungus'. Seconds later I had struck pay-dirt. Pages of the stuff on the history and uses of amadou: to stop bleeding, as a strong purgative and, intriguingly, 'the Sammi people are said to use it for a moxia'. I have no idea what a moxia is and nor does my dictionary. There were details of amadou preparation – 'Add strong urine to cover the fungus. Boil gently for three days and nights, adding urine as necessary.' – and, happily, a more savoury chemical equivalent. It had the lot. Curiously, this amadou site (www.ragweedforge.com/amadou.html) has nothing to do with fishing. It is the site of an American knife-maker. He also makes steel strikers for tinder boxes. Amadou, it seems, is the traditional and best tinder for catching a spark. So I read about that and ordered a striker and flint. I couldn't resist it. See what I mean?

These forums can be invaluable. I was going to Germany, but what licences would I need? Things had changed since I was last there. I had heard dark rumours about hours of exams and tricky questions about the number of scales a roach has got. I don't know that sort of stuff, so I posted a notice pleading for information. Within a few hours there was an answer from a Nik Stiefel, a German working in Stevenage. He gave me chapter and verse – including the welcome news that foreign visitors were excused the exam as long as they had a note from their mum. Even better, he introduced me to some of the European fishing websites. A couple of the best are Swedish. You do not have to speak Swedish, thank goodness: most Swedes speak better English than I do and, besides, what is good about these websites is not their pages about the fishing in various bits of Sweden, it is the links they give to other fishy sites around the world. These links, alas, are my downfall.

Remember *The Lion, the Witch and the Wardrobe*? Well these links are a wardrobe into another world. 'LW's Fishing Site' (www.acc.umu.se/ ~ widmark/lwfishxl.html) reckons to be 'the most complete list of fishing resources ever made on the Web'. I wouldn't argue with that: there are over 300 links here. I know because I counted them last night, which is how I came to stumble onto my future career in snail-breeding. Somewhere down the bottom of the list, amongst a miscellaneous collection of fishy flotsam, I came across BaitStick (www.baitstick.com).

I don't know why I clicked on this one. Baitstick, it seems, is a very sticky sort of glue. You dip your hook in it and then touch the hook onto a live and kicking bit of bait: they suggest a cluster of ants or a couple of woodlice or a grasshopper or a fly – a real one. What a brilliant idea. I must send off for some. A small pot costs $7.50 plus post and packing. But wait! On the same page is an earthworm. It is alive and well and wriggling – and green. It has been dyed chartreuse with BaitDye. So I looked at that and there I noticed a Wormgrowers Page. It would take a stronger man than I to resist visiting a wormgrower's page. So I didn't. Resist, that is. It is but a short step, a few clicks, from worm-growing to snail-breeding.

America's equivalent of Fish & Fly is the Fly Anglers Online Magazine (www.flyanglersonline.com). This is a weekly magazine and has quickly built up a superb archive of features and instructional articles. I stumbled into this site a few weeks ago after the postman delivered a small green lump resembling, now that I know about such things, a coil of chartreuse-dyed earthworms. It was a very old silk fly-line that had been discovered in a dusty corner of a tackle shop. It had gone very sticky. I looked in a lot of books from the era of silk lines to see what they could suggest. They suggested I forget it – or they suggested strange concoctions that I didn't really fancy asking for in the chemist. So I got my web-searching gizmo to find me anything to do with 'silk' and 'fishing' and 'lines'. What it came up with was an article on Cleaning and Restoring Silk Lines by Reed F. Curry (www.fly-anglersonline.com/features/bamboo/part87.html). This turned out to be part of a vast archive of features on traditional kit, bamboo rods and similar stuff. The line-cleaning instructions begin: 'Prepare a bucket of warm (not hot) water with 1/3 box of baking soda dissolved in it,' which is the sort of thing I can understand. I haven't tried it yet. I'll let you know what happens.

Websites do not have to be big. One of the best is the homepage of one enthusiast in Devon. The Crediton Fly Fishing Club (http://freespace.virgin.net/howard.thresher/ht/home.html) fishes a few small streams in mid-Devon but has become familiar to fly fishermen the world over. This is the web at its best: a fisherman anywhere in the world can see maps of the Crediton waters, look through a large photo gallery of pools and beats on the Yeo and the Creedy, and get information on tickets, car parking and tips. You can even fill out a membership application if you want to join the club. It is clear and beautifully simple. It is the work of Howard Thresher, a vet in Crediton. By forging mutual links, the Crediton Fly Fishing Club can be found on the some of the best fishing sites around the world.

There are little gems like this from all corners of the fly-fishing world. The trick is finding them. This spring I am going to Italy. In a weak moment I promised my small daughter we could visit her best friend who left the village to live in the mountains north of Venice. Now, these mountains were made by the same firm that put up the mountains of Osttirol, a few miles north in southern Austria where I had had some magnificent high-summer fishing a couple of years ago. With a little judicious planning I might come out of this trip smelling like Father of the Year and with a spot of fishing into the bargain. I have found some astonishingly cheap flights to Venice with Ryanair – on the Internet (http://www.latebreaks.com/airlines/ryanair/faresloneur.html). All I needed was to find some information about the fishing. On LW's Fishing Site I spotted a link to The Italian Site of Fly fishing (http://www.infotel.it/ ∼ anori/index.html). So I did that.

It is written in Italian. I suppose it is entitled to be. I was stumped. Short of getting hold of a translator, I wasn't sure what to do next. That is the other thing with the Internet: it is always worth giving it a go. I typed 'translator' into the box of the search gizmo and waited. Miraculously it came up with a translator. It lives at http://translator.go.com. It is, frankly, unbelievable. All you do is to type in the address of the website you wish to translate, choose a translation from the pull-down menu (Italian-English, say) and click the 'Translate' button. It thinks about it for a bit and then, lo! the site appears, complete with all the original pictures and bits and pieces, but with the words in English.

It is English, Jim, but not as we know it. For a start the thing seemed to be obsessed with the import of soft fruits to the former Soviet Union. Take the first heading: 'That cos' it is the peach to Moscow?' it asked enigmatically, and I could picture its left eyebrow arched in ironic enquiry, a smile plucking the corner of its lips. The subtitle was not much help: 'Pale attempt to explain the inexplicable one.' It was sounding more like Nostradamus with each utterance. And it kept banging on about these peaches to Moscow.

In desperation I got out my little green Collins Gem Italian dictionary. I could see the problem: the Italian for 'peach' – *pesca* – is also the word for 'fishing'. And in the same way, *Mosca* can mean both Moscow and fly. 'The peach to Moscow' is fly fishing. I was on familiar territory now. My grandfather had been blind for half his life. He would bash out letters on an ancient typewriter and for the first few lines they made fairly good sense. Suddenly, halfway down the page, they would lapse into impenetrable code, groups of unconnected letters sprinkled with the odd number or symbol. What had happened was this: he had shifted his hands up or down, left or right on the keyboard without realizing it. Our job was to get out a typewriter and translate the gobbledegook by using the keys above, below or sideways of the ones Granddad had struck. It was quite good fun.

Before long I was confident that 'In the peach to "sand bank" peach nearly exclusively to go up itself' was a description of fishing a dry fly upstream and not nearly as unpleasant as it had appeared. And I got on even better when I discovered an Italian website with photographs of the rivers in every region at http://www.fiumi.com/ric3.htm. A few moments looking at the Italian page on 'Fishing Licences in Europe' (http://homepages.allcon.com/ ~ zaphod/eur-flyfish/licenses/welcome.html) and I was all set for a week at the end of May. Or perhaps just a long weekend – May can be a busy time for us snail breeders.

Incidentally, you will find snail breeding at http://escargot.free.fr/ eng/snail.htm.

17

The Border Years:
'94 – Teme Spirit

It was sunny when we left Banbury. It was 7 a.m. and it was that sort of early morning sun that means absolutely nothing. As often as not it can be cloudy an hour later and raining steadily an hour after that. At 8.30 we were on Clee Hill outside Ludlow and surrounded by cloud. This also means nothing: Clee Hill is always cloudy. I have only seen it clear once, twenty years ago when we went to look at a house high up on the hill. The view as we knocked on the door that day was stunning, with the Teme Valley rolled out below us and Herefordshire stretching away into the distance. When we came back out of the front door half an hour later, we had to grope our way to the car through a thick mist. We did not buy the house. I have driven that way many times since then and, as far as I know, the cloud has not lifted since.

Another half-hour to the west and the sky was darker still. Little bits of it were beginning to fall on the windscreen. All the car headlights were on. Frankly, it was gloomy outside. And gloomier yet inside.

You won't know how we came to be here, so I'll run it past you. A year ago Father and I were on our way to explore the Ithon, a Wye tributary to the west. The route had taken us, then as now, through the lush lanes of the Welsh Marches from Ludlow to Leintwardine and Knighton, following the River Teme. It looked a lovely stream, swinging over a gravel bed through sheep pastures. I like to see a sheep pasture beside a trout stream: it usually means that the land is too poor for intensive farming with intensive fertilizers. It also means that the sheep will have nibbled the bankside vegetation down to something I can back-cast over without thinking too much, an activity I prefer to avoid these days. Thinking too much, that is, not back-casting. Still with me? Anyway, we liked the look of the Teme. I got out the *Where to Fish*. This is an excellent book for the fisherman, either for reference and research or, as in the case of the upper Teme, as a work of fiction. Three spots were mentioned under the heading for 'Knighton': a mile of free fishing,

fishing and accommodation from 'Mr Habersham' on an old Craven Arms telephone number, and the same at the Red Lion, Llanfair Waterdine (three miles upstream). We were passing Llanfair Waterdine at the time and called in at the Red Lion. No, she said, they did not have water and anyway they did not let people fish it(?), and nor did anyone else, upstream or down. I must have forgotten to take my charm pills that morning – or perhaps she had forgotten hers. We left and out of sheer perversity called at the next farm along the road, Pound Farm. By all means, he said, we were welcome to fish their water on the Teme. We took one look at the infant Teme rushing over the bright gravel and said we would be back.

A year later and here we were. We were on headlights now and it was raining steadily. There was a time when I quite liked fishing in the rain. I thought in some way that I ought to catch a lot of fish: I was suffering, I was cold and damp, and all that suffering would be rewarded. It is part of our upbringing: 'No gain without pain', 'If it isn't hurting, it isn't working', 'Nothing worth doing comes easily'. And so on. This is a dour and worthy philosophy that all too often seems depressingly true. And then, a few years ago, it dawned on me that fly fishing a wild trout stream was an awful, wonderful exception to this dreary Law of Life. On a trout stream the best fly fishing comes with the very pleasantest of conditions: a gentle breeze on a warm day in May, the cool of dusk after a hot day in summer, a late warm spell after the first cold nights of autumn. Perfect. A cold, dark day of steady rain in a nearly-Welsh valley does not appear on this list and I was resigned to abandoning the day. But, then again, we were here. If nothing else, we could explore the fishing prospects for another day.

Out with the *Where to Fish*. I tried 'Mr Habersham'. The telephone number didn't work. I rang directory enquiries and they found me a Habersham on the Craven Arms exchange – but it was the wrong one. I explained who I was looking for and the lady on the other end rather thought I must mean her nephew. She gave me his number. I accused this nephew, when I got him, of having fishing and accommodation on the River Teme. He rather thought his father might have acted for an estate that did once, years ago. It was a dead end.

By this time we had passed Knighton and reached Knucklas, little more than a halt on the Heart of Wales railway line from Shrewsbury to Swansea. A lane crosses the river here and we drove down to take a look. Even in the rain it looked inviting, a swift, shallow stream threading through the pastures past a farm. I stood in the rain outside the farmhouse door of Monaughty Poeth. For anyone looking to find a bit of fishing on the upper Teme, there can hardly be a better door to knock at.

Mrs Williams runs a bed and breakfast at the farm, and a visitor who wishes to fish can do so. And if you are not staying with Mrs Williams, you can ask if you might have a day's fishing anyway and the chances are you can, for few visitors come to fish the river. That is as it should be: the Teme is a small stream with wild trout, and more than the occasional fisherman would be out of place in the landscape. The fish are small. In the recent hot, dry summers the waters of the upper Teme have disappeared from time to time and the local herons have had a good time in the shallow pools. Last year was wetter and better fish were seen. Last winter was wetter yet and with luck there will be the odd half-pounder or better in the bright riffles and runs.

I am painting it as it is. This is a delightful, small, wild stream and its trout are much the same. On these waters you will scare more than you raise and raise more than you hook. And you will walk more than you cast. And if you think you might need more than the half mile or so at the farm, there is a network of farms and farmers strung out along the river that may, if asked nicely, let you cast your fly over their water. In Mrs Williams' kitchen I met her neighbour, Maureen Bates. She has the next water upstream. She does bed and breakfast at Lower Graig, which has just a big garden's worth of the river but her visitors can fish on Mrs Williams' water or upstream, on the waters of The Graig where Mr Fred Beavans farms up towards Llanfair Waterdine. I checked at the Red Lion again this year. They do have a few yards in the garden, it seems. Above Llanfair there is Mr Ruelle of Pound farm where we had called in last year. And so it goes on. Gwen Evans of Lower House has a fine stretch of water that is notable for a few deeper holes where fish can hide in a long, dry summer when the rest of the upper river is down to its bones.

Outside it was still raining. I was herded and penned back into my car by a pack of border collies who were just keeping their hand in until something more worthy of their art came along. Below Knighton the river is a little bigger, a little less prone to drying out and every bit as pretty. We followed a narrow lane along the northern bank and crossed to the main road on the first bridge on the river at Milebrook. A small tributary dribbles into a large pool above the bridge where the main current has a fine run with deep channels between swaying beds of ranunculus, just like on a grown-up river. Most of the water in these parts is leased to the Midland Fly Fishers – but not all. We turned onto the main road to Leintwardine and found Milebrook House, a hotel and restaurant, lurking behind a lush hedge. It was still raining, and since we had nothing else to do, we went in and asked. Yes, they had two rods on the luscious stretch we had seen above the bridge and they were available for visitors. These riches were getting embarrassing.

Halfway to Leintwardine, Lingen Bridge crosses the Teme to Bucknell. Remember Mrs Williams? Upstream – Monaughty Poeth? Well, her sister Brenda is married to Peter Davies who farms hereabouts at Bucknell House, and they, too, have a stretch of the Teme, and you can fish there for the asking and the price of a pint or so. And if you like, you can stay for bed and breakfast.

It had not been a bad morning all things considered. Practically every place we had called along the River Teme had some fishing: a field or so, a mile and a bit, whatever. And almost all were willing to let an angler try his luck for a pound or so; in some cases just for the courtesy of asking. Perhaps all fishing was like this once. I like to think so, but now more and more of the small streams have been cornered by a club or syndicate, not local men who could have fished their friends' waters anyway. I do not belong to one of these clubs, or any club, and I love to stumble across these small oases of freedom. And still it rained.

At Leintwardine we stopped at the Lion Hotel for lunch. Here the river sweeps slowly around the garden of the hotel before dipping under the road bridge. Guess what? You can fish here in the hotel garden. And just up the road, on a lane just past the last petrol pump, you will find River Cottage where you can get a ticket to fish a couple of fields on the River Clun where. . . . Enough! It was time for lunch.

We had lunch. And after a pint or so we stepped out of the Lion – and blinked in the sunshine. It was only 2 p.m. We piled into the car and headed back up the valley, heading for that weedy run and pool above the bridge at Milebrook. We called in at the hotel to pay our dues, and within ten minutes of the last swallow in the Lion, we were looking down from the bridge, watching a fish rise steadily along the deep edge where the small brook trickled in.

Perhaps not fishing all morning is good for the soul, but I doubt it. But the unexpected warmth and sunshine of that afternoon was magical. Trout were rising the length of the water, purposeful stuff with the steady rhythm that is a joy to the angler. The fish that day were small and feisty as befits a small, wild river. That first one, which Father hooked and landed beneath the road bridge, was 10 inches or so and fat and beautiful. Some of those that followed were smaller, one or two were larger, up to three-quarters of a pound, which is large enough for anyone on a river like this. There are, no doubt, larger fish in the river, but they would not have made that sunny afternoon of dappled shade and glittering runs one whit better. The sun shone all that afternoon. It shone like it had never considered doing anything else since it got up that morning. It was still shining when the fish tired of feeding around 6 p.m. and we made our way back downstream. A shepherd and his dog were watching from the bridge and we chatted about his river and then walked together to the car which shared a small layby beside the bridge with a stack of fresh-cut pine poles. It is a heady smell on a warm evening, entirely unlike the toilet cleaners that claim a 'pine freshness'. The smell may not mean a thing to you, but it took me back thirty years to a field just a mile or so to the south of this spot, beside the River Lugg above Aymestry, where a load of pale-kneed boy scouts from the 1st Boxmoor troop had been dumped on just such an evening. We were, I think, the last troop in civilization to wear the huge silly hats with four dimples in the crown that mounties look good in and boy scouts don't. Dumped beside us in the field was a stack of fresh cut pine poles, provided by the Forestry Commission in the hope that when we were looking around for things to chop and whittle with our new axes and sheath-knives, we would choose the pine poles provided rather than bits of the countryside. There is a trout in that memory too, a trout caught in the Lugg, encased in leaves and mud and then baked in the embers of a camp fire. All part of the 'backwoodsman's badge', I think. Perhaps I'll try the Lugg next year.

The Border Years:
'95 – Stitched Up by the Doctors

It started, as so many of these things do, by pure chance. My first trout of 1994 came from the River Teme, on the Welsh border – literally. I was standing in gravelly shallows in Wales but the trout was rising under the far bank in England. Well, the trout rose to my fly and the usual degree of excitement ensued before the fish slid under the net. Other fish followed on that sunny afternoon after a dismal grey morning, and it was as pleasant a start to a fishing season as you could want. I had left the car in a layby just beside the bridge. The air was still as we took down the tackle that evening and there was a sappy scent of freshly cut pine from a pile of logs beside the layby.

A smell like that can do it to you: I was back thirty-something years to a field beside the River Lugg. A large pile of freshly cut pine poles had been dumped a few yards from the river and a troop of boy scouts had been dumped beside it. The pine poles had come from the Forestry Commission, the boy scouts had come from Chaulden, then one of the newest bits of the new town of Hemel Hempstead, many hours' journey to the east. We had come, for some reason, in a furniture removal van. The pine poles had been provided in the hope that we would build our cunningly whittled and lashed camp stools and suspension bridges and counterbalanced water-raisers without denuding the surrounding woodlands.

We were to be there for a fortnight in that summer of 1962. It was the longest any of us had been away from home or family and there was a visitors' day halfway through when those parents who had cars and the inclination to make such a mammoth trek could come and assure themselves that their offspring were still intact. My parents came with a large fruitcake and strict instructions from Mrs Perman, who lived at the other end of our terrace, to photograph her son Raymond eating something, as she was convinced that he would starve without his mother to cook his favourite foods. I found that photograph last year after the trip to the Teme that had started all this off.

Raymond and I are grinning out of a faded print from a box-Brownie. There are other photographs from that visit: me as a spindly lad making my solo voyage in a canoe, the culmination of my 'canoeists' badge'. I remembered that one. Amongst other things we had to jump into the river fully dressed, take our clothes off while treading water and then climb back into a canoe. This is not an easy thing to do. But it was probably the 'backwoodsman's badge' that I got there on the summer camp by the Lugg that set me on the course to wherever I am now. One element of the 'backwoodsman's badge' was to build a shelter from natural materials and to sleep a night in it. We also had to cook a backwoodsman's meal: a rabbit or a fish, cooked without implements or utensils over a fire beside our shelter. We chose a fish. It was a trout.

It was not the first trout I had seen caught and eaten. My father had taken me fishing the summer before in Scotland. He had caught a few small trout with a murderous quill minnow armed with three trebles dragged through a pool on a burn. He had fried them in a frying pan over a small stove with some sausages and then we had driven off, crushing the frying pan which had been left to cool beneath the car. But all that was something fathers did. It was on the River Lugg that I first realized that catching a trout – and eating it – was a possibility for a small boy.

I didn't catch the trout. It was Stephen Ling. Lingo (we were painfully unimaginative with nicknames: I was Beero) was in the same class at school but was far wiser in the ways of fish. He had a fixed spool reel. He had a spoon spinner, something I had never seen and frankly could not see working. The Lugg was deep alongside the field, deep enough for an embryonic canoeist to tread water whilst removing his clothes, and there were shady bushes overhanging the undercut banks. Lingo stood in a reed bed on our bank and cast downstream, across into the shady depths. I don't recall how long it took. I think I had lost interest when he was shouting at me to give him a hand. Reared on roach and suchlike, we were not used to the sheer wayward power of a trout. Eventually it was subdued, dragged into the reeds and up onto the field. Later that evening it was wrapped in leaves, plastered with mud from the riverbank and buried in the embers of the fire in front of our backwoodsman's shelter. I don't remember eating this fish: the 'backwoodsman's badge' just required us to capture and cook it. I rather think Lingo and I survived the night in the wilderness on my mother's fruitcake.

It was a whiff of pine resin in a layby beside the Teme that had started all this, and the Lugg at Amestry was only a few miles from the Teme. This spring I visited the Lugg. I had no plans. It would be pleasant to fish that same spot but that might not be possible. I had some doubts that I would be able to find the place again. We did not doubt we would be able to find some fishing along this pleasant little river: the year before, on the River Teme, we had found a dozen places around Knighton where a farmer would let us fish his stretch for a day or a guesthouse had retained a rod or so.

We arrived at the Lugg below Aymestrey, a clean and dashing stream that tumbles alongside a young conifer plantation. A woman was walking a dog and I asked her if it might be possible to fish hereabouts. The fishing was leased, she thought, to a syndicate of doctors from Worcester. In Aymestrey I called in at the village shop and explained that I had camped and fished somewhere around there thirty years before. She said that there had been camping in the field, between the two weirs, but that had been stopped for years. She also told us that all the fishing had been bought up – even the local lads could not fish round here: it was a shame. Too right. It was the same story at The Riverside Inn, but the landlord did direct us to a farm that might have a bit of fishing up the valley. On the narrow lane to the farm I saw the old campsite beneath the steep wooded bank where thirty years before one of us Kestrels had fallen onto his head from a tree and that night peed blood in his urine. Magical days. But at the farm ahead there was no fishing. The farms had been let without the fishing. That had been let to the syndicate of doctors from Worcester – or somewhere. And so it went on. We did find one stretch of the river at Kinsham unleased – but that was because the owner would never consider letting anyone fish his water. This is deep, deep countryside, this last bit of England before the hills of Wales, another world and another time. Near Presteigne, for a moment, I thought we had struck paydirt. A hearty old gentleman and his dolphin-chested wife allowed that, although their fishing was leased, they had retained a rod, a rod that Peter and I might share – provided we told no one where we had been fishing and took no photographs. 'We don't want to be invaded,' she confided to us. I said I thought it unlikely: a few small trout from the upper reaches of the River Lugg were hardly in the same league as Kit Williams' *Masquerade* and a bejewelled hare in solid gold. She gave me a sort of look that spoke of a lifetime of wisdom or one too many sherries before lunchtime.

'We've been lucky so far,' she said, 'They don't seem to cross the A49.' I must have looked puzzled – who don't cross the A49?

'The Indians!' she confided. I was about to point out that anyone who has managed to traverse two continents and an ocean is hardly going to be daunted by crossing the main road from Ludlow to Leominster should they wish to. It isn't even a dual carriageway. But I didn't – there didn't seem much point. We just left and pushed on up the Lugg.

Beyond Presteigne the story was much the same: the river was let, seemingly to more doctors, these from Birmingham. Finally, as the valley steepened and narrowed at the top of the river, we found a farmer who had four fields where we might fish at will. Up here you could step across the river and at times, he said, the river dried up completely. I knew how it felt.

Listen: the Lugg is a pretty river. It is clean and healthy, it passes through no major towns before Leominster. But it is nothing special. It is not the Test or the Itchen. And you and I can fish none of it. And neither can the people who live in the valley of the Lugg. Just a few doctors from Worcester. Or Birmingham.

It was past lunchtime. Way past. We sat in the car in a gloom and mused on the parlous state of fishing in a country where such things have come to pass. If you had passed me clause four of the Labour Party constitution at that moment, I would have opened a vein and signed it in my own blood. We had not yet wet a line. I opened *Where to Fish*. The rivers of the Welsh Borders below Llangollen are all tributaries of the Wye and the Severn. We had tried the Wye. We would go north to the Severn and see what could be saved of the day.

Llan-y-Blodwel, despite all evidence to the contrary, is in England. But only just. It lies on the River Tanat. The entry in *Where to Fish* was typically terse:

TANAT (tributary of the Vyrnwy): Trout (good average size), chub and grayling, but fewer than there used to be. Llan-y-Blodwel (Salop). Horseshoe Inn has $1^1/2$ miles (dt £3), 3 rods per day, fly only.

That hardly does it justice. It is easy to miss the road to Llan-y-Blodwel from the south and so we missed it. From the north you approach the inn over the high arch of a narrow bridge over the Tanat. The Horseshoe Inn nestles. The village may have a name out of *Ivor the Engine*, but the Horseshoe Inn looks like something out *of Tess of the d'Urbervilles* with its black and white, half-timbered buildings. It was built a century or so before Elizabeth I came to the throne and a mildly alarming bulge developed in the north-west corner a few years later. Not much seems to have changed since then. In the days of coaches it became a coaching inn, although it is not obvious where those coaches could have been on their way to. Perhaps they didn't bother once they got to Llan-y-Blodwel. I wouldn't.

The Horseshoe Inn is clearly a popular place at any other time than 3.30 on a Thursday afternoon in April. There are picnic tables arranged along the riverside beside a splendid pool with a deep run beneath the twisted bole of an ancient tree on the far bank. And there was a fish rising in the run. Looking at water we were actually allowed to fish was a rarity that day; seeing a fish rise in it was an unlooked-for bonus. We got our tickets from Angela, the landlady, and tackled up in a fever.

I missed that first fish in the run below the bridge. I am not surprised. After the morning, I was wound up like a watch-spring, and when the fish came obligingly to my fly, I snatched it out of his mouth as sweet as a nut. But I got the second. The first fish of a day is an enormous, unspoken relief. You can relax after the first fish. The cloud of the morning had lifted, the sun had come out and it was a perfect afternoon in spring.

The Horseshoe Inn has about a mile of single bank either side of the bridge. The old smithy that had once served the coaches lies across the lane with a garden going down to the river. I always feel rather iffy about fishing up someone's garden, so we leap-frogged upstream. Here the river bottom is bedrock, with sharp ridges of rock across a swift channel sluicing into a huge pothole of a pool. A few fish were pecking at the surface where the tongue of the current slackened in the middle. They looked like small fish – especially as I could not cover them wearing thigh waders. Up in the rocky neck of the pool a single fish began to rise, tucked in between the current and a hard place where an eroded hollow must allow a fish to lie beside the tumbling water. A fly cast across the current to this spot drags within half a second and the books will tell you that a self-respecting trout will have no truck with such a fly. Happily, the trout had not read the books – or had no self-respect – for, after half a dozen casts had sent the fly skidding over its head, the trout grabbed hold.

As the fish and I settled our differences in the large pool below, another fish began to rise in the fast water of the rocky run above. Contrariwise, the 'small fish' in the body of the pool had stopped. It dawned on me what was happening: as the hatch of fly strengthened, the trout that had been feeding below were moving up, under the press of competition, into the faster water. Somehow I seem to have to learn all this stuff anew each season. After number two had been photographed and freed, I trotted the fly upstream over this eager feeder. The trout was lurking under a ledge in the eroded hollows of the bedrock, and as the fly danced out of the main current over this ledge, the large trout detached from the shadows and rose vertically towards the fly. Any trout that does this to me early on in the day, early in the season, is in no real danger of being caught. The sight of the fish coming up through the water is quite enough to set my nerves a-tingling and I will strike far too quickly. Later in the season, later in the day, I may just be blasé enough to wait until the trout has turned down again before tightening. Maybe.

And so it went on, one fish landed for one fish missed, pricked or lost, through what remained of that sunny afternoon. The last fish, from the top of the beat, was the best at around a pound, which is perfect for a rocky little river. It does not last forever in late April. By 6 p.m. it was weakening; by 6.30 the river was quiet again. We packed up, had a pint in the dark and cosy bar, and then headed for home.

Stuff them: if they leave me the Horseshoe Inn and the Tanat, the doctors can keep the Lugg.

*   *   *

After this story appeared in *Trout and Salmon* magazine, a letter to the editor complained of my intemperate view of doctors. The writer suggested that I take care never to fall ill in Hereford.

'Alone and lost in that tight little world of rock and water.' (*Posted to the Highlands*)

'This was Terry's sort of fishing: you did it sitting on your backside with almost no effort and the fish jumped out of the water to get at the thing.' (*The Duns Tew Snooker Club*)

'Limestone does something to a river... the blue-green clarity looks more transparent, the bottom clearer, than if there were no water at all.' (*Two Cheers for OFFSTED*)

'Bagworthy Water, a stream of ill-repute and chockfull of Doones at its headwaters.' (*The Doonesday Book*)

'It was the first time I had hooked two fish at the same time in a river.'
(*Boys from the Grey Stuff*)

'This was one of the chaps who Know What They Are Doing' – Andrew Ryan on the Najerilla. (*The Lost Weeekend*)

'Blokes from Banbury don't get to drive dog sleds very often.' (*Doing it Doggy Style*)

'The little fly disappeared in a fluster and a lively fish was dashing about the place.'
(*The River Roo*)

'We were not sure if pollack counted.' (*The Tangle o' the Isles*)

'He called across to me and I saw his rod bent against the background of the Cuillins.' (*The Tangle o' the Isles*)

'The tunnel spewed us blinking into the sunlight of a spacious alpine valley' – the world of the upper Dorfer. (*The Mile High Club*)

Signal crayfish – 'Like the GIs they are here for the duration. We might as well enjoy it.' (*Over-sized, Over-sexed and Over Here*)

'Jolly fat faces… in coffee houses peer down at this idiot in a tumbling mountain stream two metres below their well-upholstered bottoms.' (*The Mustard and the Fischmeister*)

The Border Years:
'96 – The Lugg at Last

I peaked too early. The zenith of my athletic career was a summer's day in 1962 when I beat Len Heron in a cross-country race. You had to know Len Heron to appreciate the enormity of this triumph. He was our hero. He was everyone's hero. He was a bit older than us. He was a brilliant sportsman at almost everything and a schoolboy international at rugby union. The only reason I was even *in* a race with Len Heron was because we were all away at scout camp and the whole troop had to run this race. It was a handicap race: we youngsters started way out in front so that we had no idea how close the pursuit was. We dogged along in the dust and sun and when we got to the final ridge overlooking the campsite there were still just two of us, Lingo and me. We looked round at a noise back down the path and there was Len Heron. He had overtaken everyone but us. I fled down the track, leaving Lingo behind. By the road at the bottom of the ridge Len Heron had passed Lingo and I could hear him catching me. It was the stuff of those awful running nightmares. My legs hardly worked as I panted up to the gate of the camp. The field lay just below the road and there was a merciful slope down from the gate, which gave me some momentum to stagger across the grass towards the river and the finishing line. I could hear his feet pounding up behind – schoolboy rugby internationals do not give up – and I glanced round to see the rhythmic swing of his plaster cast. Did I mention he had broken his wrist and was running with his arm in plaster? No? And I crossed the line.

I was fishing a small river last weekend. I waded the stream, climbed the bank and found myself in that same field. Beside the River Lugg.

I had tried to fish the Lugg last year. Then I called at a picturesque, half-timbered inn beside the bridge at Aymestrey to find that the fishing hereabouts was let to a syndicate. The landlord suggested I might try the farmer upstream but there the story was the same, and so it continued through that day, up the valley to Presteigne and beyond into the Welsh headwaters: water, water everywhere and not a drop to fish. So I gave up and went elsewhere.

And then, on a day in late April, I had a phone call: a letting had fallen vacant and that picturesque pub now found itself with a bit of the Lugg. The next day I packed wife and smallest child into the car and drove down through the orchards of Herefordshire at the loveliest time of the year.

We arrived at 6 p.m. There was just about time for a brief attempt on the river before dinner, so I left wife and smallest child to unpack and togged up. A wooded track leads west behind the pub and the Lugg rattles down a stony run alongside, deep in the shadow of a high limestone cliff. At the top of this run the Lugg comes swinging through a double bend forming two deep pools incised into the meadow. This pattern of stony run and a chicane of deep pools is repeated up the valley from the weir at the top of the pub water. These deep pools looked very trouty. At each pair of pools, of course, the channel swings from side to side. One pool is best fished from one bank, the other pool from the other, so the fisherman has to find a place to ford – not easy in the heavy water of spring. You have to concentrate. And so it was that I heaved myself up the far bank and suddenly found myself back in 1962. There was the gate down from the road, a new gate but the same slope with the steep wooded ridge beyond the lane. When I looked back where I had just fished, I saw the deep pool where we trod water whilst removing a pair of pyjamas as part of our 'canoeists' badge' and the gravelly shallows where we cleaned the patrol's greasy dishes with the handful of gritty sand that Baden-Powell confidently asserted will scour the things spotless. It won't. Not with sausages. Beans, yes. Sausages, no. We lived, as I recall, almost exclusively on baked beans and sausages for that fortnight: it was all we could cook. Even that took long enough over our small, damp wood fires. It took even longer to wash up. Food, one way or another, had figured pretty largely on my first visit to the River Lugg.

Food figured pretty largely on the second visit, too. 'Wild Venison with Wild Mushrooms and Port Wine Sauce' awaited me when I walked back down to the inn in the last of the spring sun that evening. Everything served at the inn is cooked by chef Steve Reynolds. Steve trained in Mayfair at Albert Roux's 'Le Gavroche'. It shows. It was perfect.

Valerie and Steve Bowen bought the inn some years ago. Then it was called The Crown and had been closed for several years. They found Steve Reynolds and wisely turned the kitchen over to him, while Val and Steve did everything else in and around the charming sixteenth-century inn. An old stable block was converted to make two cosy suites with the river running below the window, the intimate hillside gardens were restored and, finally, last month the fishing on the River Lugg was acquired. The result is that rarest of things: a real cosy old fishing inn serving splendid ale and sumptuous provender. You start using words like 'ale' and 'provender' after wild venison and wild mushrooms in port wine sauce. And so to bed.

There are perks in owning a riverside inn. Steve was coming fishing this morning. We tackled up on a table beside the bridge and waited for an old friend of Steve's who was to join us.

In the summer of 1962, at Presteigne, the next village up the river from that field of damp boy scouts, there still lived the most famous of Lugg fishermen. Cosmo Barrett was an upholsterer by trade, a fly-fisherman by inclination and instinct and a wizard on the small rivers of the Welsh Borders – 'he could get a fish out of a hedge'. In his workshop in Presteigne he made superb fly-rods in split cane and created a series of flies with reversed hackles that became justly famous when they were included in Hardy's catalogues between the wars. Two of these, Barrett's Bane and his Professor, are still popular today. By 1962 Cosmo Barrett had all but stopped making rods and tying flies, although he was still fishing.

Lingo and I knew nothing of all this. While Cosmo Barrett was winkling trout from the waters of the Lugg with a delicate reversed hackled number, we were attempting something similar with a small pike spoon, and at least one trout was too stupid to appreciate the difference.

But there was another newcomer to the Lugg that same summer. Peter Flint was a jeweller, a goldsmith and silversmith, with businesses in Birmingham. He had discovered the fine fishing on the Lugg a few seasons before. He had met Cosmo Barrett in his shop in the quiet little town of Presteigne and the two fished together whenever Peter visited the river on holiday. For a time Peter tied the flies that Cosmo sold in his shop. In 1962 Peter and his wife decided to give up the Birmingham rat-race. They sold up and moved down to the Lugg. When Cosmo Barrett retired, Peter took over the Barrett workshop and business, restoring antiques and selling fishing tackle.

Thirty-five years on, Peter Flint still lives hereabout and still fishes the waters of the Lugg. It would be hard to design a finer old gentleman of the river. He still uses his original Barrett split cane rod and still ties the flies that have taken so many fish from the waters of the Lugg and Wye and Cothi.

The river that morning was still high but the sun showed some promise. Peter selected a Professor with its two hackles, a white and a natural red, tied at the bend and a dubbed body of creamy sheep's wool plucked from a fence. It floats jauntily, is easily seen and, on these tree-lined streams, the hackle-shrouded hook rarely gets caught in the leaves. A jeweller's eyeglass on an improvised stalk clipped to his spectacles is Peter's ingenious answer to small hooks and fine tippets.

It is a rare pleasure to fish a river with a man who has fished it for half a lifetime and to hear stories of a man who has fished it a lifetime before that. As we fished up the Lugg he talked of other stretches up and down the river, the unsuspected fish in this pool or that spring-fed tributary, of the mayfly hatches of the past and the fish that abounded in the river. Wonderful stuff – but bloody galling as we fished on without a sign of fish through that April morning.

We still had nothing by the time Peter had to leave us. Steve and I fished on. I changed to a heavy nymph. I was fishing it deep through pools on a bend when something fairly significant latched onto the end. I don't claim to have struck: it was just there when I went to retrieve. I wanted to feel I had played some part in the catching of this fish and so I struck now. It was a mistake. The fish was doing very nicely without my help and all I achieved was to pull the hook free. That sort of thing happens on a fishless Saturday morning in April. We did not lose heart, exactly. At that time of year you usually have only to wait a little, until the strengthening sun warms the water and the action resumes. That could be after lunch or it could be some time in May. We decided to wait until after lunch. Thirty-four years before, Saturday lunch had been the high spot of the fortnight camp. It was visitors' day. My parents made the long trip from Hemel Hempstead bearing a vast fruit cake, thereby saving us from those terminal diseases associated with an exclusive diet of sausages and baked beans. Fruitcake warmed gently for three and a half hours in a moderate car is a good lunch. Good – but in truth it is not a patch on 'Crusted Lamb with Thyme and Rosemary Jus' and a pint of Otter Ale at the bar while Mr Reynolds puts it all together in the kitchen.

I had just settled down to that pint and a chat with wife and smallest daughter who had spent their morning in Ludlow, when there was a flurry at the door and Steve appeared in the bar with a lively trout in his net. He had left me choosing from the menu and had decided to have a last chuck with a dry fly in the lively little run beside the pub. The trout happened on the second cast. It is hard to give 'Panfried Breast of Chicken with a Vermouth and Herb Sauce' the attention it deserves when the trout are beginning to move in a pretty river on the Welsh border. I did my best.

The sun broke through that afternoon. The water warmed and we began to catch trout. Rises were still few and far between, so I stayed deep with a small goldhead pheasant-tail nymph that I have persuaded myself has just sufficient twinkle to attract attention in the depths of a pool still tinged with colour. A dry fly on the dropper gives me some sort of clue to things occurring below and, from time to time, will pick up the odd fish with an excess of springtime exuberance.

We spent that afternoon working upstream through the meadows above the inn, casting across the stream to the vertical bank on the outside of each bend. If we got it right, the nymph would bounce off that earthen wall to drop down into the few inches of slower water channelled hard against the bank. The little dry fly swims down the line of the current, swivelling and then steadying as the nymph straightens the tippet below, pulling the dry fly into the surface tension of the water. The dry fly creeps past, almost awash and then sinks. Usually it is a gradual process: the little fly can be seen, swimming along just beneath the surface, unable to float against the pull of the heavier nymph in the deep turbulence of the pool. Just occasionally the disappearance is more sudden. The fly is gone. The tippet, swimming close to the eroded bank, has caught for a second on an exposed rootlet and the dry fly on the dropper is tugged through the surface. You will strike at nothing. Try this for autumn grayling and for three out of four casts you will be striking at sunken leaves plucking at the tippet. In spring it is always worth a strike. And sometimes, not often, but just often enough, there is something else: a tug in reply and a gleam of a pale flank twisting below the surface. You have caught a Lugg trout.

We caught a few trout like this on that afternoon and then, as it neared the time to leave, one final fish with a taste for the theatrical rose in the run beside the black and white timbering of the Riverside Inn. I had my first Lugg trout on a dry fly.

But not, I think, my last.

Doing it Doggy-Style

It was extraordinary. I just wanted to stand still for a moment and wallow in what was occurring. But there's a fat chance of standing still with eight frenzied dogs zipping you across the snow and ice on a dog sled.

I was going fishing. For me, 'going fishing' conjures up shady alders beside a sun-dappled river or a tramp across springy heather to a distant loch. It doesn't involve dog sleds, mittens and twenty degrees of frost. And that's *centigrade*, mind you, not girly Fahrenheit degrees.

But last month I went fishing in Sweden. We were in Åre, a ski resort in the mountains close to the Norwegian border. We had done the skiing thing, wobbling about and frightening ourselves spitless whilst highly-trained midgets disguised as children of three and four years old flashed between us with sickening nonchalance.

Åre is a serious ski resort: the following week it was host to the World Cup Finals. But beyond the ski slopes and lifts of Åre there is a vast wilderness of forest and mountain. These are not the steep, pointy mountains of the Alps, these are ancient mountains, worn round and friendly by successive ice sheets. Reindeer roam the undulating snowfields of the tops and elk meander through the forests of the lower slopes. And dotted amongst this lot are small mountain lakes. There are fish in these little lakes, the arctic char, beautiful to behold and even better to eat. So wife, daughter and I set out to catch ourselves some.

There are several ways to move about this wintry wilderness. Wiry types with firm jaws use cross-country skis. Going uphill on skis looks like very hard work. Ski-mobiles are huge fun but noisy. At Åre Björnens we found another way: dog sled.

In these days, when hunting with dogs teeters on the brink of legislation and fishing is supposedly next on the antis' hit-list, there is something deliciously anarchical about going fishing with dogs.

I have read *White Fang* and its tales of ravening huskies. So I stood very still when one of Peter's dog came up and licked my hand. Perhaps it was just tasting. Then it rolled over, begging to be tickled, but I wasn't falling for that old trick. Alice is twelve and hasn't read *White Fang*, so she was in amongst the pack of excited dogs, stroking and patting and generally having a good time. Peter, our guide, had a little surprise for us. There were not enough drivers that day: I would have to drive our sled myself. Blokes from Banbury don't get to drive dog sleds very often.

Alice and Judi sat on the sled, arms and legs tucked in, 'for when you hit trees,' Peter said. Hit trees? 'Yes, you will hit trees.' I stood on the runners at the back. I learnt about steering, a bit, and I learnt about the brake. I stood on it with both feet and strained down against the sled while Peter untied us from the tree. And we were off.

That's the thing with a dog sled. It only has one gear: flat out. If you want to slow down, you stand on the brake. If you want to stop, you tie your sled to a tree. The dogs pull just as lustily for all three.

And we did hit trees. Our team was following Peter's sled but when he turned our team would cut the corner to follow and we bounced off any small tree in the way. Interesting sort of travel.

It is hard to spot a lake when you get there. It looks much the same as the rest of the countryside under half a metre of snow. We tethered the dogs and walked on another few metres. Peter said we were on the lake. To prove it he scraped away the snow and began to bore a hole in the ice with a giant auger. Ice is hard stuff. It takes ten minutes of hard work and a lot of panting to drill down through a metre of the stuff. Then the auger broke through and a gout of water slushed out onto the ice. I took the auger and went off to make my own hole.

I will not dwell on that fishing. Ice fishing is great fun because of where you are and how you got there. The fishing itself is simply jigging a maggot near the bottom. The fish, when it came, was not big. It was not even an arctic char. By an uncanny coincidence it was a burbot, a fish I had never seen before because the burbot is extinct in Britain. And it is hardly a native to a small lake halfway up a mountain in Sweden. The burbot is the only freshwater member of the cod family. Like the cod, it has a large and oily liver, a valuable delicacy in a frozen land. Some time ago the herdsmen of these mountains had seeded the lakes with burbot to ensure a source of this oil. They are still here.

21

Out of Print, Out of Mind

I finally got my hands on this first one in a tackle shop near Hereford just last weekend, but I have sort of known it for years before that. I bet you have, too. Whenever you see those tasteful, vaguely antique prints of fish in tasteful, vaguely antique pubs and restaurants, you can bet your socks they are reproductions from Lydon and Fawcett, the illustrator and engraver of *British Fresh-Water Fishes*, written by the Reverend William Houghton.

I did not buy the book for its illustrations. Frankly, they are horrid. The original edition of 1879 may have been exquisite, but you can hardly expect works of art from something printed in Hong Kong in 1981 and sold in Hereford for a knock-down sale price of £5. I bought it for the words of the Reverend W. Houghton, which no amount of poor printing can tarnish.

In every great fishing book the man is clearly visible behind the words. You fish with him on his river or listen to his boatman as he rows across the loch. But you do not meet the Reverend Houghton on the bank, rather you find him in his study in the rectory of Preston-upon-the-Weald Moors in Shropshire. I see him as rather dusty with an academic stoop and the rather endearing habit of chuckling softly at his own obscure classical jokes. I fancy he wears one of those quilted smoking jackets and perhaps a silly skullcap with a tassel. These days he is more of a scholar than a fisherman. Unlike many fishing scholars, he is charmingly frank about the limits of his own knowledge, and for each species he quotes the opinion and technical description of Dr Günther of the British Museum. The effect is rather like Beachcomber calling on the authority of Dr Strabismus of Utrecht (whom God preserve). The dear old Reverend excels in the literary line. He has scoured the classics for references to each fish and translates from the originals for our edification. Here are Fascinating Facts, Lore and Legend and a Gourmet's Guide to British Fish all tumbled into one. We learn, for example, that 'the expression "to gudgeon a man," i.e. to deceive him, may . . . have reference to ease with which so delicate a morsel as a Gudgeon is swallowed'. The Reverend then supports this conclusion with a similar expression in French. But wait! We then learn that

Latham in his Large Dictionary observes: 'Of Gudgeons having been swallowed with particular ease there is no very good evidence; though there is a good deal in favour of the Loach having been so treated. The Loach is said, in most notices, to have been not unfrequently tossed off in toasts, or swallowed in a glass of wine, by the gallants of the Elizabethan period.'

Pass the port, Reverend, and tell me another one.

* * *

There is a man of a very different stamp behind another angling classic. I can never read *The Practical Angler* by W.C. Stewart without conjuring a vision of Field Marshal Montgomery of Alamein: '. . . most works upon angling,' he asserts in his downright, hectoring way, 'being rather amusing rather than instructive. The angler will not find this the case in the following volume: if he finds nothing instructive, he will certainly find nothing amusing; and we found our claims to the attention of the angling community solely upon the ground of information we have to convey . . .'.

He is quite correct in both particulars. *The Practical Angler* is supremely confident, thoroughly practical and – straighten up, that man at the back there! – an admirably logical manual for border rivers, anglers, for the fishing of.

It is a fascinating little book. Stewart prides himself on his thoroughness towards his fishing. He records his catches and methods and systematically varies his flies and lures to measure their efficacy. Take a good long look at those figures. There are some surprises. On one occasion a fellow 'well-known angler' was bragging about the fish he had caught. Nothing surprising there. He claims to have: 'only caught four trouts, but that they weighed half a pound each. The statement naturally excited surprise and suspicion. Such an "average" in that particular stream was unusual on any day . . .' . They went on to rifle through his creel when he was distracted and found only two-ounce tiddlers. But look, on the waters of a Tweed tributary in the golden age a century and a half ago, what 'naturally excited surprise and suspicion'. Four half-pound fish.

Later he describes his own highest average using a minnow, 'because the largest trout taken by rod and line are usually caught by it'. So how large are these trout?

We once took with the minnow, between Bowland and Stow, twenty trout, the whole we got that day which weighed fifteen pounds, and we never got such a large average size of trout in any of the other tributaries of the Tweed, or even in Tweed itself.

And this is using his preferred minnow tackle with a treble trailing '. . . at least three inches behind the minnow... The object of having it so far behind the minnow is to catch, by the outside of the body, those trout which bite shy or miss the minnow.'

Well, it would.

*   *   *

There could hardly be a greater contrast between fisherman than between W.C. Stewart and Arthur Ransome. Stewart, realizing at the age of just twenty-five years that he is the finest trout-fishing machine that nature has assembled to date, sees it as his clear Calvinistic duty to enlighten such heathens as fish otherwise. Or at the very least to pity them. An older and infinitely wiser Arthur Ransome would simply smile and go off fishing. Alone if possible.

Stewart instructs you how to fish. Ransome tells you what it is like to be a fisherman.

Rod and Line is a famous collection of weekly articles Ransome contributed to the *Manchester Guardian* between 1925 and 1929. I have just flicked through to the beginning of my copy to check those dates and half an hour has passed as I stopped to re-read one well-loved piece – and then just another. And so on. Each little gem is about four pages long, which is enough to let you read just one more. I will give you only one quotation from this delicious book: you will understand why. It is from a piece entitled 'On Giving Advice to Beginners':

The better a fisherman is, the more conscious is he of his imperfections and consequently the more shy of giving advice to others. He is also likely to have learnt that the chief pleasure of fishing is to be still beginning and, unselfishly, he will be very unwilling to steal from a beginner any of the delight of finding out for himself.

And I envy anyone opening a copy for the first time.

*   *   *

There will always be a place for the straightforward 'How To Do It' fishing book. In Ransome's time (or soon after) there was one of the finest ever for the trout fisherman. *Modern Trout Fishing* was never going to be a title to wear well through the years, but W. Carter Platts' superb attempt to cover all branches of the sport was in print for the next twenty years. What is so special about this book, unique perhaps amongst practical manuals on almost any subject, is that much of it is *more* valuable now than when it was written sixty years ago. Pish-tush and fol-de-rol! How can this be so? I will tell you.

Carter Platts begins his preface: 'This volume is the result of an honest effort to describe, with such impartiality as I am capable of, the many and various legal methods of catching trout with rod and line in common usage today in the British Isles.' And he does just that.

There is something very strange in the soul of the British angler that eschews one method or other as being 'too easy' and hence 'unsporting' and then spares no effort to make the difficult, sporting, method easier. I have never understood this – any more than I can understand why some folk take up cycling for exercise and then get the lightest, most efficient bicycle they can buy in order to reduce the effort of cycling.

There is none of this nonsense from Carter Platts. Here you will read of the delights and wiles of worm fishing. I know other books talk of worm fishing but they can never refrain from saying that, whereas worming in a low summer river is frightfully OK because it is jolly difficult, worming in a flooded river is very far from OK because it is easy. No one seems to make this distinction in salmon fishing.

With an even-handedness that I have seen in no other fishing book, before or since, Carter Platts tells us about worming in a flood, upstream nymphing, fishing a minnow on a fly rod, dobbling a bait though a bush, fishing the dry fly, spinning for Thames trout, trotting a stonefly creeper and several other things we would all find very satisfying without wishing our mothers to hear about them. He is full of humour and enthusiasm, and each time I read a chapter about some method I have yet to try, I have to get up and walk around the room a bit while I think about it. I tingle. I have already planned an assault on a Thames trout. I'll let you know how I get on.

*   *   *

I once devised a golden rule of thumb for examining any new book on fishing. It is this: look in the index under the letter 'K'. If the entries thereunder consist of 'knots', 'Kennet, River' and 'Kite, Oliver', put the thing down: it is just another fishing book. The best book on fish and fishing to have been published in the last thirty years scintillates with fascinating insights and information, trivial or deep, but never dull. This book has just two entries under K. They are 'Kemal Ataturk' and 'Kidney-stones, treatment for'. And you can readily see that herein you are going to find something new, something you have not come across in lesser books on fish and fishing. I will tell you the name of this book. It is *The New Compleat Angler* by Stephen Downes and Martin Knowelden. You will have seen it. You may well own it because fifteen years ago it was one of those books that fishermen were given as presents by aunts or wives or daughters. But you may well not have *read* it.

There is a reason for this. First, anything with a title harking back to Walton is apt to be a bit of a Christmas Present of a book, designed for the giver more than the receiver. Secondly, the book is big with huge and beautiful illustrations. This should be a bonus but it tends to reinforce the first impression: you turn the pages and admire and decide to read the bits round the edge some other time. It is not a book you can curl up with. Thirdly, it covers the whole panoply of British fish from perch to salmon, through charr to eels and bream and beyond. Modern fishing, like much of modern living, has tended towards the specialist. We are stillwater flyfishermen or we are carp anglers or we are nymph fishermen. *The New Compleat Angler* does not even confine its scope to fishing. In fact there is precious little on the subject of how to catch the things at all. But then there is everything else. You can open the thing on any page you fancy and there you will find something new and fascinating and funny about fish, the universe and everything.

*   *   *

Where *The New Compleat Angler* is high, wide and handsome, *Fishing a Highland Stream* is just the opposite. It is a small and intimate gem. It is not concerned with fishing in general or even just trout fishing or even fly-fishing for trout on small rivers. It is a personal account of one man's love affair with one small, rocky stream.

The River Truim is a spatey tributary of the Spey. Forty years ago John Inglis Hall glanced at the Truim as it passed beneath the railway line that was carrying him north to a sporting hotel on a salmon river. The salmon river was a disappointing mistake and, remembering an isolated hotel beside a blue stormy loch with a thin river beside the railway line, he got off the train at Dalwhinnie. It is that scene where the hero glances just once at the heroine in a party of friends. They hardly notice each other but we saw that glance and also we know they are the stars of the film, so We Know What Will Happen In The End.

Fishing a Highland Stream is a scrapbook of their affair, this man with this river, over the next ten years. As he describes how he fishes it, stone by stone, run by riffle, up from its confluence with the Spey, we see the stone where: 'I came upon a salmon . . . resting before a move upstream, and walked to within a yard of it. For this wholly insufficient reason I always expect to find a large trout there but never do.' We see the stickle where, 'five years ago, in the field on the left bank, I was bitten by a small white horse which crept up behind me quietly, meanly and with malice and nipped me hard on the left cheek of the bottom'. Not exactly 'a cigarette that bears the lipstick traces: an airline ticket to romantic places' – but you get the drift. You will see the Truim through the eyes of a man who loved it and you will love it too. It is irresistible.

Mr Inglis Hall chose, whenever possible (and quite often when it was not possible), to fish with a dry fly. It was how he liked to fish. What that young and zealous Scot, W.C. Stewart would have made of this romantic and in-efficient notion I shudder to think.

More or less what he would expect of an Englishman, I imagine.

*   *   *

Only two of these books are in print at the moment. *The Practical Angler* has just been published in a beautiful leather-bound and boxed edition by the Flyfisher's Classic Library. This includes a new and thoroughly researched biography of Stewart. The Flyfisher's Classic Library (Tel: 01626 834 182) is also reprinting their edition of *Rod and Line*. They are not cheap. But then nor is a first edition in immaculate condition of some of these. No matter: there have been several editions of most of them and you can buy a good, readable edition of any of them for somewhere around £10 (and some of them for much less).

Ronald Coleby of Carlisle is one of the most knowledgable dealers in old sporting books. I asked him for his valuation for each of these books. The first figure is what you might expect to pay for one of the cheaper editions. The second figure is the value of a first edition in good condition.

Rev. W. Houghton, *British Fresh-water Fishes* (originally in two volumes), 1879 – £14 (mine was £5 in a sale) for the 1981 reprint; 1st edition up to £600.

W.C. Stewart, *The Practical Angler*, 1857, continuously in print up to 1961, so lots around at £10; 1st edition £175.

Arthur Ransome, *Rod and Line*, 1929, many editions, some in paperback, which you can find at £2; 1st edition £70.

W. Carter Platts, *Modern Trout Fishing*, 1938, very popular in its day and plentiful now at around £7; 1st edition £18.

S. Downes and M. Knowleden, *The New Compleat Angler*, 1983, originally published at £9.95 and you can still find new copies at this or less.

J. Inglis Hall, *Fishing a Highland Stream*, 1960, broadcasts on BBC radio prompted later editions in 1987. You can find as new copies at £8; 1st edition (slightly different title) £20.

There are several dealers who specialize in books on fishing and sporting subjects. They will have most of these books in stock.

River Roo

I saw the little River Rhiew for the first time three years ago, in the last weeks of the trout season.

We had decided to take ourselves off for a day of trouting to the tributaries of the Severn that run in from the west. A series of pleasant little streams leak out of the Welsh hills upstream from Shrewsbury. The first of these, the Vyrnwy, is big enough to have respectable tributaries of its own: the Tanat, the Cain and the Banwy were listed on page 125 of *Where to Fish* (1994–95), and for a season or so I had been working my way down the page. We arrived at the village of Llanfair-Caereinon on the River Banwy on a warm, dry day after a warm, dry summer and found that the Banwy at Llanfair-Caereinon was also warm and dry.

And so we headed south and discovered the cool and plentiful waters of the River Clywedog at Llanidloes.

But we did not discover them right away. First we had to get out of Llanfair-Caereinon. I don't know what you do round your way for amusement of a weekend in late summer. We have village fêtes, we have car-boot sales and horticultural shows. In Llanfair-Caereinon they were having a sale of trailers. Llanfair-Caereinon is not ideal trailer-sale terrain. The narrow streets and lanes had become hopelessly jammed: folk arriving with trailers to sell had become inextricably entwined with those who had just bought trailers and hadn't quite got the hang of manoeuvring them yet. And the people who didn't have trailers felt obliged to offer advice to the people who did. And sometimes the advice helped and sometimes it didn't, and one or two who had trailers just unhooked them after a bit and left them in the road. They had had enough. It was a warm, dry day and not getting any cooler.

We finally emerged from the mêlée into narrow lanes between high hedges winding south through late summer. We rounded a bend in the lane and found ourselves in one of the prettiest corners I had seen in all my puff.

Berriew is a village of black and white. Half-timbering things seems to be something of a local pastime and painting the wooden bits black and the other bits white seems to be the other. And they do it so well that they were voted 'Best Kept Village in Wales' in 1970. Also in 1972. And 1989 and 1990. A modest sign records these triumphs: it is the only thing not painted black or white. The tiny centre of the village is enclosed by the church, the Lion Hotel and the Corner Shop and beside the shop is the bridge over a river. On that warm, dry day we bought an ice cream at the Corner Shop and stood on the bridge, looking down at the river.

The bridge at Berriew spans a rocky cleft. Upstream, the river tumbles down a series of small waterfalls, plunging into deep, rocky pools where the currents boil. Downstream the river flows serenely over a gravel bottom, between broad, lush banks overhung with the occasional willow. You would hardly think it could be the same water that has just been banging about between the rocks on the other side of the bridge. We stared down into the water from the high bridge, as fishermen do, looking for signs of life. I thought I saw something wafting in the depths of the pool below the last waterfall, but then fishermen always think they can see something in the depths of pools. It looked as nice a little river as one could wish and all the nicer for being unsuspected.

Looking back, I can't remember why we did not stay there and fish, but I suppose we were on our way to somewhere else, and besides, we knew nothing about the little river other than its name on the map – the Rhiew. Even that was uncertain: the spelling differed with the map. And so we climbed back into the camper van and plunged back into the lanes that lead south towards Newtown and Llanidloes and the Clywedog.

But the picture of that chocolate-box village with its lovely little river stayed with me. Back home I looked up the River Rhiew in *Where to Fish*. It is not there. Nor is Berriew or the Berriew Angling Club – the name I had seen on a hand-written notice on the door of the Corner Shop. And so that was more or less that for the next two and a half years.

*   *   *

It had been a gloomy spring. All the fine and splendid things I had meant to do at the beginning of the new season had been washed away in the floods of Easter and the cold grey days that followed. On another cold grey day I was fretting and watching the weather forecast. It promised more of the same for England, with a fresh north wind thrown in and worse towards the east. But in Wales it would be warm and dry. It was the 'warm and dry' that did it. I vaguely remembered what 'warm and dry' felt like and I fancied that warm and dry was what I needed most. Then I remembered that other warm and dry day in Wales and so the next morning Father and I headed back to Berriew.

It was still there. Nothing had changed. The forecast had been spot on: the sun had broken through the clouds on the Welsh side of Shrewsbury and was now shining hard as we climbed out of the car beside the Corner Shop. The river looked as picture-booky as before, with the light dancing in the splash of the falls above the bridge. We went into the Corner Shop to pursue our enquiries. Mr Lawton runs the corner shop and post office. Berriew Angling Club, he told us, has about 2½ miles of fishing on the river Rhiew from the main Welshpool–Newtown road, through the village and up into the fields beyond. Splendid. And could we get a day ticket to fish this water? No, we couldn't.

The annual subscription for the Berriew Angling Club is £10 and at 10 a.m. that spring day its two newest members stepped out of the dark of the little Corner Shop into the bright sunshine.

There was nothing to be seen rising on the river, so we parked the car across the bridge and tackled up in a desultory sort of way. The Rhiew is the sort of stream that makes you feel very silly wearing chest waders most of the time, but I didn't know that yet, so I put on chest waders. I couldn't find my scissors. Proper fishermen don't use scissors: they clip off the nylon between their front teeth, but nature did not fashion me for a fisherman and my front teeth don't quite meet in that way. So I trudged back to the Corner Shop – which sold everything but nail scissors. Eventually Mrs Rees found a pair of nail clippers in a drawer, not for sale, and handed me those in exchange for a trout to be delivered at the end of the day, demonstrating a heartening spirit of faith in both of us.

A small lane follows the river downstream, past The Talbot, a small pub, which is lovely, and the Andrew Logan Museum of sculpture, which is horrid. A second bridge spans the river with two fine, soaring brick arches and a diddy little tunnel for the lane. This tunnel was dripping alarmingly, which was not surprising when we discovered that what was dripping down on us was the old Montomeryshire Canal from its aqueduct above. We walked to the end of the Berriew beat beneath the main road from Welshpool to Newtown. A meandering mile or so downstream the Rhiew joins the River Severn and here the Rhiew slows and is barely recognisable as the dashing little river we had followed from the village. It was deep and lined with sunken willows. And in between those fallen branches a fish rose.

At another time I would not have bothered to fight my way over the barbed wire and along the fallen trunk with its sprouting withies and twisted branches, but this was the first rise of the season and it seemed somehow symbolic of something-or-other. Besides, I had chest waders on, which was just as well as I lowered myself down through the new root growth and hoped to touch bottom before I was beyond the point of no return. The fish had not risen again. I was standing up to my nipples in a watery copse of willow wands. I flopped the line forward just beyond the rod tip as best I could. Nothing much happened. I flopped again. I had invested so much effort in getting into this position, there seemed nothing else to do. And after perhaps a dozen flops the fish rose again and grabbed the fly.

It was not a big fish. Also, it was a grayling and out of season. And yet I felt a ridiculous sense of triumph.

We worked our way upstream, casting dry flies at likely looking spots in the absence of another rising fish. This is my favourite form of fishing. Taking fish on the surface is always fun because everything happens within view and there is sound and splosh and sparkle, and even if the fish does not connect, at least you know it tried. If the fish are already rising, you know exactly where they are and where to place your fly. When they are not rising you have to predict these things from the flow of the currents across the lumps and bumps of the river bed and its banks: where the food will be concentrated, where the fish will feel safe. You bung your fly there and often nothing happens but sometimes it does and when it does it feels as if no fish is safe with you around. This is a good feeling for a fisherman.

We worked our way upstream towards the village, rising the odd fish from the runs and glides below the bridge. They were all grayling in this stretch, close to the wider waters of the Severn. Above the bridge the river swings down a rocky cleft into the deep pool where, three years before, I had seen, or imagined, a wafting of a larger fin in the depths. Large fins do waft hereabouts. Berriew must be 140 river miles from the tide but salmon make their way each year to this pool and fight their way up these miniature falls to the headwaters beyond. And for their £10 a year the members of the Berriew Angling Club can have crack at them. We stood on the bridge and watched the pool. It was not a salmon that was dimpling the surface amongst the white bubbles from the falls. Father edged under the bridge and cast into the froth and bubble and the little fly disappeared in a fluster and a lively fish was dashing about the place. It was our first trout: a nice little fish of 8 ounces or so.

The pools above are hard and deep, lined with bedrock and I have never done well with a fly in such places. Perhaps the absence of the gravel and small stones reduces the habitat for nymphs and larvae, but I suspect that anywhere that is scoured clean of gravel and small stones has a few pockets of quieter water where a fish can lie safe in a spate. There is a problem with this theory: these same falls and hard plunge pools are favourite spots for worm fishermen who swing their weighted baits into the white water and let the turbulent currents search the depths of the pool. Later that afternoon, as we stood on the bridge for a last look at the river before heading home, a local angler was doing just that. But his worm wasn't doing any better than our flies.

We had lunch on a rock in the river and then fished on upstream into the afternoon. Above the falls the river swings alongside some pretty succulent gardens, and the mowers, muted by the cold, wet spring, were in full cry on this rare day of sunshine. The Rhiew slips into Berriew as quietly as it slips out. A white painted footbridge crosses the river and below this the water trots along beside a wall before swinging around a long, slow bend. Trout love lies like this and so do I. Somewhere along the narrow band of current on the outside of the long bend there will be fish. On a good day, on a good water there will be fish jostling for position the length of such a bend, but if there are fish to be had anywhere on a river, they will be there. The man with a dry fly starts at the bottom where the current breaks free to spread across the stream and works his way up until the fish and his fly collide. The fish that day was waiting for the first cast at the very tail of the run, so Mrs Rees had her trout and I still have the nail clippers.

Beyond the footbridge the river flows between wooded banks and the fisherman must wade up the shallow river that rattles from side to side across a gravel bottom. There are few obvious pools and deeps where a trout must lie, but you should have your eye in by now and there are deeper runs to be found, echoes of the ledges and clefts that form the falls through the village. We fished on upstream. There were medium-sized olives fluttering above the water, but if fish were rising to them, I missed them in the dappled shadow on the bouncing water. We worked our way beneath the trees, dropping flies wherever the water deepened, and often nothing happened and sometimes it did.

That is how it is on the little rivers of the Welsh borders. I wouldn't have it any other way.

23 ♋

Fishing with Mr Fernie

Thirty years ago, almost to the day, Bob Farrer and I were hitch-hiking up the A1. We each carried a bed-roll and a guitar: it was the middle of the sixties. The Stones were singing 'This Could Be the Last Time' and the Animals had just released 'We Gotta Get Outta This Place', a chorus the two of us belted out at the top of our voices as we walked though the dark streets of Darlington where our last lift had dropped us. Darlington at dusk made you sing that sort of song in those days. Perhaps it still does.

The next day we managed only a few miles northwards. It was getting dark again. We were tired and hungry and miserable just outside Berwick on Tweed. A pub stood beside the road in the middle of nowhere. Its name was written in white letters on the roof. It was, I think, The Black Cat. I was ludicrously under age but Bob, a couple of years older, was very nearly legal, and besides, he had one of those blue jaws that we all envied at school. It looked like he had been shaving for years. I don't suppose the landlord of The Black Cat gave a hoot either way. We ordered a pint of bitter each. It was one of the great pints of bitter.

Now, I am not a connoisseur of beer. I can tell that some beers are different but I would be hard pressed to claim that one is very much better than another. Except for that pint in the Black Cat in the summer of 1965. It was a colossus of a pint. It towered above other pints. I was stunned. It may, of course, have been the moment – it sometimes is – but I think it was the beer and I committed the name of that brew to memory for future reference. And then, sometime during the next thirty years, I forgot all about it.

Until a couple of weeks ago. I was driving through the border town of Galashiels. There in front of me was a small pub, The Salmon. On the window was the simple legend 'Dryborough Heavy', the name of that long-forgotten, perfect pint.

That is the thing about the Borders: so often they are just something to get through on the way to somewhere else, the Poland of the British Isles. I had been to Scotland dozens of times since that drink in the Black Cat but, it seems, I had never stopped long enough in the Borders to have a second pint of Dryborough's. Until a couple of weeks ago. This time I had come to the Borders to fish. The man I had come to fish with lives and works a few miles north of Galashiels.

David Norwich makes some of the finest fishing rods in these islands in a labyrinth of a workshop below his white cottage at Fountainhall. A small track in front of the workshop leads down to the Gala Water, the bright stream I had glimpsed from time to time beside the road from Galashiels. It is a magical spot in June, fresh lush green, just becoming overgrown in that slightly intimidating way that looks as if it might get out of hand soon. Out in the meadows it was a hot, bright afternoon but down in the stream there was shade enough to give a chance of fishing. There were flies, too, honking great things that looked for all the world like mayflies. And mayflies they were: the small Gala Water has one of the best mayfly hatches in Scotland but that does not make it a good mayfly hatch. And the good Scottish trout on that June afternoon were ignoring the mayflies as some soft southern aberration. They were doing just as good a job ignoring the Yellow Sally stoneflies that fluttered across the current, but something was being sipped in the shady runs beneath the trees.

Every fly fisherman should, from time to time, take himself off away from any water to a small copse beside a meadow. In high summer the air thereabouts will be full of flying insects. Few of these will be aquatic. They wouldn't know what to do in water. Except drown. Gala Water, or any similar stream, is just a copse with a river running through it and many of those same insects will end up on the water. You won't see them though, because they are usually dark and, not being designed to cope with water, they will all be trapped in the surface film. But the trout will see them. A black fly with a sparse parachute hackle imitates this perfectly. It sits awash in the surface and, just like the natural, it is impossible for the angler to spot. But if you tie the hackle round a vertical tuft of white polywing (or almost anything white) you can see it for miles.

Of course, sometimes they ignore the Black Parachute as well, but not that afternoon on the Gala Water. The trout up here can be huge, up to two pounds, but usually they are not. A half-pounder is a fair fish. Anywhere.

Down in the stream, encased in green, it is easy to believe you are the only anglers to have found this water. But from time to time you see a steeper bank where the ancient path of a railway used to share the valley with the river and the road. Then the 6.15 train from Waverley would be packed with Edinburgh anglers on a holiday morning. It took an age, stopping at every halt to drop anglers like beans in a trench along the threads of the border streams: at Heriot for Heriot Water, at Fountainhall and stations south for the Gala, a change at Stow for those off to Lauder and the Leader Water to the east. At Galashiels the fishermen for the Yarrow, Ettrick and the Tweed itself would change, but anyone heading for the Teviot would stay on past Melrose to Newtown St Boswells and on to Hawick or Roxburgh where another change would carry the few remaining fishermen on to Jedburgh and Jed Water. It took, in the early days of the century, three changes and as many hours to reach the Teviot that runs beside the old Jedburgh line. It must have been a fine, frustrating, exciting, exasperating excursion, with anglers of all sorts and stations, the variety of tackle and talk. It has all gone now. But as David and I stood on that desolate old railway track beside the Gala, we saw upstream a glint of light on a waving rod. He was dressed in a tweed jacket and a squashy hat, with an old-time creel across his shoulder and a wading staff cut from the hedgerow. He was working his cane rod upstream and, apart from his waders, he could have been left here by the last train before the Great War.

I found the fisherman's train from Waverley described in a splendid little book David showed me later that evening. *Dry-Fly Fishing in Border Waters* was written in 1912 by F. Fernie. I had not heard of F. Fernie. Neither, perhaps, had the angling world of 1912, because the book was given an enormous 'Introduction' by one J. Cuthbert Hadden, who must have been something of a celebrity brought in to bolster F. Fernie. They needn't have bothered: J. Cuthbert Hadden's is an overblown literary cream-puff of a piece, whereas Mr Fernie's book is a little gem.

It is all the more valuable for the visitor because Fernie himself was a visitor, albeit from Edinburgh, when he came to fish the waters of the Tweed. You might think that the best way to fish a river is to fish it as the locals do, the height of arrogance, or at least folly, to do anything else. Not necessarily: '. . . in a district where everyone has fishing at his door, few people consider it worth while to fish, except at the most likely times. Thus one might hang about the Tweed in the neighbourhood of Peebles for the whole of a June day without seeing a single angler until the evening rise, perhaps at half-past seven or eight o'clock.'

And that was in old money, before the clocks went on in summer.

Things haven't changed. The locals still go out at 8 or 9 p.m. and this can be discouraging for a visitor who isn't about to sit around all day on his fishing holiday. Don't be discouraged. That *is* the best time to fish. It is not the *only* time to fish. Let us talk of the Tweed around Peebles.

The Peeblesshire Trout Fishing Association has an awful lot of it. On and off it has about 14 miles of the main river, so you are going to find a fair amount of variation, but it is typically a broad and rather shallow river. Perhaps 30 yards or so wide and you could cross at many points in thigh waders. And at many other points you couldn't. About that deep. There are holes, one of them deep and thrilling between rocks beneath a slightly self-conscious castle. But for the most part the river is broad and steady over a pebble bottom. And it is clear. Somehow the word 'clear' never seems to do these days: it has to be 'gin' clear or 'crystal' clear, as if clear on its own meant just a little murky. Well, it is clear. And if you can't see the trout, it isn't the water's fault. They can see you alright. We stood on the footbridge across the river at Lyne Station where once the train had stopped. A few rings disturbed the surface and an impressive bulging bow-wave ploughed upstream from the shallows beside the bank. You can see why a three-pound leader is regarded as rather obvious on the Tweed in summer.

Now, you can catch trout on a bright sunny morning in June on the Tweed by fishing a wet fly across the broad current at the head of the long pools. But they will be very small trout. Mr F. knew all about that. At a time when the dry fly was considered just a thing of the soft south, he wrote, '. . . and yet I venture to say that no successful angler in the town of Peebles, in the months of May and June, would use anything else on the Tweed except the floating fly, at any rate up to dark'.

On the long smooth glides of the Tweed it is easy to spot a rising fish. It is easy to cast across the broad stream to cover the fish with a small dry fly. The hard bit is fooling the fish. It is all too easy to change the fly for another . . . and another . . . and another, as the fish rises serenely if irregularly on the cushion above a rock, edging slightly across the current as the casts drift over-head. It takes an act of faith, or about an hour of such futile casting, to abandon these obvious rises and look for something catchable. It is hard to see a rise in the sparkling, bouncing riffle at the head of the pool, and we didn't see one – but that is the place to fish the dry fly on such a clear, bright day. Up there in the faster water the leader is all but invisible, the fly is moving faster and must be grabbed or missed, and, more to the point, any fish up in that current is there to feed rather than fiddle about frustrating fisher-men. Of course, on such a day there may not be a fish up in the fast water feeding. But usually there is. And so there was this time. Not a big fish, 12 ounces perhaps. The anglers of the Tweed can get pretty sniffy about fish of 12 ounces. They shouldn't. Of a memorable summer day, Mr Fernie tells us of eight trout by lunch time *weighing a little under four pounds*. A half-pounder seems to be about the standard for the river then. And perhaps now. It is a good standard for wild trout anywhere, but there are fish much, much bigger than that in the Tweed. And late June and July is the time to try for them.

There is something about fishing at night. You don't get a lot of night in the Borders in June and July but these are the two months when such practices are, grudgingly, allowed on this salmon river. And then only until 1 a.m. After that you are up to no good. If you are taking this seriously, you will not arrive at the water until dark – say 11 p.m. – but this would be rather pointless because the other fishers of Peebles will have been at the pools since dusk, because this *is* the best time for fishing these waters. We started at 9 p.m. on the long flat pools between Horsbrugh Ford and Manor Bridge. Other figures were moving through the long dewy grass. A pod of trout were rising below the bend but they were sipping steadily at something invisible in the surface. They were not buying what we were selling, even the black parachute. You can still change you flies at this time – and we did – but you are better to change your fish. A lone rise, more than a sip, occurred a dozen yards downstream. It was a better fish, or perhaps it just felt better as it ploughed off into the gloom under the far bank; everything feels bigger and stronger at night. The trout came to the net and David grasped it to remove the fly. 'A stockie,' he decided. There is a stocking experiment on the Tweed this season and, for some reason, the stocked fish feel slimier than the natives. He flipped the fish over in the light of the torch and pointed out the tiny spot of blue dye that marks all stocked fish. These may be taken by the fishermen, while any native fish must be returned.

Before it got too dark, we beefed up our leaders from the fine stuff we had been using during the day. The sips and rises from midstream were lessening, but in their place were crisp, crunchy rises, heard rather than seen, hard against the far bank. This was sister to the Bustard fishing I had first tried on the deep, slow waters of the summer Eden. We put on big flies. I tried a large red sedge. The man in the tackle shop in Innerleithen recommended a Dancing Leslie: I hope and believe that is a dapping fly. David uses a Goofus Bug (size 10–14). With its dense hackles and humpy back of deer hair, it makes a mouthful to tempt the four- and five-pounders that are taken from these waters every season. You wade up the centre of the river (and chest waders make this a lot less fraught), casting tight into the banks. The fish can lurk within an inch or so of the grass or tree roots.

It did not last long when it happened. I heard a crash of a rise from the gloom of the river upstream and David's rod tip was visible, bent extravagantly against the last light of the sky. Then it dipped suddenly into the silhouette of the trees and things went quiet. Very, very quiet. It is how a rod-maker registers despair.

* * *

I started this with beer. I must finish it with Moules Marinières. I have eaten the definitive Moules Marinières: they were cooked for me by my daughter's pen-friend's mother in their home overlooking a mussel-bed near Perpignan and they were as good an argument for having daughters and pen-friends as you could wish. And in the years since then I have eaten other Moules Marinières and had come to the conclusion that perhaps you have to eat them overlooking a mussel-bed near Perpignan. Not so. You can eat them in the Traquair Arms Hotel at Innerleithen as well. And when I return to fish the Tweed, the Yarrow and the Teviot next year, I intend to eat a lot more.

Mustard and the Fischmeister

I first went to Monschau for the mustard. We were staying with friends in a flat bit of Germany near Bonn and we fancied a day out. 'Visit the mustard-mill in Monschau,' they said. So we did.

It is still a joy to drive in rural Germany: the roads are perfect, traffic scarce and the wooded Eifel hills rose suddenly out of the plain as we poled east towards the Belgium border. The lie of the land is perverse to English eyes used to countryside shaped by glaciers. The meadowland is on the top of the rounded hills with the slopes becoming wooded and ever steeper as they descend to rivers and streams running in tight valleys, unsuspected from the rolling plateau above. Take the road into Monschau and you find yourself looking down through trees into somebody's chimney-pot.

The mustard-mill was powered by a small stream, the Laufenbach, which tumbles down the steep side of the valley. As the houses of Monschau spread up the valley, each staring down the other's chimney, they simply built over this stream until much of it now runs under the beautiful jumble of black and white half-timbered houses and cobbled streets of Monschau. You glimpse it from time to time as you climb up Laufenstrasse to the mill: peer down between the bakery and the house next door and there is a wild mountain stream tumbling crystal water from pool to pool – and there is a rise!

The rise was not the 'blip' of a tiddler. It was the purposeful sip of something that knew what it was about. I followed the sound of the tumbling water two houses upstream. There was another pool and four resident fish, each around the pound. I could not believe it. But each gap showed the same picture: a rocky streambed 6 feet below the road level and great, fat fish. And so we reached the mustard-mill.

The mustard-miller is a character, a great bear of a man who can chat fluently in four languages – so long as the talk is of mustard. On the subject of fish he could speak nothing but German. I don't speak any German at all. He could see I was excited and we both went out to look at the fish in his mill-stream. We mimed the difference of appearance and behaviour between trout and grayling. I *think* we may have mimed the difference between rainbow trout and brown trout but I could be mistaken there. I mimed me fly-fishing and he nodded, 'Why not?' This was all so easy.

But it was also November and the close season, and so I had to content myself with gathering information for a trip in the spring.

At the tourist information office in the town centre I was given the phone number and address of the secretary of the local association that controlled all the water. She could provide all the necessary permits and tickets we would need the following April.

It is three hours' drive from the ferry at Dunkerque to Monschau on the Belgian–German border. All but the last 15 miles are on motorway. We arrived at Frau Brandenburg's gate before noon. As we went to knock on the door, a head appeared through a hole in the concrete path just in front of us. The head wished us '*Guten tag*' and disappeared. The Brandenburgs' house is on Laufenstrasse, built over the stream, and Herr Brandenburg was repairing the tunnel through which the Laufenbach tumbles down to the town.

Frau Brandenburg speaks no English – no matter. By the usual channels of smiling, nodding and rummaging through the dictionary, we found we would need a day ticket (about £8), a regional licence (£3.50 and a passport photograph) and 'an international Certificate of Fly-Fishing'. This last was a bit of a poser. I had no certificate to prove that I could fish with a fly. Nor did my father or anyone else I knew. I showed Frau Brandenburg an out-of-date Welsh Water Authority fishing licence and she wrote down the number. My father showed her his Salisbury Angling Club ticket and she wrote down that number and everyone seemed to be happy with these formalities. I have no idea what that was all about.

The river in Monschau is the Rur. It is not one of Germany's premier trout streams. There are plenty of fish, trout and grayling, in the town and the mile or so of wooded valley below, but they average under the pound, for this is a stony, upland stream. There are larger fish, much larger, in some of the rocky pools, particularly in the centre of town where the tourists lean over the footbridges; they shout and helpfully point out the monsters you are missing.

This is the bizarre fun of fishing in Monschau. The town is preserved as a living museum, visited by millions of sightseers each year. It is as though someone had taken the ancient, pretty bits of Stratford-on-Avon and tried to shoehorn the lot into a narrow gorge on the Welsh Usk.

As you pick your way up this wild mountain river, over slippery rocks and through fast runs, you can glance up to see jolly window-boxes and ancient balconies hanging just above your head. Jolly, fat faces munching sticky cakes and hot chocolate in coffee houses peer down at this idiot in a tumbling mountain stream two metres below their well-upholstered bottoms. In the river you are in a wild world of pools and riffles and sparkling brown trout in difficult lies. Walk up a set of stone steps and the river becomes no more than a scenic prop in this model village. It is an extraordinary experience.

The Rur at Monschau is best fished early in the season. In April and May there is plenty of water in the river and fewer tourists. In June there will be less water and the somewhat overcrowded nature of the town with its influx of tourists in the summer can overstrain the normally efficient German sewage system. The result is abundant algal growth on the smooth rocks, which makes wading very dicey, and a definite sort of 'something in the air' over the river under a shimmering noon sun.

I never did get to try for the subterranean monsters of the Laufenbach, the small tributary I had first glimpsed under and between the houses. That was out-of-bounds, kept as a nursery stream to provide a natural stocking of the main river, a sensible provision in this sensible country.

Fishing the Rur at Monschau is fun. Thirty miles to the south-east flows the River Kyll. This is a more serious proposition altogether. The beautiful River Kyll flows south through the heart of the Eifel to join the Mosel (or Moselle, if you are in France) close to the Luxembourg border. In its middle section, from Gerolstein to Kyllburg, it is well known for its trout. It is better known for its superb grayling. In England such a status would ensure that day tickets for the visitor were either non-existent or cost a king's ransom. Yet the whole of the premier middle Kyll can be fished by the visiting angler – in fact it is cheaper than fishing the humble Rur! This could make the river impossibly over-fished. It doesn't – for there is an eminently sensible stipulation.

Each village controls its local stretch of water: tickets are only available to visitors staying at least two nights in a guesthouse or hotel (or occasionally a campsite) within the village. The whole village benefits from the revenue of the river and it is little hardship for us visitors from Britain – we would have to stay somewhere, anyway.

We parked in front of the post office in the small riverside village of Birresborn. Father had been practising the phrase for 'Can we a fishing ticket buy here, please?' He launched it at the first man we met outside the post office, It had a remarkable effect. 'Yes,' the man said decisively, and immediately led us across the square to the inevitable sticky-cake-and-coffee shop, the Cafe Blasius. This, it transpired, was where all such business was carried on.

We provided the sticky cakes and coffee and he got out the tickets after re-commending a guesthouse where we might stay. By luck we had happened upon the 'under-fish-master' of the village (the 'over-fish-master' was some-where else). Over coffee we proffered our fly-boxes and he nodded, smiled, frowned and shook his knowledgeable head over the contents. What emerged from that conversation was a revelation to me.

In Germany, as in much of continental Europe, the 'status' or regard given to trout and grayling is the reverse of that in Britain. Here in Britain the trout is often portrayed as discerning and wily: one poor cast will put him down. The grayling, by contrast, is somewhat artless and will come time and again at a fly. Grayling flies, in as much as they are different from trout flies, are usually cruder, flashier beasts, often with a red flag to attract the slow-witted grayling. The grayling itself is regarded as vermin on some trout streams.

Even where both fish co-exist there can be a twinge of disappointment when the hooked fish reveals itself as 'just a grayling'. A book written by the chairman of the Grayling Society is entitled *Grayling – the Fourth Game Fish*, a fair assessment of its status in Britain.

Not so in Germany. In fact, the reverse is true. These flies, we were told as he rummaged among our collection of patterns, would certainly catch the trout (the implication was that a piece of toffee-paper on a hook would serve), but for grayling we could use only those, my smallest and most nat-uralistic. And we would have one chance only with the grayling: the stupid trout might try time and again in an effort to hook itself. And so on. Odd.

But then on the River Kyll the grayling are not like ours. A fish of 47 cen-timetres – over 18 inches – was landed while we were there. This is a serious river indeed!

The river at Birresborn is unexceptional to look at. It is perhaps 15 metres wide but with considerable variation. It has a bit of everything by way of fea-tures, without any one feature giving it a particular character. The gradient is gradual but not as even as a chalkstream; it has fast runs falling into slower, deeper pools beneath high banks. There are no spectacular waterfalls but there are long sections of broken water over stone and boulders. There are wide flats with a smooth current over a pale gravel bottom where the large shadows of grayling hugging the bottom can be seen in the clear water, edging upstream ahead of the wading angler.

Beneath one such glide there is a feature that never fails to excite me, for it always holds good fish: an old constructed embankment forces the stream round in a long, smooth curve, speeding the water as it gently constricts it. The result is a long curve of faster water against the outside of the bend.

There are good fish on the angler's side of the fast water, and the gradual speeding of the current from the slow water at his feet to the fast water across the river's width allows a dry fly cast up and across to travel a long way before dragging. There are better fish on the far side of the fast water, in slack pockets of water hard against the embankment. A fly cast over the fast water would drag instantly but there is no need: the lies are so close to the fast stream that a fly in that main current will be grabbed as it bounces enticingly past these lies. The result is a series of good fish lying the length of that curve.

It was at the lower end of this curve that we positioned ourselves on our first evening. We had shared the three-mile beat with four other anglers, two Belgians and two Dutchmen (such is the reputation of this water). Over lunch at the streamside the Dutch anglers had waxed lyrical about the evening rise they had experienced the previous day.

Now, I have heard of evening rises the previous day before. Often. I have waited for them the next day. Often. They are never quite as my fancy paints them. 'Seven o'clock,' insisted the Dutchman. And we thanked him because one does not like to call a foreigner a fibber to his face.

So there we stood, on the inside of a bend of the river Kyll on an evening in early summer.

You really cannot trust a foreigner: there was not a hint of a rise until 7.05 p.m. – when there was a distinct 'slurp' at the head of the run, then another below. In a few minutes there were rises pock-marking the length of that long curve. We were hooking and releasing good fish in a frenzy of activity – fifteen fish in one glorious half-hour without shuffling more than a foot or so upstream. And then, just as suddenly, it was over. The sky was still light, there had been none of that frenetic changing of flies in the semi-darkness. We thought perhaps we had put our fish down, but on the flats above and below the long curve the rings of rising fish were becoming sporadic and soon they stopped altogether. The river was still again.

It had been the classic evening rise.

It is a long way to go for a good weekend and one perfect hour. I thought it was worth every mile.

And I did bring back some really good mustard.

25 ♌

The Tangle O' The Isles

There are 280 hills over 3000 feet high in Great Britain. They are known as 'Munros', after Sir Hugh Munro who published his *Tables of Heights over 3000 feet* in 1891 – which is a pretty soft way to get 280 mountains named after you, if you ask me.

Climbing one of these hills is known as 'bagging' a Munro. For over a century Munro baggers have been collecting Munros like other folk used to collect cigarette cards. You can bag them one at a time or you can see how many you can do on one week's hols. You can take a lifetime to bag all 280 if you wish. Folk who have climbed all 280 Munros have legs like very old turkeys, all muscle and sinew. They also have a way of looking serene, as if contemplating some inner distant horizon, which is rather irritating for everyone else. They have a tendency to commit Morris Dancing. I do not say this as the result of research: I have never knowingly met anyone who has climbed all 280 Munros. Nor is it the result of personal experience: I have never knowingly climbed a Munro myself. It is pure prejudice.

Likewise, there are about 150 islands around the coast of Great Britain that have a freshwater loch or pool containing trout. Some do, some did but now don't and some never have. The troutful islands are called 'lochisles' because I have just called them that. Catching a trout on one of these lochisles; is not called anything at the moment because, although people have been catching trout on islands forever, they didn't know they were 'lochisles'. 'Netting' a lochisle has a rather unsavoury ring to it; 'Creeling' is too ootsy for words. We'll see what turns up.

To bag (or whatever) a lochisle you must catch a trout from some freshwater on the island.

What follows is the first attempt on the **World 5-day Lochisle Record**.

* * *

The ferry from Oban to the Western Isles would not sail for another five hours. Philip decided he would like a pair of forceps. It didn't sound like the sort of thing that would take five hours. Either Oban would sell forceps or it wouldn't. Almost everyone we met thought Oban did sell forceps but opinion was divided as to where. We tried the chemist. He had seen forceps further down the street. So we tried there. They sent us to another shop, and so it went on. When we started it was just a whim to fill a few moments, but gradually it took on the flavour of an Arthurian quest. We would re-pass people in the street, they would ask how it was going and make further suggestions. It had become terribly, terribly important to find forceps. We exhausted the shops of the High Street and the square. We had taken to questing along back streets when Philip noticed the door to a vet's surgery. We asked the receptionist if she knew where the vet bought his forceps. She went to find him. He might have been in the middle of an operation because he came out carrying a pair of forceps. We were so near. We asked where he bought them. He said that they were delivered by a medical supplies company. I thought Philip was going to break down. I think the vet did too: he offered Philip the pair of forceps in his hand and refused any money. I did wonder what happened to the hamster under surgery though.

A curious thing occurred as we walked back through the town. We were passing a hotel doorway when a shower of stuff came raining down onto the pavement from a third-floor window. They were medical supplies: blister packs of pills, capsules, ointments and sticking plasters. Hundreds of them. We wondered whether our search for forceps had somehow conjured this shower like manna in the desert. There were no forceps however.

The Caledonian–MacBrayne ferry left Oban at 2.50 in the afternoon. It winds along the narrow strait between Mull and the lovely Ardnamurchan peninsula, slipping past Coll and out across the Hebridean Sea towards the Western Isles. We reached Lochboisdale at the southern tip of South Uist five hours later. We were under starter's orders. We drove off the ferry at 7.40 p.m.: the starting pistol had sounded and the clock was running.

We bumped off the ferry ramp and turned hard left up the steep drive to the Lochboisdale Hotel. This is called research. We carried two fishing guides in the camper-van: Bruce Sanderson's *Rivers and Lochs of Scotland* and *70 Lochs – A Guide to Trout Fishing in South Uist*, a little gem written by the man I knew we would find in the bar of the Lochboisdale Hotel. If anyone could advise us where to fish first on South Uist, it was John.

What we did, an hour later, was to leave South Uist without dampening a fly.

Anyone planning an attempt on the World Lochisle Record is going to find himself juggling with mileage, arcane ferry timetables and SUNDAY. It is perfectly legal to fish for brown trout on a Sunday in Scotland but in places it is just not done. One of these places is the Western Isles. Three of these islands, South Uist, Benbecula and North Uist (and some little ones along the way), run south to north, joined by causeways. In the south of South Uist, where we had just landed, you could fish for trout on Sunday and no one would turn a hair. In the north of South Uist and Benbecula, Sunday fishing is frowned on, but provided it is done discreetly, you will be tolerated as an ignorant and Godless creature more to be pitied than chastized. In North Uist they will shoot first and pity you after that. You have to know these things. It was Friday evening. If we fished the islands in a logical sequence, we should reach North Uist on Sunday and be stuffed. We drove north, along the length of South Uist, across Benbecula and North Uist to the outlying island of Baleshare.

I have a rule – which I never follow – not to judge any place where I arrive late in the day after a long journey until the next morning. We had not slept for thirty-six hours when we arrived at Loch Mor on Baleshare. We were far from convinced that we *had* arrived. On my old Ordnance Survey map the thing was slightly smaller than Rutland Water. What we found was a shallow depression filled with rocks, weed and some unappetizing algae. We fished it fruitlessly anyway and then walked all around looking for another, better, Loch Mor. It was the only one they had. When I had phoned the North Uist Estate for permission to fish, the factor was sceptical about fish in Loch Mor, but in Bruce's *Rivers and Lochs of Scotland* we had read 'nothing for the glass case but good sport and something for breakfast'. We didn't want something for a glass case, just a trout from the island of Baleshare. We didn't get one. In a shallow depression of our own we drove back on to North Uist to find a place to sleep.

*   *   *

Saturday, 6 June

We woke to a steel-grey morning. Rabbits scattered into a warren of burrows in the sandy turf. We had slept near Loch Hosta on the north-west coast of North Uist. Look for rabbits by the lochs of the Western Isles and you have a fair chance of good trout. Rabbits like the sandy turf and so do the trout: the sand is crushed shell, neutralizing the naturally acid waters of the peaty terrain. We tackled up, walked around to the windward shore and cast.

Nothing happened. For a bit – then I felt a long draw and tightened into something that would have done very nicely for a couple of breakfasts. That first fish from Loch Hosta was a beauty. Of course, it would have been a beauty if it had had galloping acne and a squint: that is how it is with a first fish. But it really *was* a beauty.

We had bagged North Uist and our first lochisle. It was time to move on. We drove south the way we had come, heading for the small island of Grimsay, off the causeway that connects North Uist to Benbecula.

We were heading for Loch Caravat in the middle of Grimsay. Bruce's book suggested that we 'follow the outlet stream east over the moor to reach Loch Caravat after ten minutes'. We did that. And then we fished. We fished all round that loch, including 'The north west bay . . . in the vicinity of the small island and on either side of the promontory', which Bruce reckoned 'is the most productive'. We did not have a tug. On the way back across the moor we passed the crofter who lives below the loch. We told him we had not had a tug. He was not surprised: there are no fish in the Loch. His neighbour said there never had been. When she had fished as a girl, they had always gone across the island to the loch beside the road. So we did that.

The road circles the coast of Grimsay. From Killin, at the eastern tip, we could see the small island of Ronay, which has three or four lochs, but we could not afford the time to find a boat and get across. Another time, maybe.

The road threads between Loch Fada and Loch Hornary. Hornary is long and narrow with high, rocky shores. Fada is broad and open and shallow. They are *both beside the road*. We began to fish Fada. There is something about a broad stony bottom. After you have been fishing for a while, it creeps into your mind that fish don't like broad stony bottoms: they feel vulnerable and are easily scared by a line plonking down over their heads. You start to think of those deep, craggy coasts where fish lurk in the comforting depths within inches of the shore and zoom up to grab the fly. It seems so obvious: the woman had been talking about Loch Hornary. So we crossed the road to Hornary.

There is something about fishing a steep rocky shore. After a fishless hour you realize that on a steep shore you are high above the fish and very visible as you cast. Experience tells you that the productive areas are always the broad shallows where the fish can cruise. It seems so obvious: she meant Fada. So we crossed back. And so on. It started to rain and I was all for giving up. Philip insisted we stay for a bit longer on Fada, which is the reason he catches more fish than I do. But this time it was me that felt the line draw away and I pulled up into a fish. Which fell off the hook. We had agreed that a fish was only to be deemed caught when it was in the net or in the hand. It was not a nice moment.

There was nothing to be done but to keep on keeping on. I do not find this a pleasant way to fish. If I had wanted to fish like that, I would have become a salmon fisherman. An hour later the line slid away through the same hole in the surface and I tightened into a second fish. I do not think I have played a fish more carefully. We had bagged Grimsay and lochisle number two.

You may have spotted a slight drawback to lochisle bagging. It was dawning on us: on islands where the fishing was splendid we would catch our trout and leave. Where the fishing was poor we spent hours. We had spent quite some time where there were no trout at all. On the other hand, the vagaries of the ferry meant that we could not leave North Uist until Monday morning. On Sunday we could only fish on Benbecula and South Uist. So, for the rest of Saturday we buzzed off and fished, in the rain, for fun. That evening, in the Creagorry Hotel, a man was committing grievous bodily accordion music. This was similar to fun – but not very.

* * *

Sunday, 7 June

We had parked the camper van in a fold of the hill above Loch Caslub on the north-west coast of South Uist. John Kennedy's book calls Caslub dour. We didn't need dour. A cold north-east wind was still blowing, as it had since we reached the islands. We were looking for something easier to open the batting. I was looking in the book for something a little more encouraging when Philip came back from an early morning walk above the loch. He had seen something rise – a rare enough event in that time of cold north-easterlies – and he was going to catch it.

And he did. It was a pollack. We were not sure if pollack counted. We didn't think they did. So we headed off to Loch Naid.

Loch Naid lies a little walk north of the road from Caslub to anywhere else. John Kennedy describes it as, 'another loch where the angler just cannot fail to catch trout'. I suppose it comes of being a child of the sixties, the streak of anarchy that lurks in the soul of anyone who was eighteen in 1968 when students took to the barricades across Europe and North America. It was an age of rebellion and it left its children rebellious. We chafe against authority: it irks us to be told we cannot do something. We just naturally go and do it. So we did. We failed to catch a fish in Loch Naid.

In one arm of the loch we had spotted the tell-tale detritus of a failed fish-farm: split floats leaking polystyrene, rusty fittings and peeling plastic. We were to see the same throughout the islands where European development cash has brought boom and bust and shattered the delicate ecosystem of another loch.

Time was getting on. The next morning we had planned to leave the Uists on the first ferry to Berneray, Harris and Lewis. We could afford just one more loch on South Uist before heading for Benbecula and the north. We headed south and turned down the small road to Loch Skiport. We making for Loch Teanga in the hills of the eastern coast, hoping that a change from the flat lands of the west and north would bring a change in the fishing. An islet in a roadside loch was ablaze with pink rhododendron. It looked positively indecent after the flat moors under grey skies.

A narrow arm of Loch Teanga reaches to the roadside: this was no time for rambling and exploring: we had to catch trout right speedily. We just walked to the edge of the heather and simply plopped flies down into the water. We would worry about climbing down the near-vertical slabs to the water's edge in the unlikely event of something sticking to the other end of the line. This is the non-smoker's equivalent of putting the rod down to light a cigarette. Within seconds I had a sharp little take and a feisty little fish was on the end. I called across to Philip to get a camera but he was just as busy. This was how we had pictured the whole adventure. We had driven 600 miles and fished our socks off for two days for a bare handful of fish. Suddenly, on Loch Teanga of blessed memory, we had thirteen fish in one hour. We became blasé. We got out the dapping rod and they came up for that. This was fun. Two blokes pulled up in a van and watched. It was Sunday. We wondered if they were religious vigilantes from North Uist. It turned out they worked on a fish farm at the end of the road and had never actually seen fly-fishing. They watched, incredulous, as we put back those 10- and 11-inch fish. Could they have some of those for tea? Of course they could. So that was the end of that. We fished on for twenty minutes without another touch.

The world seemed a brighter place on the road from Teanga, across the causeway to Benbecula. The sky was still grey, the wind cold and north-easterly. Also it was raining. But there was a roseate hue to the dripping scenery.

Benbecula, we figured, would be a doddle. We had fished on Benbecula before and had good steady sport on a loch in the middle of the moors in the east of the island. We approached Loch nan Clachan from a different direction this time, striking directly across the moor along a peat track. Nan Clachan is a big loch and it was easy enough to find in the maze of lochs and lochans.

We fished it for a few minutes until, moving along the shore, we spotted the real nan Clachan a short distance away across the heather. So we fished that. It was quite similar to the *real,* real nan Clachan which we discovered a little way beyond this second nan Clachan. So we fished that. Within a few minutes Philip was into a nice little trout. It had the same strange greenish hue we had found on nan Clachan fish the year before so we didn't bother to search for any other nan Clachans in the vicinity. We fished happily, and damply, along the shore as the sky darkened on our second day in the islands.

We had bagged four lochisles out of five islands: another seven lay beyond the next ferry.

*   *   *

Monday, 8 June

You know those autobiographies where old blokes are recalling their child-hood? They gives pages of verbatim dialogue of what the doctor said to Mummy whilst the boy author, aged three, was listening from his bed, deliri-ous with measles, or hiding behind the door in the butler's pantry. How do they remember all that stuff? I have difficulty remembering what I had for breakfast. So you will only get the gist of the conversation that morning. Think yourself lucky.

The conversation was of lavatories: Philip wanted to know if there would be a lavatory at Otternish. It seemed very important to him. It was 7 a.m. on a cool grey day after our third night in the camper van. We had come to the Western Isles on a mission – an attempt on the World 5-day Lochisle-Bagging Record. We were feeling pretty confident of scooping the World 5-day Lochisle-Bagging Record: we had trained our young bodies to the temper of Toledo steel. Also it was the first attempt, so we were bound to get it.

The first two days should have been easy. So far all the islands we had vis-ited were joined by bridges and causeways, so there had been no need for ferries and timetables and sea-legs and so forth. But it had not been easy. It had been wet and cold and we had fished far into the long summer evening before going back to the van for supper.

About these suppers: I take it we are all agreed that tinned cassoulet is the single greatest gift of French cuisine to a hungry world. That rich mélange of haricots, onions, saucisse de Toulouse, bacon and bits of a goose after a hard day's fishing is unquestionably the puppy's privates. Up to a point. A cas-soulet three nights on the trot, so to speak, is possibly beyond that point – a cassoulet too far. It does things to your insides, things that are incompatible with life in a small camper van.

There *was* a lavatory beside the isolated waiting room at Otternish. It may not be there now – its disappearance not the result of the cassoulet but of the causeway. A monstrous finger of rubble was inching out beside the slip at Otternish towards the island of Berenay. Within a month or so there would be no ferry to Berneray.

There are two lochs on Berneray. Bhruist, the largest, is a fine-looking loch nestling between low hills and the sand dunes of the west coast. Its waters are arguably the finest in the islands, spring-fed through the bed of the loch and sweetened by the alkaline sand. It is a shame there are no trout to enjoy it. There have been trout in Brhuist, fine fish that grew rapidly to over 8 pounds, but the loch has no feeder streams and the fishing lasts only as long as the oldest trout. Bruist was last stocked a dozen years or so ago. If there were any trout in the vicinity when we worked our flies along the grey fingers of bedrock, they would have been very few, very large and very, very old. We learnt all this from Don Alick MacKillop. Don Alick and Gloria have a comfortable B&B below the loch. The estate, he told us, plan to restock Loch Brhuist with local trout in the spring of 1999. In a couple of years they will be monsters.

But not now. We had started the day with another elusive lochisle.

We caught the next ferry back to North Uist. As we came closer to the slip, we could see the ferry from South Harris arriving ahead of us. It would unload and depart, leaving us stranded at Otternish for another three precious hours. We bemoaned our plight to Gloria who was riding the ferry with us: she explained it to the captain who promptly got on the radio. We were stunned to watch the large South Harris ferry close its loading doors and back away from the slip, allowing our ferry to slide past and dock. No one would call Philip and me beautiful. But between us, it seemed, we could muster a *milliHelen* – the unit of beauty required to launch a single ship. It was a proud moment.

South Harris is quite different from the Uists. The sun shines for a start, something we had not seen for three days. There is more grunt to the land-scape, with towering masses of rock tumbling down to the sea. There are rivers that look like rivers and in these blessed outer isles a river has salmon. This is altogether more serious stuff. It means that wandering hobbledehoys like ourselves could not just pitch up at any water we fancied and start fish-ing with the blessing of a single estate factor. Some estates own whole river systems, others have a swathe of hill and lochans, and some just a single loch. Many owners hereabouts are happy to allow brown trout fishing, particularly on lochs without a run of migratory fish. And some are not. And some, let's be frank, will never know. The trick is to know which is which. There is a man who can do this trick. His name is Donny Maciver. Everyone calls him Donny. He is to be found in the Sports Shop in Stornoway. Give him a call. That's what we did, and armed with his knowledge we set about bagging the bits off Harris and Lewis. It had become clear that lochisles were harder the smaller they got – harder to get to, harder to get back from. And harder to find fish where spawning streams are short, iffy or non-existent. We decided to knock off the smaller bits first.

Scalpay lies off the east coast of Harris beyond Tarbert, and we had missed the ferry. But we had only missed it by a matter of months: now an elegant bridge swoops across the narrow Kyles of Scalpay.

It was raining again. A track climbed beside a steep little burn and so did we. Loch an Duin, at the top of the track, spread away to the east. I have rarely seen a troutier looking loch. A steep cliff on the southern shore gave depths of dark promise. The northern shore was shallower, the little bays studded with islands and skerries where the fish would forage in the productive shallows. The whole thing said 'TROUT'. It was, of course, lying through its teeth. But it took the rest of that day for this to dawn on us: each corner and bay looked troutier than the one before and we managed to convince ourselves that the reason we had seen nothing so far was that they were all holed up in this bay – or perhaps the next. We climbed into the hills and fished the skein of lochs that stretched to the east. It was cold and wet and so were we. We didn't understand it: Bruce's book had assured us 'modest brown trout in all the lochs, with the chance of a few larger specimens'. We were commencing to have doubts about Bruce. We retired, bruised and baffled, back across the bridge and limped into the Harris Hotel. Which is what we should have done first.

In the Harris Hotel we met John Morrison. He told us what had happened to Loch an Duin. It was a depressingly familiar story of a failed fish farm, a tilt in the delicate balance of nutrients and a catastrophic algal bloom. The fish farm had gone and so had the fishing. There are still trout in Loch an Duin – a 5-pound fish had been taken that season on a deep worm – but the population of young fish, two, three and four to the pound, had gone, leaving a few old giants. The chances of us catching one of these in a few hours were vanishingly small. We needed a Scalpay trout. As to the other lochs, Mr. Morrison was doubtful but he would make a phone call. If there were trout to be had on Scalpay, John MacLeod would know where. And if he had only been in, he might have told us.

It had been a disastrous day without a single lochisle bagged. We sought solace in the bar of the Harris Hotel.

It is surprising what several of pints of solace will do for the spirits of damp fishermen. It is alarming what a fourth cassoulet will do for their digestion.

*   *   *

Tuesday, 9 June

We could not phone John MacLeod until the afternoon, so we decided to make a dash for Great Bernera, 45 miles away, off the north-west coast of Lewis. Before the bridge had been built everything had been ferried across to Great Bernera in a rowing boat and landed on the beach, including the post office van, the only vehicle on the island up until then. That was forty-three years ago. Forty-three years can do things to a bridge in this climate. You'd want to check a bridge after forty-three years. The bridge to Great Bernera was closed for inspection. We could see that: they had opened a dirty great hole in the single width roadway so that they could climb down and inspect its bits. We must have looked pathetic, standing there, weeping, at the end of the bridge. They climbed out of the hole and waved to us to drive across the bridge – which we did, with our wheels *just* straddling the dirty great hole.

This time we asked first, in the general stores at Breacleit. Where could we catch a trout in a hurry? There was some discussion amongst the knowledgeable lady shoppers and we were sent to little Loch Ionail: 'turn left at the school and follow the post van'. Which we did. And lo! we caught trout. In the rain. Thank you very much, the shopping ladies of Breacleit. We had bagged another lochisle.

We were dashing back to Scalpay when the sun broke blearily through the clouds. We were passing a rocky little loch, one of the ones that had no migratory runs, where we might catch a Lewis and Harris trout and no questions asked. We tumbled out of the van and ran down to the shore. I had an electifying tug on the first cast and a minute later Philip had a fine little 6-ounce fish and soon I had another. Fishing was fun again, so we carried on until the fifth or sixth fish came, spluttering and protesting and generally making a bit of a fuss at the surface. It was a small sea trout. It was in the wrong loch – or we were. We left a bit smartish.

We had bagged two lochisles in a couple of hours and we were on a roll. As we rolled down to Tarbert, we looked for a phone to ring Mr MacLeod while the dice were still hot. He told us of a small loch hidden in the hills above Loch an Duin – which was looking as trouty as ever. We scrambled up the cliffs on the southern shore and headed into the hills beyond. Loch Tarsuinn, when we found it, was small and steep-sided and weed-choked and looked as unpromising as an Duin had looked trouty. We felt like a couple of bullies, two blokes with big rods setting about this quiet little loch that no one had disturbed for years. Just give us a trout and we'll leave you alone – right? We felt more like bullies when we caught one. It was the smallest trout I have ever photographed. And possibly the most precious.

We were elated. We had caught fish on three islands that day. There were other lochisles off the coast of Harris and Lewis but they would wait for another expedition with more time and a boat. The ferry to Skye left at 7.30 the next morning and we would be on it with seven lochisles under our belt and just one day to go.

*   *   *

Wednesday, 10 June

We docked at Uig on the north-west tip of Skye at 9.15, Wednesday morning. We had arrived on South Uist at 7.40 on Friday evening, four and a half days before. Our self-imposed target was to bag as many lochisles as possible *and be back on the mainland* within five days of arriving. We planned to catch the last ferry from Armadale at the southern end of Skye at 7 p.m. This was due to land at Mallaig on the Scottish mainland at 7.30 – with a bare ten minutes to spare. To be on the safe side we would try for the earlier ferry at 5.30. We had eight hours.

There is plenty of fishing on Skye itself but there are also several islands with lochs studded around its coast. Only one of these has a scheduled ferry service from Skye. Raasay is a long finger of swooping hills set in the seas between Skye and the Applecross peninsula of Wester Ross. The next ferry for Raasay left Sconser, on the other side of Skye, at 10.30.

It was a perfect day. The sun shone, desperately trying to make up for the previous four days of downpour, and a stiff breeze blew the tops off the waves as the ferry pushed across the Sound of Raasay. The nearest loch to the ferry lies in the Raasay Forest. Bruce Sandison describes this Home Loch – Loch a'Mhullinn – as 'great fun to fish', and goes on to suggest Black Zulu, Red Palmer and Peter Ross. 'All Raasay lochs are fished from the bank,' he says. We called at the Isle of Raasay Hotel to get advice and permits. The fishing on Loch a'Mhullinn, it turns out, is free. We drove up through the towering pines of the forest to the loch.

It is not obvious when you get to Loch a'Mhullinn. You expect to see water when you get to a loch. What you see at Loch a'Mhullinn is rhododendrons. They were magnificent rhododendrons, a riot of pink and magenta in the June sunshine. But no sign of any water. We could hear water, the sounds of paddling and splashing from behind the screen of rhododendrons. We walked back down the lane to a small gap in the shrubbery where a flotilla of canoes was fussing in the shallows like a brood of ducks. A narrow view of the loch was visible down the tunnel of rhododendrons. There are islands in Loch a'Mhullinn and presumably a far shore, but we could not see them. They too were festooned in rhododendrons. We decided to walk around the loch, to find the spot where Bruce had had great fun fishing his team of flies from the bank. It took a precious hour or so to fight our way round through the tangled shrubbery and we never once saw the water. There is no gap. We did spot a broken plastic boat tied to the bank and by sliding down through the bushes one of us could stand, teetering, on this and flip something of a roll cast onto the water. This is not great fun. And after a while we gave up. We were getting desperate. We gambled all on the long drive to a cluster of hill lochs at the northern tip of Raasay.

There are no rhododendrons around Loch an Uachdair.

Here the breeze that had ruffled the sound was screaming off the open sea and ripping the surface. It was hopeless. After another hour we abandoned the attempt. We packed the rods away and drove disconsolately down the length of this beautiful island to catch the ferry back to Skye.

The road to the ferry passes through Raasay forest. We had twenty minutes until the ferry was due. We looked at each other. There was time for ten more minutes on Loch a'Mhullinn. It was Philip's turn to teeter on the sunken boat. With just three minutes to spare before we *had* to leave, I heard a shout from beyond the rhododendrons. There was a splashing in the water beside the sunken boat: Philip had caught a miraculous Raasay trout. We hurled the kit in the van and raced the ferry along the shore to the slip.

We landed back on Skye at 3.45 p.m., two and a quarter hours before we had to check in for the last ferry from Armadale at the southern tip of Skye.

We had chosen our last loch with care. Loch Mor na Caiplaich is an unremarkable loch in low hills above Sligachan where all roads in Skye must meet. Wherever we had fetched up, we would have had to pass this spot. With eight Lochisles bagged, we were feeling pretty damned invincible as we squelched across the sodden moorland. The sun still shone from a clear sky and the view, south to the stark grandeur of the Cuillin Hills, took one's breath away. So did the wind, still pushing out of the north-west but now with the mountains of Skye to contend with. For the last time we settled to the familiar pattern, working along the coast of the little loch, leap-frogging from feature to feature, from one rocky outcrop to the next, working the deeps or shallows according to fancy. It was Philip's day. He called across to me and I saw his rod bent against the backdrop of the Cuillins. It was a brave sight.

It was all but over. We stumbled back to the van, packed the rods away and headed for Armadale and the ferry.

I don't remember which of us spotted the little 'B' on the timetable above the 7 p.m. ferry. We looked at the legend at the bottom of the page. The little 'B' meant 'operates only during July and August'. It was 6.30: the last ferry had left an hour before. It was not quite over yet. We swung the van round and headed back for Kyleakin.

At 7.25 we crossed the infamous new bridge to Kyle of Lochalsh.

We had caught trout on nine lochisles in fifteen minutes under five days.

26 ℒ

Snob

A trout lies in a gravel hollow etched by the clear water funnelling into the pool. The armour-clad form of a stonefly nymph tumbles into view amid the bubbles. Before it is swept on its way, the trout tips up into the current and grabs the heavy morsel. A major error. As he turns to settle back in the lie, he finds himself attached to a fine nylon line and being hauled unceremoniously towards the sunlight. There is panic and pandemonium for a few long minutes until, exhausted, he feels himself slid across the surface. In the relative calm of defeat, the trouts's tongue squeezes the traitorous stonefly nymph impaled against his palate and a wave of relief suffuses his exquisite speckled body: 'An artificial – thank heaven for that – just for a moment there I thought I had been caught on bait.'

The English have a talent for snobbery. Many saner nations consider the best imitation of a stonefly nymph to be a stonefly nymph. But not the English fly fisherman who regards bait-fishing with lip-curled horror and then spares no effort in his search for arcane materials to create a 'fly' that looks, feels and moves like a stonefly nymph.

There are, of course, many fishermen around the globe who fish only with a fly. They may think fly-fishing is more challenging, artistic, satisfying or exciting. They may just think it is more effective. But some Englishmen, incomprehensibly, have regarded fly-fishing as morally superior to other forms.

You think about these things on the River Dove. It was here that Charles Cotton, dilettante scion of Derbyshire landed gentry, first pointed the finger of scorn at bait-fishing for trout, which he asserted was not 'so cleanly nor (as 'tis said) so Gentile a way of Fishing as with a Flie'.

I had never fished on the Dove. I had always assumed that so historic a stream would be parcelled out into private syndicates and clubs with the occasional manicured hotel water. And so it is for much of the beautiful middle reaches below Hartington. But most rivers, however prestigious, have odd pockets of nostalgic sanity where a bit of fishing can be had for the price of a couple of pints passed across at the farmhouse door. The problem for the travelling fishermen is to find them without spending frustrating hours and days wandering down the wrong lanes to knock on the wrong doors. So I will mark your card on the understanding that it goes no further.

I am a bit iffy about mentioning Bank Top Farm: the last thing I want is anyone fishing there. Some places can be fished communally, anglers nodding when they meet, exchanging a word or so in the fishing hut and so on. Upper Dovedale is not one of these places. It is a place for quiet solitude. It is the most secretive, secluded little river I have ever fished.

Limestone erodes quickly, dissolving into a tight little steep-sided valley, with the bright stream twisting through the bankside alders. Now, bankside alders are not everyone's idea of a good time. They have catkins in a most virulent form, little round ones shaped like those strange carved utensils you find in craft shops for delivering honey from jar to plate. Unlike most catkins, these dry and endure and entangle any fishing tackle that comes within their gravitational field. These alders, and the steep undercut banks, envelop an angler working down in the stream. It is delightfully intimate.

Up here, above Hartington, the river is small, often only inches deep, but there are deep holes in the limestone bed where chest waders are the only way to avoid hoisting up out of the bed to get round an undercut alder hole.

Beresford, once the home of Charles Cotton, lies a few miles downstream among the ramblers and Kagouls of the middle reaches. The fishing lodge with the entwined initials of himself and Issac Walton still stands beside the waters of the Dove. But these are not the only angling ghosts that haunt the river. Above Hartington, on the single track, much-gated lane that follows the river up to Pilsbury, a ruined cottage nestles in the valley. Local lore has it that the cottage was once the home of Canon Greenwell before his association with the waters of the Tweed and the fly that bears his name.

Don't rush off to Bank Top for a fishing holiday. File it and forget it until you fancy a quiet day of contemplation and improvisation among the dark alder roots on this most English of trout streams, home of that most English of angling vices.

27

Conway Twitter

Something pretty strange started appearing as we drove along the valley of the Dee near Llangollen. Enormous butterflies were clinging to the white-washed walls of cottages alongside the road. Huge things with a yard of wingspan: tortoiseshells, fritillaries, all sorts. One farmhouse across the valley was festooned with the creatures. Eerie. Why butterflies? And why here?

'Wasn't Merioneth known as the "Butterfly County" at one time?' said my father. He delivers these obscure rhetorical questions with the implication that, surely, anyone with half a claim to an education has such facts at his fingertips. He does this to me all the time. I sometimes suspect he makes them up as he goes along, but it is difficult to call his bluff without a working knowledge of Merioneth. The butterflies continued to infest the buildings alongside the A5 as we drove through the pretty town of Corwen, crossed the Dee and headed north-west towards Snowdonia.

We were on our way to the River Conway. The Conway is famous for its migratory fish; whether sewin or salmon depends on whichever is in the ascendant: these things come and go. At that moment it was salmon. Betws-y-Coed is the centre of the salmon fishing. The upper waters of the Conway join the A5 from the south-west, 5 miles above the town, and the two drop down into a tight, wooded gorge. But the narrow gorge just ain't big enough for the both of them and the road crosses the river and soon begins to climb up on the other side. A layby on the left has a transport café in an old caravan. It is splendidly seedy. You can watch the bacon for your sandwich frying on the stove as you chat to the owner about the fishing on the river below. The water was high to be sure, but it had been a lot higher this year and he had had fish at the weekend. Big bacon sandwiches and hopeful chat such as this are just what fishermen need. We slithered down the steep, slippery slope of grass and bracken that falls away from the layby, down into the rocky gorge.

It is a magical spot. The swollen waters were carrying rich colour, twisting with ominously little noise through the ruptured rock (I apologize for the alliteration: it is impossible to avoid in Wales). It is a place of deep pools and dark currents between steep sides. The whole scene shouts 'SALMON'.

It is, of course, lying through its teeth. The Conway Falls a mile or so above Betws-y-Coed are impassable to the migratory fish that wait hopefully at their base. They may not have much longer to wait – or they may. For several years now a fish pass has been planned, promised, imminent and shelved. Earlier this year I was assured that this was to be the year. It isn't. Perhaps next year. If and when it arrives, it will open up many miles of good spawning grounds on the upper river and its tributaries. For now the upper river is left to the hardy little brown trout of the Welsh mountains. It was for these little gems that we had come to the river. And the gorge, for all its beauty and power, was not a place to be wading unseen with a wet fly. We had walked some way down through the beech woods without seeing a rise to aim at. Perhaps we might return later in the day. For now we scrambled up the wooded slope and back into the daylight of the A5.

A stone cottage stood on the far side of the road. I recognized it. A small sign on the side of the house reads 'Fishing Tickets'. The National Trust has the fishing on most of the waters of the Conway above the falls and Mr Ellis issues tickets on four beats. Two are on the Machno, a tributary that enters the Conway hard by the falls. You can fish on the Conway itself, in the gorge below the layby and its café, a mile or so down to the Conway Falls, and that will set you back £2 for the day. There are times, I am assured, when North Wales bakes under a summer sun: these are the times to pay a visit to the gorge of the Conway, deep in its cool woods. But not today. Today it was chill and the little sun there was came in fits and starts – we needed all we could get. It was a day for the open waters of the upper river where the high waters of the last few days would hopefully be receding first. For £3 we could fish on the whole of the upper river, 8 miles or so from the lip of the source in Llyn Conway to the A5, and most of this double bank.

The upper Conway is a perfect example of a stony mountain stream. It was built by the same firm that did the Dart up on Dartmoor, the upper Eden high in the Pennines and any number of unregarded gems that tumble down the mountainsides of the west of Scotland, Wales and the South West. The banks are wooded but, in the curious way these things have, they are rarely wooded on both sides: where the current cuts deep under the roots of scrubby oaks and rowan on one bank, the other will be nibbled close by sheep and perfect for casting. There are large boulders to squeeze the tumbling water into narrow channels, waterfalls in the full range of sizes, small, medium and large, deep still pools and long rocky riffles in a range of depths to suit all tastes. Occasionally the sun would burst through and it was perfect. Nearly.

Look up the river: you are looking to the south-west and pretty soon your eyes are watering in the stiff little south-westerly wind. We would fish downstream. The water was a rich dark brown, not thick with sediment, but stained like very old tea in the pot.

I am not a natural wet-fly fisherman. I lack faith. With rising fish I am happy enough: I can see the things and they are feeding. I can cast for hours without a touch, as long as I can see something to go at. It is different when nothing moves. Soon I have the suspicion that my flies are swimming in a fishless desert. That first tug of the point fly, the one that tells you that you are not alone in the river, is vital for my equanimity. Thankfully it was not too long in coming. A pool, deeper and slower than most, was divided by a large rock. As the flies swung over between the far bank and the rock, something lively attached itself to the line and danced up the pool. A trout of 8 or 9 inches: fat and fine. It was enough. There were fish to be had that day in the River Conway.

The received wisdom in peaty water (and I have never seen one peatier) is to fish flies with flash, a touch of gold or silver. But with a faith as threadbare as mine I prefer to stick to a team with a pedigree. My tail fly, the one that does 90 per cent of the work, is usually a small Endrick Spider. This is a fly to inspire confidence. The body is, to all intents and purposes, a pheasant-tail nymph, copper wire and all; the hackle is a sparse collar of partridge hackle, the soft, pulsating 'life' behind many of the great north country spider flies. What a combination! If you can't have faith in that, you may as well use a net. A brighter Partridge & Yellow goes on the middle dropper and a black gnat or black spider on the bob, where smaller fish who have lost the will to live are wont to hurl themselves. If you want to catch the maximum, you should, I suppose, use a long rod to steer the team through the currents. On a small stream I much prefer to use a small, light rod that lets the small mountain fish show what they can do and, if there is a rise, I can snip off the droppers and fish dry.

And so it went. We wandered up the stream, through the small village of Ysbyty Ifan, taking small bright fish from the wind-riffled pools. It was not my first visit to the upper Conway. I had come before in May, when the rivers of the lowlands were just coming on song. But not in the Welsh hills. It was a cold day and the waters of the Conway had that grey clarity that looks devoid of all life, like the eyes of an oldish cod. We had fished all morning and not touched a thing. The trees had had barely a hint of green on them and the water, when I turned over a rock to look for any sign of life, was bone-chilling. It is a mistake to come to these high streams until the weather has warmed the water into life. I had meant to come again in summer and had not got round to it. Now, in September, the river was cooling down again. But it was not too late.

Half a mile below the village there is a long deep pool where the trees, for once, line both sides. The pool was full of the brown water and the lower branches of the bushes trailed in the currents constricting the surface flow. Where the trees ended, the pool widened. There, at the edge of the faster water from between the flooded foliage, was a rise. And again. A fish was feeding on one side; another fish worked the opposite side. We had walked miles of the river and not seen a hint of a rise, yet here were two feeding fish and now others were working the pool below them. I switched to dry fly and floated, twitched, hurled everything I could think of at those fish. I could see nothing on the water. One fish pricked itself on a nymph: another scared itself spitless coming to a black gnat. Nothing stuck. Father watched with the air of 'if only I was allowed to have a go'. He had a go and I watched with the same sort of air. We both gave up. We went off to different bits of the river where fish were still resolutely not rising and then snuck back. There they were, still at it and still untouched by us. I have seen it time and again and do not understand. Why, on the miles and miles of river we had seen, should the fish rise at this one spot? And not just one fish but several. It leads to the disquieting thought, on those days when nothing is happening, that somewhere, round the next bend maybe, the surface would be snap, crackle and popping like breakfast cereal. You can walk a good few weary and fruitless miles in the grip of such thoughts.

The trout in that pool tired of the game before we did and we were left to work our way back down to the car, picking up a small fish here and there from the tea-stained depths on tea-stained spiders until the sun finally disappeared behind a grey sheet from the west. And then in the failing light, one fish feeding surreptitiously behind a drowning branch fell to a parachute Black Gnat.

I don't know. It was a close decision that could have gone either way. But I *think* we won on points. It certainly felt like that as we drove home.

Over-sized, Over-sexed and Over Here

I went fishing last Saturday. It was bright and cold at 9 a.m. when we met in the car park beside the River Windrush in Burford. There were four of us, each hoping that we would *not* catch what we had come here to catch.

For fishermen hoping not to catch something, we were certainly going at it in a big way. A purist might complain that our methods were a little unsporting, but no one could say we weren't trying. Julie was using baited fish traps she had lowered into the river the night before. Andy was staggering up the bank under the weight of a large metal backpack. It had dials and switches and looked like one of the more technological ways of going to war. He was electro-fishing. Vaughan's method was elegantly simple: earlier that morning he had wound down the sluices on the weir above the town, draining the river by the car park to a shallow trickle. And I had a bucket with a glass bottom for peering into that shallow trickle. One way or another we had that bit of the Windrush fairly surrounded.

Vaughan found the first one in a piece of old drainpipe among the rocks and rubbish. Mud and sand slithered from the pipe as he lifted it and there, staring up with pointy little eyes, was what we hoped we wouldn't find: an American signal crayfish.

Why is that everything that comes from America is bigger, more aggressive, eats more, grows quicker and breeds faster than its European equivalent? They said something of the sort about the GIs during the war, and the grey squirrel, the mink and the rainbow trout are much the same. It is certainly true of the signal crayfish, which is the reason why signal crayfish were imported into Britain in the late 1970s to be farmed for food. It was believed that they could be kept under control. Alas, like grey squirrels, rainbow trout, mink and GIs, they soon showed an alarming tendency to wander. Worse: the signal crayfish harboured a fungal plague to which they were tolerant but which wiped out our smaller, less precocious native crayfish. As crayfish farms sprang up throughout southern England, so, stream by stream, the native populations began to die and disappear. In some rivers this was spectacular, with reefs of red corpses littering the bed and piling up at the margins. Elsewhere they just weren't there any more.

They just weren't there any more in the Windrush. No crayfish of any sort had been seen on the Windrush for a decade.

Last spring one of the first projects to re-colonize native crayfish was begun on the Windrush, a mile or so above Burford. You do not simply lob native crayfish into the water and hope. These are valuable creatures, rare and getting rarer. Cages of precious native crays were planted along the river bed. These were experimental 'canaries' to check for the presence of plague and other problems. Their six-month quarantine was passed successfully this winter and full-scale re-colonization was to begin this spring.

And then a Burford fisherman reported finding a large, red-clawed crayfish at the end of his garden – which is why we went fishing last Saturday. We found more. Not many, but enough: one was 'berried' – a female heavy with eggs – and two were babies. Eighteen months of effort, preparations for the reintroduction of natives, may now have to be abandoned.

Just how those American signal crays came to the river beside Burford car park may be the saddest chapter in this sorry tale.

When escaping signal crays began to colonize certain southern rivers, not everyone shed a tear. The local boyos, who had been used to catching a plateful of natives for the barbecue, now found something larger and juicier in their traps, something that would fetch £5 a pound in the export market without the bother and expense of farming the things. One or two boyos went into trapping in a big way. In the Thames region the National Rivers Authority began to issued consents to trap signal crayfish, hoping that ruthless trapping would check, if not wipe out, these populations of interlopers. A happy thought – and impossibly naive. What trapper will deliberately wipe out his own source of income? Unless, of course, he is lucky enough to know of other rivers where signal crayfish have set up home – perhaps because he put them there one dark night. This is 'ranching'.

How much the spread of signal crayfish is the result of escape or the result of deliberate seeding by unscrupulous trappers is unknown. But the number of populations found beside bridges and car parks is awfully suspicious. Either way, the damage has been done: the native British crayfish may well be doomed.

But let me leave you with a cheerful little thought: there is evidence that the average size of the trout, barbel and chub increases on rivers that have been invaded by signal crayfish. Like the GIs, they are here for the duration. We might as well enjoy it.

Sea Trout Sampler

The worst thing you can say in our house is, 'You're getting to be just like your grandfather.' That pulls you up short, I can tell you.

My grandfather was a farmer in Templecombe and a famous curmudgeon in that part of Somerset. His legendary selfishness and audacious meanness would take your breath away. Also, in later life he developed a huge and bulbous nose, which has always left me super-sensitive to the threat of becoming like him (you never know with genes). Grandfather was also a life-long church bell-ringer. Now, they are always looking for new ringers in our Oxfordshire village but for years I refused even to try it in the fear that bell-ringing might somehow release the miserly campanologist with a massive hooter lurking in my heritage.

But then my daughter announced that she was getting married and the parish put out another plea for ringers for the millennium and I thought how splendid it would be to peal the bells at Emily's wedding and so, ten months ago, I pulled my first bell. And, sure enough, I have become a fanatic.

Which explains why, at 9.00 on Monday night – the moment when the first fly was to be cast in the National Sea Trout Festival Challenge, I was still 300 miles to the south, climbing into the camper van with ringing ears and sore hands. Monday night is bell practice night.

The National Sea Trout Festival was taking place on the sea trouty waters of the Annan and the Nith around Dumfries. The festival consists of a lot of fishing for sea trout and a fair amount of talking about sea trout. And most people, I would say, are there for the fishing. I am not a sea trout fisher myself: I have fished for sea trout and I have caught sea trout, but rarely at the same time. But I know people who are sea trout fishers and I can tell by the way their eyes go when the talk gets round to Cleughead and Mount Annan beats of the Annan and Drumlanrig Castle on the Nith that this sort of fishing does not come along every night of the week. You get to fish these beats (and others just as resounding) if you enter the Challenge.

The Challenge takes place over five nights of fishing, from 9.00 in the evening until 4.00 the next morning. Staying awake for a couple of those nights would be challenge enough for me, but the challengers are there to catch sea trout and there are prizes awarded for the most sea trout and the largest sea trout and so on, and you may think, reading between the lines, that this is a fishing competition. And you would be right. It is. Sort of. The difference is in the spirit rather than the letter. Listen: Kevin and Nick had not met before the Challenge. They found themselves sharing Cleughead on Wednesday night when Cleughead came into life. At 9.45 Kevin was into a sea trout on Luce Flats Pool; by 10.15 he had had four more. He called to the marshal, who had been watching all this from the bank, and asked him to fetch Nick from upstream to take his place on that magic pool. Within minutes Nick had a sea trout, the first he had ever taken on a fly. That is the spirit of the challenge. In that hour before dark both Kevin and Nick had caught five sea trout, the limit score for any challenger in one night: after five sea trout, you are fishing for fun. The Challenge is taken seriously, the competition is not.

And certainly not by me, not this year. This year I was dipping my toes in to see what the water of the Sea Trout Challenge was like. So it didn't matter too much that I was setting off from home as the Challenge got under way six hours' drive to the north. I would arrive beside the waters of the Annan as the fishing stopped in the early hours of the morning. I would have had a night without sleep to get in step with the challengers who had fished through the night.

Things do not always go according to plan. On Sunday it had rained long and hard on the waters of the Annan and Nith. The rivers had risen high and dirty and fishing on that first Monday night of the Challenge was abandoned. Fishing the swollen waters in the dark would not only be dangerous, it would be pointless: the sea trout would not take a fly in such turbid soup. So there was to be daytime fishing on the Tuesday and everyone could get a night's sleep on Monday night. Except me.

So on Tuesday morning I climbed into Anthony's battered Land Rover and, as he took me down to the Kirkwood beat of the Annan, he explained the organization of the Challenge. Anthony Steel has been the driving force behind the Festival since its beginnings in 1997. He handed me a folder of large-scale colour maps, one for each of the five beats to be fished, with meeting points, pools, car parking and beat boundaries clearly marked. As he guided me through the arrangements, I caught a whiff of the prodigious problems in organizing such a do. Look: it is midnight, it is pitch black, it is in the middle of the broad waters of the River Annan. A bloke has a fish attached to the end of his line. It is a sea trout. It weighs about two pounds. He nets the fish and releases it. And later on everyone believes this story. You see the problem? Or he could kill the fish to prove the point and there would be one less sea trout left to spawn in the river – which isn't much of a festival for the sea trout. The solution has been to recruit an army of volunteers from the local fishing fraternity to act as marshals. Each marshal stays within range of one or two fishermen and can be called by a blast on a whistle to verify each fish before its fate is decided. Over 200 sea trout were caught during the four remaining days of the Challenge and three-quarters of these were released. Also, of course, when it is midnight and pitch black and the middle of a big river you have never waded before, it is quite a comfort to know there is someone standing within a whistle-blast.

Down by the water at Kirkwood we met Kevin. Kevin is a dedicated sea trout fisherman from Carlisle. He has lived all his life within 300 yards of the Sheepmount Pool, where the Caldew meets the River Eden. The Annan was still high and coloured and the fly-only rule of the Challenge had been relaxed for this morning of off-the-record fishing. So the 5½-pound salmon and the plump sea trout that fell to his Flying-C in the next few minutes would not count in his Challenge tally.

I stumbled through the rest of that morning, walking the banks of the Annan under a warm sun, through Lower Hoddom, Upper Cleughead and down to Mount Annan where I would be fishing that evening. The river was dropping rapidly. A trio of fishermen was fishing the fly on the waters of Lower Hoddom and as I passed on the opposite bank, one of them straightened into that nonchalant pose that migratory fishermen adopt when they have a fish on. It is an eloquent pose and says, 'It's no big deal, it happens all the time and could someone, no hurry, get the net I left with all our gear at the top of the run because I didn't for one moment think there was a chance of connecting with a fish in this lot. Plenty of time, though.' It was a sea trout and I think we all enjoyed that fish. It gave us hope for the evening to come.

At noon the fishermen gathered at Barony College for an old-fashioned fry-up and the other festival event: the National Sea Trout Conference. The conference this year was to be on 'Improving the river habitat for all game fish' and had brought together experts in the field from everywhere in the British Isles. I wish I could tell you more about this splendid and worthy event, after thirty-two hours without sleep, I dozed off in the back of the camper van.

It was 7.00 that evening. We gathered beside the fishing shelter on the Mount Annan beat. The challengers who would be fishing together had met at lunch. Kevin was there, a salmon and a sea trout ahead on the day. Jonathan had come from South Africa on a fishing odyssey: the week before he had been on the chalkstreams of southern England, next week he would be on the Derbyshire Wye. His uncle, Philip, had joined him for the Sea Trout Challenge. A young man, Nick, had caught just one sea trout in his life and that was on a spinner. And there was me.

Fishing would not start for another two hours. Until then we would walk the water with Scot, a local expert on this beat of the Annan. He would point out the best pools and runs for this height of water, the hidden holes and underwater ledges to avoid. He could advise us on flies and tactics and the best beer to be found in the surrounding pubs. We listened hard.

Mount Annan beat has about $1^{1}/_{2}$ miles of double bank fishing, which can swallow five anglers with ease. Jonathan and Philip decided to take the upper section around Brydekirk Bridge. Kevin would start at the bottom of the beat, at Sand Pool and the island. Nick lowered himself through the trees beneath the wooded centre section of the beat and waded out beyond the furthest branches. And, for the moment, I watched.

Fishing – and especially sea trout fishing – is a combination of experience and luck. In the days that followed, over the lunches when the challengers would meet, bleary-eyed, to mull over who had done what on the previous night, who would do what that night, two names began to emerge. Kevin and Nick. By Friday lunch time it had all but become a two-horse race. The smart money was on Kevin. He was one fish ahead of Nick. He had been catching sea trout for eighteen years. He fished a Waddington of his own pattern, the fly that had taken countless sea trout. He had taken the five-fish limit on Luce Flats two days before and then invited Nick to take over the spot. If experience counted for anything, Kevin was money in the bank.

But if anyone had been watching with me as Nick edged out from beneath the trees on Tuesday night, they might have wanted to hedge that bet. Nick, who had caught just one sea trout before, had something else. His first cast swung round across the rocks of the side channel and the line went taut. That's the sort of thing you need.

It was not a sea trout. It was a fine little brown trout of around the pound and just the thing to get the rod bending. Nick slipped the fish back and fished his way down the rocky run in the last of the evening sun. As he moved out of sight around the long bend, I eased myself down into the water. I was armed with a shrimpy little Irish double on the point, a Cinnamon & Gold on the dropper to flash through the water still heavily tinged with colour. I fished out towards the faster water across the river and worked my way downstream. The sun had gone, the light was leaking from the sky and, in the deep shadows under the trees behind me, trout began feasting with crunchy little rises. Not huge fish, but fish – if you know what I mean. I can only fish fruitlessly for salmon or sea trout for so long if there are brownies rising all round me. This was so long. No one was watching. I reeled in and replaced the big double with a Black and Peacock Spider in trout-sized 14. On the dropper I tied a Golden Olive Bumble, a fly that has no business on a river, but for some reason has always been good to me. It was not, after all, a competition. I turned and side-cast these flies into the tunnel beneath the trees: at last I felt I knew what I was doing and before long a small brown was skittering across the surface. I was so absorbed in this game that I quite forgot about the challenge and the marshals – so when a voice called from the dark trees on the bank and asked how I was getting on, I jumped and felt guilty, as if I had been caught doing something behind the bike shed. I couldn't see the man in the shadows but I reeled in, replaced the spider with the shrimpy double in the last of the light and dutifully turned and cast into to the main current across the river.

Good grief! There was a violent tug and before I had time to do much about anything there was a frothing commotion on the end of the line. In a moment I realized this was no brown trout. I also realized that I had not brought a landing net with me.

It was a sea trout. Not, in truth, a big sea trout but, at 13 inches, big enough to count in the Challenge. And I realized I had also forgotten to bring my whistle. I was alone on the dark river with a sea trout in my hand. I manoeuvred my camera from its case with the other hand. I held the fish as far from me as I could and hoped the flash and the autofocus would do the rest for posterity.

I slipped the lovely silver thing back into the water. It was smaller than many a brown I have caught but there is, when all is said and done, something very special about a sea trout in the night. I caught no more before I climbed from the river in the darkness and crawled into my sleeping bag in the van.

I slept until morning. I looked out at the river and wondered for a while whether I could stay for just one more night. Then I started the engine and headed for home and my daughter's wedding. I couldn't take the risk: a man who can get addicted to bell-ringing would stand no chance against the beguiling addiction of sea trout at night on the River Annan.

*   *   *

P.S.

That night the river came alive: four of the twenty challengers caught the limit of five sea trout in the hour or so before dark. By Friday, Kevin had nine fish, Nick had eight. On Friday morning the heavens opened again and the rivers rose. That night Nick Isles caught two sea trout; Kevin caught none.

There is talk of next year's National Sea Trout Festival moving to Wales – or the West Country. Either way, Nick and Kevin will be there. And – having run out of nubile daughters – so will I.

First Love

G.E. Moore was not, to my knowledge, a fisherman. He was a philosopher. He specialized in Ethics and it appears to have been a nice line of work to be in because he only wrote a couple of books in a lifetime of endeavour. And they were not big books at that. The second was a slim tome concerned with how we can decide whether an action or a state of affairs is 'good' or 'bad'. G.E. Moore was not by any stretch of the imagination headstrong. He does not plunge. Something like half the book is taken up in considering whether when we say an action is 'good', we are saying anything about the action at all. It could be, he says, that we are merely making an assertion about our feelings towards it: when I say 'christmas pudding is nice' and you say 'christmas pudding is horrid', we are not really disagreeing about christmas pudding. We are saying 'I like christmas pudding' and 'I don't like christmas pudding', and both can be true at the same time. We are simply describing our feelings towards christmas pudding, and not describing the christmas pudding at all. We are describing ourselves. Riveting stuff.

I mention all this because I have an uneasy feeling about what follows. And in describing the differences between fishing for trout in rivers and on still-waters, I find I am saying more about myself than about fishing.

It was a day in late July four seasons ago. Somewhere, elsewhere, the CLA Gamefair was in full swing. I forget where. I was on a small river in Cumbria. It was a sunny day just like the days before and the river was low. The banks were high, steep and wooded so that the river felt intimate and private. I had worked my way up a long section of boulder-strewn riffle of the sort that you are always advised not-to-overlook-because-there-are-these-holes-and-hollows-in-which-good-fish-can-lurk-unsuspected-by-the-casual-angler. Well, I suspect these fish like the very dickens on that sort of water but I cannot off-hand recall finding one. I did not find one on that sultry late morning. At the top of the long riffle was a bridge arching high over the stream and beneath the bridge was a pool. The pool was shaded on both sides by tall, leafy trees but in the middle the current passed serenely under the sunlight before slipping down between the first of the tumbled slabs of red sandstone that formed the riffle. I could see this pool for some time as I worked my way upstream. I was hoarding it like I used to save the yolk of my fried egg till last. There were small movements among the line of bubbles that drifted down the pool.

On another day I would have worked up to the pool and started fishing, but it was a warm morning and the movements among the bubbles were the first signs of fish. I did not want to squander them. Besides, I needed a pee. You would think that, standing in a river to the tops of one's thigh waders, one is in an ideal position to pee. Not this one. This one is English and finds that peeing is only satisfactory, damned near only possible, when done against something – like a tree. I am uneasy in the middle of a field, let alone a river. Is this a throwback to scent-marking ancestors in our arboreal past? Or just English inhibition? Or just me?

Relieved, I surveyed the pool from the wooded bank opposite the tail of the pool. There was nothing difficult about getting to the fish. I could wade between the boulders at the tail of the pool and from there it was an easy cast to cover the hint of activity in the middle beneath the overhanging trees. They weren't overhanging much: I'm just trying to make this sound a respectably tricky cast. In fact, it was dead easy. I sat on a boulder and, just for once, I did what I always tell everyone else to do but never seem to be able to manage myself. Nothing. I was a much better fisherman when I smoked. I made it a rule to get into position for a cast and then get out a cigarette. I was never a very adept smoker and I found it impossible to smoke and do anything else, so the fish and I had five or ten minutes to get used to each other before anything else happened. There was time to spot other, subtler, rises and for the scene to forget my arrival. Five minutes without a cigarette is a very long time. But on this occasion I was feeling expansive. I pulled off some line and rebuilt my leader, sitting on the boulder, watching the fish. I tied on a new fly and got everything just so. And then I cast across to the bubbles. Nothing happened for a couple of casts but I was in no hurry, so I let them drift over the lip of the pool and cast again. And then the fly just disappeared in a tiny disturbance.

It was not a huge trout but it was a *good* fish. There is little more to tell. It did nothing spectacular: it fought its weight around the pool, in and out of the shade and came soon enough to the net. It weighed exactly one pound. I really have no idea why this fish has stuck with me for four seasons. It was just perfect. Everything I love about fishing a river was there.

First, I knew where the fish were. This has always struck me as a major drawback of stillwaters. The fish can wander all over the shop and it doesn't take long to convince me that I am fishing over water untainted by trout – a thought that quickly erodes any perseverance I had to begin with. Which brings me to something I read in last month's letters page. Mr D.A.L. Birrell of Great Dunmow read Chris Tarrant's article on catching the huge lake trout of Lake Nueltin in Canada's Northwest Territories and he prays 'that our sport of game-fishing be protected from people who use Humming Bird fish-finders and down-riggers . . . '. Well, Mr Birrell, I have seen Nueltin lake: it is the size of Wales and 100 feet deep and if you were to go there, you had better use a fish-finder if you want to find fish. If you stay in Great Dunmow, you are in very little danger from the people who use them. And, incidentally, game-fishing is just as much their sport as yours; rather more theirs, in fact, in the Northwest Territories. Sorry about that, but it really needed saying.

There is no need for a fish-finder on rivers like the Caldew. Even if the fish are not obligingly showing themselves, there are really only a few places where any self-respecting trout will be found on a river. And what's more, they stay still. If you see a fish on a stillwater, practically the only thing you can be sure of is that he will be somewhere else in a minute's time. Not so on a river. As long as you don't scare him, he will stay there or thereabouts for days, years sometimes. And if you don't get him this time, you can try again an hour or so later, or tomorrow. You can get quite attached to some fish when you are river fishing. I have had the closest relationships with trout that lie beneath brambles.

There is something about a trout beneath brambles. They are often sizeable fish because it is such a very good lie. And because it is such a good lie they feel secure. I can remember one on the River Otter, about a foot or so down-stream of the metal footbridge which marks the end of the private water above and the public water below. Budleigh Salterton society consists of vast phalanxes of elderly ladies (I don't know the collective term for elderly ladies) who walk their dogs between Budleigh Salterton and Otterton. They trip-trap over the bridge like so many Billy Goat Gruffs (I don't know the collective term for them either) and helpfully point out to the stalking fisherman the shoals of trout working their way upstream through the silkweed. These trout are mullet. But there are trout. And the one that lives under the bram-ble by the bridge is impervious to pointing and dogs and so forth. He is also impervious to deception. He rises boldly but always follows the morsel down-stream, tilting back a little to examine it before taking it crisply. I start my fishing at the bridge and have a go at him. The cast under that bramble is difficult enough to cover his lie about one cast in four, which means you may cover it two or three times for each fly lost in the bush. Occasionally he rises to my fly but seems to double over it as if, at the last minute, he had spotted the ball had gone but couldn't avoid the late tackle. I have never so much as pricked him. I return to him after fishing down the river and have another go before packing up. Deep down I don't think I want to catch him anymore. We have become too friendly. You don't get that sort of thing on a stillwater.

As destructive to my confidence as not knowing where the fish are is knowing where they are and not being able to get there. This is a problem on all waters but it is worse on stillwaters: there is so much more of it to see and so much more of it out of reach. If you are a bank fisherman, the whole thing can turn into a long-distance casting competition, an enterprise I am ill-equipped to join. Or you can wade out, which always seems rather puny with the whole of Blagdon Lake in front of you. Or there is boat fishing – which is an expedition and there is someone else and paraphernalia and a spare can of petrol and I can't be doing with it. And still the fish seem to be rising just out-side range. So you row over there and then they aren't. River fishing is not immune from this. Sometimes it can save the day.

One of the delights of fishing a new, and especially a small, river is that each run and riffle might have a better pool or run just above or just around the bend, and if they are not rising here, well then, they may be rising there because each bend and pool has its own pattern of shade and current and bottom. Loch Corrib is a fine and famous trout water, and splendid days with many splendid fish may be had there. I know, because I've read about them. But there are other days when nothing happens and then, on a big water like Corrib, nothing happens as far as the eye can see in any direction. The place has switched off. Rivers can switch off, too, but most rivers, particularly small rivers, have such a variety of conditions that somewhere, perhaps round the next bend, something will be happening.

On a cold day in early autumn on the upper Conwy it was a pool below a slow moving run through a tangle of scrub willows. Not a fish had moved throughout the day on this rocky little river, but in this one spot we discov-ered fish feeding steadily every time we passed. On the Lowther in high summer the water is thin and clear in the broad moorland valley that flanks the hills of the Lake District. But then the river drops through a hidden gorge above the village of Askham. It is another little world in the gorge. A cool one at that, and there are always fish to be found rising in the dappled shade. Shade is often the key in summer. The long pools of the Eden all but stop in the summer. The fish are still there but they can only be taken at night when they can be heard crashing after the moths and insects that infest the night over the river. During the day nothing stirs. You look for shade and movement and you're lucky if you find either. At Sandford, below the Black Bridge, we found both. It was not a feeding frenzy, you understand. At the most you could claim that feeding occurred, but it was enough to take a fish from a long hot day.

Looking back on all this and considering perfect fish and fishing, I am forced to recognize something I had not seen before. My pleasure and satisfaction in fishing is not involved in any way with Endurance in the Face of Adversity, with rugged derring-do, with Guts, Determination and the Will to Win. The fish from the bridge pool of the Caldew was not difficult, it was not long sought, it was not huge. It was not, in short, a triumph. It was a small, intimate pleasure – like a phrase of jazz for piano, bass and drums that is not a virtuoso piece but simple and perfectly harmonious. A stillwater is, for me, too big a stage. There is always something of the unexpected about catching a trout in stillwater. It is hard to claim you planned to catch *that* trout there. This, of course, is the thrill of fishing a loch, that at any time on a long and heroic day a monster may rise from the deep and the fight is on.

My pleasure in river fishing, like the pleasure in playing a piece of music, is not the pleasure of the unexpected. The dots were all there on the page, the trout was there to be caught. My pleasure in small rivers is orchestrated. The surprise comes when it works.

31 ✒

A Day on the Dee

I have always rather admired salmon fishermen, in the same way that I admire a circus contortionist: it's not something I want to do, my body doesn't work that way, but I am always impressed that anyone does it at all. Personally I need hope, and lots of it. I need some sign that any moment a fish will grab my fly. Ideally, I want to see feeding fish or, failing that, at least some small sign that the unlikely might happen. A tug, say. Or a flash at my floating fly. Something. Anything to reassure me there is Something Out There.

But salmon fishermen are made of sterner stuff. Their faith is founded on the rock of conviction. It is not something that withers and perishes in a few fishless hours. They know that patience will be rewarded, if not now, then in the hereafter – this afternoon, say, or tomorrow, or after the next spate, or next season, sometime. And so, firm in their faith, they have no need of signs, they do not crave reassurance.

Not so. They're as bad as the rest of us.

We had only been on the riverbank a few minutes when a much-bewadered figure came into view. He asked how we had got on and we explained that we had just arrived. We asked him how he had got on.

'Oh, just one,' he said, casual-like. The salmon fisherman who has just caught a salmon bears a striking resemblance to the man whose wife has just produced a baby. There is the same inane grin: there is the same pretence that this is, after all, an everyday event, nothing to make a fuss about, and at the same time there is the same unbearable urge to tell people all about it. It is very mean not to ask the new father or the proud captor for more details. Over the years my wife has trained me in the correct interrogation of a new father. I have been given a standard procedure. The questions are: Sex? Weight and size? How long did it take? Where did it happen? How are they doing? Any amusing anecdotes accompanying the event? With the slightest modification the same questions will do very nicely for the salmon angler bursting with pride at the bankside. It was, we learned, a fish of about 6 pounds taken just above Duncan's Pool and being rather red it had been released.

The details of this fish were passed back and forth up the river for the rest of the day, changing and recycling so that it seemed at times that several fish had been caught. There were many salmon anglers on the water that day and each one we passed asked the same hopeful, fearful questions. 'How have you been getting on then?' Hopeful that someone, somewhere was catching fish to show that there were fish to be had; fearful that someone, somewhere was catching fish to show that they were on the wrong fly, the wrong depth, the wrong pool. Craving reassurance but dreading the good news.

There is much innocent fun to be had at such times.

'How have you been getting on then?'

'Oh, I've had a couple and Paul's had three, I think.' A rainbow of emotions dances across the face of the salmon angler: envy, hope, joy, hatred – they're all there.

'Any size?' he asks, biting the bullet. I am enjoying this and quite prepared to string it out for a bit but Paul is getting uneasy. He reads the lesson in church from time to time and entertains some hopes of going to Heaven, and besides, he is a salmon fisherman himself and cannot stand such gratuitous cruelty. 'Pound and a half,' he says, 'not bad for a grayling.' The tortured salmon fisherman relaxes, his countenance clears. We are grayling fishermen. Probably harmless.

Nobody fishes the Welsh Dee for grayling. Not in early October. Not when there is water at the end of a splendid salmon season. Not when a rainstorm the night before has raised the river a couple of inches and tinged it with colour. And this is strange, for the Welsh Dee is almost certainly the finest grayling water in England and Wales, possibly in the British Isles. I knew all this and yet this was my first visit to the fishing around Llangollen.

We nearly didn't come. The night before, we had heard, the heavens had opened and brought traffic to a crawl and then to a standstill on the A5 near the Dee. I had planned an early start from Oxfordshire but with the rain lashing down at 6 a.m. the chances of finding the river fishable were very slight. At 6.30 I had a brainwave. Tickets for the Llangollen Angling Association are available from D.M. Southern, Newsagents, in Llangollen. Newsagents are about at 7 a.m., so I phoned the shop to beg a report on the water. Mark Southern is a fisherman himself and understands people wanting to know about rivers at that hour. He asked me to ring again at 7.30 – when he would be less busy and when there would be enough light for him to see the river.

I glanced out of the window by my phone: it was still pitch black. Silly me. At 7.30 he reported the river up a fraction with a tinge of colour and miraculously fishable. We set off.

At 10 a.m. we were beside the water. The sun was shining onto trees in the richest of autumn colours, reflected in the big waters of the Dee. This is a big river.

The Llangollen Angling Association has about 7 miles of the river, most of it double bank, around the town. The majority of this is available on a £3 day ticket for trout and grayling, which must make it some of the best value grayling fishing in the country. How a notorious cheapskate like myself could have missed this all these years is beyond comprehension. The fishing below the Chain Bridge Hotel allows worm fishing from 16 June: above the hotel the trout and grayling fishing is fly-only. Just above the hotel the spectacular Horseshoe Falls supplies the water for the Shropshire Union Canal that starts here. And so did we.

Above the falls the river is broad and serene with a hint of a faster channel on the far side. The morning was warming in the unexpected sunlight, and as we watched, a small rise appeared in the channel. Nothing much, but a bubble remained on the surface, which I always associate with feeding grayling. Then another rise, further back, which was worth wading for. Almost everything hereabouts seems to need wading. Wading comes in two sorts on the Llangollen water. There is deep wading where the river is relatively slow because it is deep. The bottom is usually gravel, which is just as well, as you are up to your armpits and almost afloat. Then there is shallow wading. This is worse. It is shallow because the river bed is crossed by bands of hard slate set at about 45 degrees to everything. Here the current is faster and the angled rock is slippery, sliding away into deeper holes. On that Saturday each of these rock barriers had a salmon fisherman perched upon it, fishing the deeper plunge pools below.

I eased out into the slow run above the dam, far enough to avoid the glorious chestnut trees behind me. By dint of dipping my elbows into the water, I managed to get a cast across to the rising fish which eventually did the decent thing and grabbed hold. It was a sprightly little rainbow trout. Mark Southern had come down the river to see how we were getting on. He was standing next to Paul on the river bank. I was rather proud of my little fish, pleased to have caught anything on that day after the storm. I called out that I had a rainbow. 'Yes,' he said, 'we put a few of them in here for the disabled.' I don't know why, but somehow I felt as if I had shot a sitting bird. Nothing definite, but not quite a gentleman. We moved upstream.

Three hopeful salmon fishermen were angling away on Duncan's Pool and we exchanged stories about the 6-pound red fish landed earlier in the day. Walking upstream from Duncan's Pool, the river swings round to the right, running broad and deep between steep, wooded banks. Occasional rises could be seen under the trees on the far bank. We clambered down the bank to wade across but the water under our bank was too deep to attempt. We ruminated as anglers ever have as to the truth that the rises are always to be found under the far bank. We had seen nothing under ours. At the top of this broad and deep run a water pipe is slung across the river under a cable, and we had been told that the water was fordable here. It is, but only just. It is not comfortable wading, for it is deep, chestwaders only, and encumbered with thick trails of weed deep below the surface. Once on the far bank we found that rises were now to be seen under the bank we had just left. But not under our bank. Either we were scaring the fish under our banks or the rises close by were impossible to spot amid the foliage. Either way we were getting nowhere. The solution in the end was simple. Moving back to the ford beneath the cable we waded precariously out to midstream and set off gingerly down the middle of the river.

It was a happy discovery: a tongue of wadeable water stretches down the centre of this magnificent run. To each side the river flows in deep channels beneath the steep wooded banks where the fish can lie protected from everything – except Paul and me. From midstream we could see tiny, discreet rises under both banks, and casting from midstream was a piece of cake compared to trying to thread the thing through the trees.

And so on that sunny October day we made hay. I worked my way down until the height of water threatened to lift me off my feet, then I turned and worked my way back upstream, floating a small dry fly down the channels. Paul was working downstream, drifting a nymph down the channels. We met in the middle, several fine grayling ahead of the game.

And that is the essence of the thing: we had solved the puzzle. If we had not found that tongue of gravel hidden beneath the coloured waters, if those waters had been a little bit higher or I had been a little bit shorter, if we had not seen the tiny rises under the far bank, if several other things, then we might have come away without a fish, and perhaps that will happen the next time. It often does. But not this time. This time it was all smiles and a deep satisfaction in those beautiful grayling from a beautiful autumn stream. But I have a nagging suspicion that Paul would have traded the whole lot for one red 6-pounder.

32 ♌

The Mile-High Club

Don't you just hate canned music?

And this was canned music of a particularly virulent strain. It was loud: it was a brass oom-pah band playing the 'Radetzky March' and going ta-ta-TUM, ta-ta-TUM, ta-ta-TUM-TUM-TUM in the way it does. Also it was filling my hotel room as I staggered from the shower in the bathroom. It seemed to be coming from behind the curtains at the far end of the room, so I went looking urgently for the speakers and some sort of control knob.

Lienz is a small town in southern Austria, the capital of Osttirol, the small enclave of the Tyrol on the sunny southern side of the Alps. A few miles to the west and to the south lies Italy, and the Italian influence could be seen in Lienz in the pavement pizzerias and ice cream cafés among the shops and restaurants that lined the town square just below my window. In the middle of the square there was a bandstand and thirty blokes in pointy hats with feathers and long white socks and they were giving it ta-ta-TUM, ta-ta-TUM, ta-ta-TUM-TUM-TUM on a variety of huge silver instruments.

It was all rather splendid. Why a noise should sound horrid when believed to be coming from a hotel sound system and splendid coming from thirty blokes in white socks, I have no idea. It just does.

The band played on into the evening as we ate dinner overlooking the square and the sun set behind the rocky pinnacles of the Dolomites that dwarf the town of Lienz. We were eating with Günther Wimmer, owner of the Hotel Sonne and dedicated fly-fisher, who described the rivers of the region.

Something like this: Lienz lies on the Grosse Drau – the big Drau river – which drains the southern slopes of the Hohe Tauern, the mountain range that divides the little world of Osttirol from the rest of Austria. Draining the highest mountains in Austria has its good points and bad points.

On the good side, these mountains get a lot of snow that melts in the warmer days to provide steady flows of cool water. On the bad side, these mountains get a lot of snow, which accumulates as glaciers around the high peaks, grinding bits of these peaks to a fine silt. When a glacier melts, the water that floods the river looks like dirty milk. Günther loves the fishing of April and October when there is no meltwater of any sort and all the rivers run crystal. This is the time for the local aficionados to pursue the huchen, the huge salmonid peculiar to the rivers that flow into the Danube. Huchen live only in the main river hereabouts, which is a huge comfort for anything that lives in the tributaries: huchen are big, up to 50 pounds in the Grosse Drau, and you don't get that big living on flies.

Not that anything would have been able to spot a fly in the Grosse Drau at the minute. It was the second half of a splendidly hot August, and the River Isel we had followed down from the high Alps looked like someone had emptied a large dairy into it. Now, I know a lot of places that are not at their fishing best in August; I was gloomily convinced that this was another one.

Not so. High summer is the time of the best trout fishing in the streams of Osttirol. And that makes it very good indeed. Only one or two of these mountain rivers run from the glaciers. The others trickle from the high pastures and snow fields or seep from crystal springs in the limestone of the Dolomites. These cool, rich waters in the side valleys, Günther assured me, were at their best right now. Right now a warm, soft rain had commenced, sending the silver band marching from the dark town square, oom-pahing as they went. It was a powerful, stirring sound, not at all what one might expect from men in long white socks.

Next morning the Kleine Drau sparkled along a perfect Tyrolean valley dotted with wooden farmhouses, every balcony heavy with flowers. Ridiculously steep meadows were being mown by hand and soft-eyed cattle swung mellifluous bells as they grazed. We pulled down a track and parked on a gravel bank with the river glinting through the birches. Italy was not far upstream and the Italian influence was there in Günther's tackle.

It was the coolest fly-rod I have ever set eyes on. Italian tackle design is not fettered by tradition: they will try anything, and from time to time, like the lever-wind Vivarelli reel to which I am wedded, it works. Günther's rod was made by Francesco Palu of Udine. The handle was long and thin and leather-wrapped with a second reel-seat a short distance from the butt. It was telescopic, but unlike other telescopic rods I had seen, each section could be locked in either the 'extended' or the 'folded' position. Günther could fish with a rod of anywhere from 7 feet to 13 and with a variety of actions – some of which might cast a fly tolerably well. I was about to try the beast when Günther's mobile phone rang.

While Günther was thus engaged in running a hotel, I wandered down through the trees to the river's edge. There is a bluey clarity to limestone waters. The Little Drau was rattling past at a fair old lick. At first glance it appeared an unbroken white-water rapid but there were glassy glides and calmer eddies towards the bank and behind stones. Where I was standing the main channel swept between a couple of boulders to form a deeper pool with a bottom of pale gravel. The broken, bouncing surface gave a tantalizing illusion of grey shapes swooping in the depths of the pool. As I stood and watched, one of these grey fragments swooped up towards the surface and became a fish. I was standing just a yard or two from a thoroughly rising trout.

I tried to look like a bush reversing slowly from the water's edge. Günther was still on the phone. I picked up my rod and tied on what I always tie on to start with: an Easy Rider Dun. With its hare's ear body and mixed grizzle-and-red hackle, it could be almost anything. I just hoped it could be something Tyrolean.

I stood behind the last bush and cast over the spot where I had stood three minutes before. A grey shape detached itself from the bottom and rose through the water, tilting up to the fly.

Fly-fishing is not difficult: folks are inclined to make a song and dance about it but really there is nothing to it. One cast in Austria, one bright wild rainbow trout throwing itself all over the vicinity before being slid to the hand and gently released, one angler trying to look like this sort of thing happens all the time. Piece of cake.

It was a handsome fish. The rainbows breed in these cold, clear waters and others are introduced as fry. They are chunky little items, full-finned and silvery. I was smiling the smile of a man with a pounder on his first cast when Günther came and put the thing in perspective with another two from the same pool.

A man could do very nicely with just a nondescript dry fly on the Little Drau in August. We did. Günther, Hansjörg and I worked our way upstream, casting over any hole between the rocks of the riverbed. The Little Drau is composed entirely of rocks and holes between rocks in roughly equal proportions, so there was plenty to go at. Before long I began to see runs and channels and pools in the bouncy confusion and concentrated on these. At no point did I see a rise. Günther did and cast to them and caught fish. I didn't and cast and caught fish anyway. There were fish everywhere.

Through the trees on the left bank we could see cyclists coasting downhill on a path that follows the Little Drau into Lienz. It looked an idyllic way to travel, bowling along with an occasional turn of the pedals to show willing. Something was not quite right: they all seemed to be coasting downhill. In my experience cycling is done mostly uphill with little bits of downhill in between. This universal freewheeling seemed against the laws of God and man – a nice trick if one could work it, but I didn't see how.

Hansjörg knew how. The Little Drau begins life in the neighbouring province of southern Tyrol (which is in Italy – following some jiggery-pokery over two world wars which no one felt up to explaining to me). A special tourist ticket from Lienz railway station gives you a one-way train ride across into Italy and the hire of a bike for the pleasant 50 kilometre downhill cycle-track that follows the river from its source to the confluence with the Isel at Lienz. Now, this is my idea of cycling, with a little cast now and then along the 10 kilometres of fishing belonging to Günther's Hotel Sonne.

Towards the top of Günther's beat, the river swings through bigger pools with deeper channels. Big rainbows lie in the depths of these channels but they were not to be tempted to the surface for a small dry fly. Günther showed me the fly for the job: a pale heavyweight nymph with a silver head. The heavy silver bead was threaded, not onto the hook but onto a brass pin, which was then bent and bound into the dressing, another cunning idea from Francesco Palu.

The problem in these swift waters is to get the fly down to the fish and then to discover when the fish has the nymph in its mouth before it hasn't anymore. And here the telescopic rod comes into its own. Günther had been fishing dry with four of the sections housed inside the butt. Now he extended the rod to its full 13 feet. He had a fine leader of little more than the depth of the channel. The heavy nymph was not so much cast as swung upstream into the head of the run. Günther steered the fly down the deep channel, holding the rod high with the fly-line barely touching the water. As the fly passed him, I saw the line twitch sideways and Günther lifted into a fish that dwarfed the others we had taken on the dry fly. He took three of these beauties from that channel.

That long rod swimming a fly between the rocks had suddenly begun to look very familiar. In the fast streams of northern Spain I had seen fishermen swim a weighted worm down such tumbling runs: the vertical line reacts instantly to any touch of a trout and a lift of the long rod does the rest. The same technique in the trout streams of France is called fishing '*au toc*', which describes the little tug of the trout as the bait of worm, grasshopper or grub hurries past its nose. And what is the difference between a grub and a thumping great nymph? Show me an expert with the deep nymph and I will show you an expert clear-stream bait-fishermen. And that is indeed an expert.

It was time for Günther to go and do whatever hoteliers do. There are half a dozen fishing hotels in Osttirol, ranging from the big and plush to cosy little B&Bs in ancient, flower-decked farmhouses. All have several beats on the rivers and streams of the mountains. Summer thunderstorms are common in the mountains and a local downpour can flood a river, leaving the next valley unaffected. These fishing hoteliers have a sensible arrangement of reciprocal fishing: each can send guests to another's water, so a visitor to one hotel can fish on most of the waters of the region and always with the water in prime condition. Hansjörg and I took a small road on the northern side of the Little Drau and began to climb.

These sides of these alpine valleys are steep, and the small rivers that tumble down them look quite unfishable. We followed one of these up to the small village of Außervillgraten and its cosy inn, the 'Niederbruggerhof', an old farmhouse stuffed to the gunnels with the usual flowers. The Neiderbruggerhof is another fishing hotel with over 20 kilometres of fishing on the Villgraten and Winkeltal brooks in their hidden valleys of the high alps.

We stood beside the waters of the Villgraten. We were both, I think, a bit daunted. Hansjörg is Austrian and had, at least, to pretend he knew how to fish the thing. I am English and had no idea. It was fast. The banks were steep and stony and the whole thing resembled the log flume ride at Alton Towers. I felt in serious need of a pool but the Villgraten did not run to pools. I had asked Günther how I should fish the Villgraten. He had replied airily that I should fish it with English wet flies and so I had put on a team of three flies. We climbed gingerly down into the water. The flow was fierce and pushed at the back of my legs as I felt my way across the hidden boulders. It was no more than 5 or 6 yards wide, and casting across the thing seemed rather pointless: I could almost reach that far. Immediately below me was a little bridge, beneath which the water rushed before plunging over a little weir. I could not see how a trout could hold the current unless nailed down. I rolled the line across to the far side and watched it whip across to hang below me like a pennant in a gale. Upstream Hansjörg was doing much the same. I clamped the rod between my knees and got the camera out for a photograph of him before one or other of us fell over and was swept away. As I faced upstream, peering through the viewfinder, the little rod between my knees was wrenched round. The reel may well have screamed (as, I understand, it is meant to do at such times in these stories) but I couldn't hear it above the sound of the river. It was, of course, a trout.

It was a fine little mountain brown trout of 12 inches, all speckles and spots. Hooking it had been a lucky accident – as is so much of fishing. The trick is to learn the lesson. And we did. We learnt to get the flies to search every quiet corner slowly, slowly. That first fish had taken a fly hanging in the current. So we lowered the flies down the current to hang in each possible lie before they were allowed to swim down to the next spot. The tugs began, at first unexpected and then anticipated in similar spots. And soon other fish followed. By the time we scrambled back up to the riverside meadows, my legs were suddenly tired from the press of the current. I had had enough. I stood on a small footbridge over the torrent in the alpine twilight and watched Hansjörg take the best trout of the afternoon from nowhere in particular in that dashing little river.

I had learnt a lot on my first day in the Tyrol. Here endeth the first lesson.

* * *

I joined the Mile High Club the next day.

There was no fuss: no one gave me a badge or a tie or anything. As far as I know, we do not even have a funny handshake. We just have this smug sort of smile that lets others know – we have caught a trout at something over 5280 feet.

It was August. I was in Austria, in the little world of Osttirol. I had spent the first day on the Little Drau and its tributaries, pulling handsome wild rainbows from the cold crisp waters that tumbled down the valleys at an alarming rate of knots. But that was just for starters.

It had been a long hot summer and the River Isel still ran murky white with meltwater from the glaciers in the mountains of the Hohe Tauern. At times like these we intrepid mountain types take to the hills.

We took to the hills in quite a big way. Actually, we took to the hills in a *very* big way. The Kalserbach is a sparkling mountain river that tumbles from the slopes of Großglockner, and hills really do not come any bigger than Großglockner. Not in Austria, anyway. 'Groß', according to my Collins Gem German dictionary means 'big'. I would go along with that. I couldn't find 'glockner' in the dictionary, but whatever a glockner is, this one – three times the height of Ben Nevis – is a big one.

We reached Kals, the village at the head of the Kalser valley and the start of the classic ascent of Austria's highest mountain. Nowadays you can drive a little further, alongside the bouncing waters of the Dorferbach to the hamlet of Taurer. So we did.

It is hard to feel an intrepid mountain type in the Hotel Taurerwirt. It is far too comfortable. It has a solarium and a splendid balcony restaurant, a sauna and tennis courts and things like that. It also has the Dorferbach, the river that sweeps along the alpine meadow that surrounds the hotel. We tackled up as we waited for our guide.

Our guide was ten years old and one of the best I have fished with. He was keen. Well, he would be: these are fast and furious waters and his father, who owns the hotel, only lets him go fishing if he goes with a visiting fisherman. We were the first for a few weeks and Christoph was straining at the leash. Also he was not expensive. I got the feeling he might have paid us his pocket money just to come along. And he was good: I have never seen anyone better at spotting fish in the swooping, twisting waters of a fast mountain river.

We crossed the river on a little wooden footbridge below the hotel. Christoph was quivering like a young dog that has spotted a rabbit in the next field. We loosed his leash and he was off up the river. We followed, watching carefully to discover how one sets about fishing the wild waters of the Dorfer.

Christoph worked his way upstream, peering intently into each back eddy and slack behind the boulders on the bank. He had seen something in the bluey waters. He pointed and, like a dutiful guide, suggested I cast to whatever he had spotted. I hate it when guides do that. If you catch the thing, you get the feeling they did it. If you don't catch the thing, you get the feeling you messed it up. And so does the guide. Besides, there was something in the way Christoph was quivering like a pointer in the presence of a partridge that told me this was his fish.

He flicked a fly a little upstream onto the slack water. It was not a prodigious cast: there was no need for one. Just a flick to get the fly on the water. Nothing happened. So he flicked again, and again, until the fish gave in to the inevitable and rose to snatch the little dry fly from the surface. That fish was a study in simplicity. Christoph used one fly that day and caught fish up and down the river. The fly was a size 16 Royal Coachman with a cul-de-canard wing for buoyancy in the tumbling water, a natural grey-brown feather under white for visibility. Christoph ties his own Royal Coachman, a skill he learned from a party of Dutch anglers when they came to fish at Taurerwirt. When they come again he will learn to tie another pattern. Then he will have two patterns and he will have to decide which one to use and wonder whether it wouldn't have been better to use the other one and he will be in the same quandary as the rest of us. I envied him his temporary simplicity. I also envied him his fish.

So he found one for me. Downstream the river flows through a stand of ancient conifers. There is deeper, slower water on a lazy bend where he had seen a good fish in the small pool behind a rock. Once. I was standing above the rock. I could do little more than flip the backcast between the trees and flop the fly onto the slowly twisting slack. I could see nothing – but Christoph had commenced to quiver again. He had seen a grey shape emerge from the bank and recede. After a few more flops I saw it too and then the shape rose to the surface and grabbed the fly. The fly was not remotely like a number 16 Royal Coachman. Nor was the fish remotely like the next one to grab Christoph's Coachman. We were standing on another footbridge. I thought we were just staring, like all fishermen do, at the water sweeping beneath. You do not look to see fish in water like that where I come from. Christoph was flipping the Coachman upstream, steering it over the deep water beneath the bridge. I wasn't really watching. Suddenly the rod buckled down over the rail on the bridge and it was not obvious how things would proceed from this point. It didn't look like the sort of fish you could dangle.

Hansjörg took the rod whilst Christoph and I climbed over the rail and clambered down the bank. I reached up and passed the rod down to Christoph and he set about the business of getting the fish into the net. It was quite a business, but then it was quite fish: a perfect wild rainbow, over $1\frac{1}{2}$ pounds, from a high, wild brook. It was a pleasant walk back through the forest to lunch.

We ate a splendid lunch on the balcony gazing down the Alpine valley amid the peaks of the Großglockner and thought it pretty fine.

The river, meanwhile, had been changing. The heat of the noonday sun on the ice fields above had brought streams of meltwater cascading down the valley sides, tinging the waters of the Dorfer. In any other stream of the high Alps, fishing would be difficult for the remainder of that day. But the Dorfer is not like any other stream of the high Alps: the Dorfer has something very special for the fisherman. But it is another thousand feet higher up the Dorfer valley.

The Daba gorge starts just behind the hotel. Here the Dorfer has carved a narrow slot, twisting its way deep through the limestone. The exhilarating path that threads the gorge is carved into its vertical sides. The Hohe Tauern National Park is for walkers, but with a powerful special permit a car of a certain sort can make it up this track if it has a driver of a certain sort behind the wheel. Peter Rogl, owner of the hotel, fine fisherman and father of our guide, offered to drive us up into the world of the upper Dorfer beyond the gorge.

It is quite true what they sing: they do 'love to go a-wandering along the mountain track'. Smiling folk of all ages and sizes were plodding up the track as we crunched past and then squeezed the car into a rough-hewn, twisting tunnel that burrows up through the mountain.

The tunnel spewed us blinking into the sunlight of a spacious alpine valley. The river rattled and bounced over a broad bed of pebbles and gravel. We did something similar down to an ancient cattle bridge. The water here was tinged with melt but nothing to stop a good fish rising below the bridge. I cannot claim the trout did not see my fly. No trout has ever looked closer at one of my flies. It rose confidently beside the thing and followed it for several yards downstream, viewing it from every angle before sinking every bit as confidently. That happened twice more before we both tired of the game. Above the bridge a trout had inhaled Peter's Royal Coachman without a second glance and was unhooked by Christoph, who had been sent on the retrieve. With its heavy speckling of small black spots and a few of red, it looked uncannily like Christoph's rainbow of the morning, but this pounder was a wild brown of the high mountains. It was our first mile-high trout.

Peter took us higher up the valley, driving at a cow's pace along the track through the small birches and pines. We would have gone a lot faster but we were stuck behind a herd of doe-eyed cows with definite views about the right of way in an alpine valley. And so we came to the Kalser Tauernhaus.

The Kalser Tauernhaus is a mountain refuge hut belonging to the German Alpine Club, which sounds rather brave and manly, the sort of thing you might stagger into, out of the blizzard that has your support team pinned down at base camp on the south col. The Kalser Tauernhaus is not really like that. Not in August. It is a cosy old stone farmhouse with a sun-drenched terrace where one sits beneath a parasol and sips ice-cold beer. It has a rather good menu. It knocks spots off a thermos of tea in a cobwebbed, corrugated-iron fishing hut.

The secret of the Dorfer valley and its superb summer fishing lies a little walk upstream from the Kalser Tauernhaus. Here the last tributary, the Laperwitzbach, rushes in from a cleft in the valley walls, milky with glacial melt after a day in the sun. Above this confluence is a small miracle: the Dorfer barrels crystal-clear down the valley. Up here it is called the Seebach – the Lake stream. The lake in question is the Dorfer See at the far end of the valley, but the river doesn't flow from the lake. Not quite. That is the secret of its success. The water from the lake seeps away through its bed of porous limestone and emerges, filtered and crystal clear, as the little Seebach, ice-cold and unsullied through the hottest summer.

And so we set to fishing the Seebach, flicking small dry flies into the slack pockets and eddies in the prescribed alpine manner. And at some time in that late afternoon in August I joined the Mile-High Club.

Mine was not the biggest trout from the Seebach that afternoon: that was caught by Christoph in the customary manner of all small boys with only one fly in their fly box. Christoph's big old brown was the biggest fish but it was not the best. The best fish fell to his father. *Salvelinus Fontinalis*, the brook char, is not a demur fish. It is not a shrinking violet. In fact, violet is just about the only colour it doesn't have. Lurid yellows it has. And orange and bright green. There are red spots with blue rings. And the inside of its mouth is a rather off-putting black. It is not a small mouth. Peter's fine little fish was barely a handful but it had a mouth of a fish four sizes bigger. And teeth to match. A brook char from the Seebach is altogether a little bobby-dazzler.

It was late evening in the high alps. We walked back down to the Kalser Tauernhaus and had a celebration schnapps as the colour drained from the peaks to leave them silhouetted against an evening sky. It had been another good day. I had my mile-high trout; I could get a mile-high char some other time. We drove slowly down the valley and emerged from the tunnel shaft onto the track. A few straggling happy wanderers were still trudging along the path through the gorge. I didn't hear anyone singing 'Val-de-ree, Val-de-ra' though.

*   *   *

In the days that followed I fished other waters of Osttirol. There were fish I will always remember: a trout from the crashing white water of a gorge, spotted from high on the track above, which rose through the froth and bubbles to take a dry fly. I even caught my char. It was in the Schwartzach, a stream of the mountains along the Italian border. The little char rose against all the rules amongst a shoal of grayling in a broad and pleasant pool and took pity on me when I had lost all hope of catching an Austrian char. I was grateful to this lovely creature – but it did not compare with the brawling braggart of a fish from the mile-high waters of the Seebach. And it's there that I want to catch one. Next time.

Hello Dollaghan

Once upon a time, as all stories should start, antelope and buffalo roamed the plains to the west of Sicily. They do not roam there now. Those ancient plains now lie 600 feet below the surface of the Mediterranean. But we know they were there once because the men who hunted the antelope and buffalo left images of themselves and the beasts they hunted painted on the walls of a cave. In 1949, on the small rocky island of Levanzo, a dog chased a rabbit under a rock ledge. The dog did not reappear and the owner followed it beneath the ledge and crawled into the narrow entrance of a cave. And there, in the deep recesses of the limestone, he discovered those paintings of men and animals, animals that could never have lived on a small rocky island surrounded by the Mediterranean. It was a glimpse of a lost world.

The other day I was looking at something similar.

The Ballinderry River runs eastward through the lush dairy farmland of Co. Tyrone, through Cookstown and on towards the vast freshwater sea of Lough Neagh. A legendary fish once swam the Ballinderry in huge numbers, and in the small town of Coagh its ancient hunters, like those of Levanzo, have left images of their quarry etched into the limestone.

Actually, the hunters were not *that* ancient. The limestone where they plonked their best fish and proudly scratched round its outline is the capping stone of road bridge in the small town of Coagh, and the chances are that these trophies were carved in the 1940s and 50s. But the fish they were recording were the stuff of legends. They were Dollaghan.

Dollaghan are a species of trout peculiar to the waters of Lough Neagh. Like sea trout, they begin life in the small streams and after two years they begin to smolt, developing a silvery coat and slipping downstream to find the sea. They do not get there. What they find first are the rich waters of Lough Neagh. Here they feast on the freshwater shrimps and the other beasties of the lough until they become fat and frisky, at which time they may move down the menu to the fish course. Lough Neagh has its own fodder fish, the pollan, a small whitefish, kin to the gwyniad of Wales and the Lake District and the powan of Scotland. The flesh of this innocuous little creature was once thought to be soporific. It was 120 years ago that the Rev. W. Houghton tried a plate of fried pollan and was warned by his boatman, 'You must move about, Sir, soon after eating them, or they may send you to sleep.'

The dollaghan move about. In August and September, sometimes in July, they re-enter the river of their birth and make their way upstream as three-year-old fish of $1^{1}/_{2}$–2 pounds. That is a fair fish but it is nothing like the lumps of things that are etched on Coagh bridge. These are the dollaghan that had spawned and returned to the lough for another season of fast food. Each time a dollaghan made that journey, it would double in size, a four-year-old fish returning at 3–4 pounds and a fish on its third journey hauling 8 or 9 pounds upstream.

* * *

I rather fancied catching one of those. So I phoned John Todd. John runs Gillaroo Angles, a company that advises on game angling holidays in the province. He has written a guidebook to the game fishing to be had there. He knows about these things.

Like sea trout, John said, the dollaghan like a bit of rain. It was raining when I met John in Belfast that morning. It was raining a little harder as we drove west along the M2 out of the city towards Antrim. At Randalstown the motorway crosses the first of the rivers that feed Lough Neagh.

The River Main flows into the lough through the grounds of Shanes Castle on the north shore of the lough. This is famous salmon water. A few miles to the west the salmon are flogging their way south from the sea up the River Bann. At the lough they turn left and then take the first turning on the left – they can't miss it – into the Main. We could see one or two of them, large silver shapes heaving themselves from the water, tinged brown from the rain. And in the River Main these fish were just as likely to be dollaghan.

John was optimistic, as is only right and proper in these circumstances. So was Alan Kirkpatrick, water bailiff on Lord O'Neil's fishing at Shanes Castle. In these waters, where a salmon is as likely as a dollaghan, fishermen use the same flies for both. A team of two small shrimp flies worked, I was advised, 'brave and slow' across the current. I nodded wisely but without the slightest idea of how one might fish a fly 'bravely'.

I need not have worried. Everything I did on the River Main that day felt pretty brave. The Main is a big river, getting bigger by the minute, and it has some of the nastiest wading I have stumbled across. Rounded boulders of irregular size are positioned at the correct distance to trap an unwary foot. I got my foot trapped between most of them down the long, fine pool beneath the bridge.

It was raining harder when Alan, John and I met in a soggy enclave by the river. There was an air of gloom. Alan didn't think it looked very hopeful: conditions were against us. John hadn't wanted to mention it, but he had been pessimistic from the start. I have heard this stuff before.

We drove west, around the shore of Lough Neagh. Somewhere in the grey gloom we crossed the River Moyola where battalions of dollaghan may, for aught I know, have been advancing unmolested.

That evening we were standing on the bridge in Coagh looking at the carved outline of that long-gone dollaghan. Beneath the bridge the Ballinderry ran coloured. Beside the bridge stands one of the friendliest little hotels you will find beside any river. It was not much of a competition.

Hanover House is not at all convinced that it is a hotel. It has just three rooms but they are big and comfortable and sometimes you can stay in one if you ask the lovely Merlyn or her brother Colin beforehand. Don't just turn up. The secret of the Hanover's success is around the back in a huge friendly bar that serves the town as a pub and a restaurant that feeds the folk for miles around. It was in that bar on the banks of the Ballinderry that I met the man who has done more than most to save the dollaghan.

*   *   *

The year of 1951 was a great one for the dollaghan. Records were being broken right and left. On one evening in the late summer of 1951 a Ballinderry man took 87 pounds of dollaghan before retiring, bored, from the game. It was around this time that the outlines of huge trout were recorded on Coagh bridge. The feeding in Lough Neagh had never been richer and the fish were returning fatter and finer than ever before. Everything, you might have thought, was oojah-cum-spiff. It was not. Lough Neagh is surrounded by rich farmland, and none is richer than the dairy country of the Ballinderry. Farming was changing and the growing richness of Lough Neagh was a symptom of these changes, with an increased use of fertilizers and the production of slurry. Before long, Ireland's largest lough was suffering from a nasty case of eutrophication, with massive algal blooms and increased bacterial activity. In 1981 the lough all but died. And in the rivers round about the increasing use of silage brought an epidemic of fish-kills from seepage.

And then the rivers of Northern Ireland were *drained*. They were drained close unto death in an insane scheme that is now used as a textbook example of how the thing should never be done. Redds were ripped from the rivers, nursery areas and holding pools reamed out. It was a ruthless age. And somewhere in the middle of all this death and destruction the dollaghan disappeared. You could hardly blame them.

I fib: the dollaghan did not *quite* disappear down the plughole of extinction. But it was close. The last vestiges of the once-great runs of dollaghan were returning from the lough to find their rivers in ruins. Worse, fishing clubs and people who should have known better were re-stocking the depleted waters with farmed brown trout without a migratory gene in their chromosomes. Ten years ago the unique dollaghan was within a season or so of its final run upriver.

And then came the Ballinderry River Enhancement Association and its director, Alan Keys.

The first task was to save the genetic inheritance of the dollaghan. The Moneymore River is a small tributary joining the Ballinderry just above Coagh. It had never been re-stocked. A few precious Moneymore dollaghan were electrofished as they returned to their native stream. The hens were stripped of their eggs and the Ballinderry Fish Hatchery was born.

There is a satisfying justice in the beginnings of that hatchery. The Ballinderry flows through rich dairy farmland and some of the worst polluters of its waters were the cheese factories along its banks. The hatchery's first fish tanks were made from long stainless-steel cheese vats, donated by the Dunman cheese factory following a successful pollution prosecution. It was inspired improvisation. Improvisation has become a hallmark of the hatchery's success: fish are still transported in the luxury of a stainless-steel something-or-other-gleaned-from-a-cheese-factory-and-mounted-on-a-trailer, eggs are planted out into the rivers in artificial redds cobbled ingeniously from Tupperware food boxes.

But re-stocking is no solution to the problems of pollution. Ten years ago ignorance and indifference led to twenty to thirty major fish kills each year from silage and slurry seepage in the valley. In the past three years there have been only two such fish kills. This miraculous transformation has been brought about largely by the children of the Ballinderry. Children have always been encouraged to visit the hatchery. A thousand children a year are shown round the tanks of growing fish and fry. They have the horrors of silage and slurry graphically explained. And all these children have parents and many of these parents are farmers.

The ravages of dredging and drainage have taken longer to redress. For years the Ballinderry River Enhancement Association has been moving heaven and earth and prodigious lumps of rock to create spawning redds, nursery areas and holding pools along the river.

*   *   *

The Ballinderry River beside the Hanover House had fallen to something more manageable. I had one last day at the dollaghan.

There are two ways to catch sea trout – and dollaghan – during the day. In the first, the fisherman swings small silvery doubles, flies sporting a touch of blue about them, through the heads and tails of the pools. Or he may work these flies through the deeper, stiller pools found on many of the rivers of Northern Ireland. This is similar to fishing for sea trout – and dollaghan – during the prime taking times of dusk and dark, only it is done with less faith and belief.

There is a second way. It was how I caught my first sea trout on the glinty, wooded waters of the Devon Avon. I was fishing a small dry fly for the small brown trout that infest the rivers of Dartmoor when something far more vigorous grabbed the fly and went looping around the pool and zipped off down the riffle towards Bantham and the sea. I hung on to the other end and pulled back in the direction of Loddiswell. In the end we compromised on a shingle bank two pools downstream. I had my first sea trout.

We started that last dollaghan day on the little Moneymore, the tributary of the Ballinderry that had spawned the rebirth of the dollaghan. Alan and John were to provide the main thrust of the daylight attack working downstream with method one. I was to make a light flanking movement, moving upstream, testing each small rise to find what lay beneath it.

I claim a small victory on points that morning. The Ballinderry Hatchery seeds about $1\frac{1}{2}$ million fed fry into the river each year in addition to those that are spawned naturally. I asked Alan to estimate what proportion of the trout parr in the river would become dollaghan. He guessed three-quarters. By that estimate I reckon I caught and released several dozen dollaghan by the end of the day. Many of these parr had curiously 'flattened' noses, a characteristic feature of wild dollaghan and visible in the adults I had seen in the hatchery.

I was cheating: a dollaghan is only a dollaghan when it comes back from the lough. Like sea trout, they prefer to make this journey in the dark and dusk, and that was the time, said Alan and John, when we would catch one.

It was a perfect evening with pink edges to the clouds and a faint breeze. Other feet had flattened the long grass beside the river down from Coagh. That was a good sign, said Alan: the locals know when the dollaghan are there to be caught. We were making for a bend where the fish paused above a boisterous riffle – a fine throw for a dollaghan – but in the dusk we could see another figure there beside the water: it was waiting, not fishing. It was Cecil. This was an even better sign, whispered Alan. Cecil is an expert. He travels from Belfast and rarely leaves the water without a fish. If Cecil had come, then Dollaghan were sure to follow.

So we fished. We fished long and hard.

Hours later the light had gone from the river. So had Cecil. Dollaghan had not occurred. We slunk back in silence. It was well along towards midnight and the lovely Merlyn made us a meal and mercifully opened the bar for us.

There are 10,000 dollaghan that run the Ballinderry and the rivers of Lough Neagh. This has not been the story of one of them.

Whisky Chaser

It isn't me, you understand, but I have this friend with a problem. We will call him Philip.

I have just spent five days with Philip in a small camper van, fishing the islands of the Outer Hebrides. You get to know a chap after five days in a small camper van in the Outer Hebrides. You discover things perhaps best undiscovered.

I discovered that Philip has a problem: he has a Whisky dependency.

I don't mean he is an alcoholic. Philip and I are both forty-eight. We were teenagers in the sixties and a slight tendency to substance abuse is an understandable, almost endearing, feature of such folk. Certainly nothing to be ashamed of. Philip's addiction is something quite different and a lot more sordid.

Each morning he would wake up and announce his firm resolve to fish throughout the day with three respectable, honest loch flies: a Grouse & Claret, say, and a Black Pennel with perhaps a Golden Olive Bumble on the top dropper. Flies that you could fish with a bright eye and a clear conscience – flies you would not mind your mother finding in your fly box. And I'm sure, each morning, he meant it.

And so we would set out to fish. The wind blew from the north under a grey sky and sometimes it was raining and sometimes it wasn't. And nothing rose. So we would work our way around the convoluted coasts of a loch, casting steadily at any point that took our fancy until something happened. It did not always happen straightaway. When Hemingway sat down at the typewriter and wound in a clean sheet of paper and stared at it, I bet the matchless prose did not always happen straightaway. So he would have a little drink, and perhaps another, and then maybe another, until he became positively eloquent. That's how these things start. And so it was with Philip. He would fish his team of traditional loch flies for a while, casting serenely onto the waters of the loch. If fish occurred, then all was well; if they did not, then before long he would begin to grow restless. He would draw in the line and examine the flies, consider them gravely and then, with an effort of manly resolve, cast them out again. But I had come to know the signs: this serenity would not last. After a few more fishless minutes the line would be wound in again. A furtive look would come over him and he would turn his back as his hand crept to the pocket that concealed his fly box and its stash of Whisky Flies. Even then, some vestige of self-respect would remain: with trembling fingers he would tie that first Whisky Fly just on the top dropper – certainly no lower than the middle dropper.

With that one Whisky Fly in his team he became a different fisherman. He would cast out again with confidence, his visage cleared and his eyes once again became bright – almost *too* bright. He had once again become the scourge of any trout in the vicinity.

And that was the strange thing: it really did work. Before long his line would tighten and I would walk across to witness the splash and landing of the trout. While the fish was still deep beneath the surface there was no knowing what fly had been taken. We didn't say anything, but each time I knew we were both hoping that it would be something other than the Whisky Fly. But each time it wasn't. A man needs help to fight addiction and Philip wasn't getting any from the fish.

The day would follow its familiar pattern. A tangle in the blustery wind would be the excuse for Philip to reduce the number of flies in his team. Like some grotesque cuckoo, the Whisky Fly would gradually displace the legitimate brood of smaller, traditional patterns until only that gaudy orange construction remained on the point. And that Whisky Fly caught fish. And if it didn't, then Philip would fish the dream team, *two* Whisky flies, until they did.

Philip knows it is wrong: if the Good Lord had meant us to catch brown trout with Whisky flies, there would be some natural water beast that is one inch long, with a body in alternating bands of scarlet and silver and sporting a mane of fluorescent orange hair reaching beyond its tail. There isn't. Not even close.

I am not saying that there is anything wrong with an *occasional* Whisky Fly. I used one myself from time to time in the Hebrides and, I must say, it is surprisingly effective. But here is the difference: unlike Philip, I could stop using Whisky Flies tomorrow. I could give them up just like that if I wanted to.

I just don't want to.

Factfile

Posted to the Highlands

The fishing on the North Assynt Estate is let by the Assynt Crofters Trust.

Day tickets £5, week tickets £20, from Stoer and Drumbeg post offices and the Tourist Information Office, Lochinver.

Callum Millar, School House, Drumbeg. Tel: 01571 833269. Callum provides ghillie services, angling tuition and advice on the North Assynt Estate. He has two boats on Loch Drumbeg.

Anne Gould has retired and Maggie and Dennis Campbell now run the Cruachan Guest House, Stoer, Lochinver, Sutherland IV27 4JE. Tel: 01571 855303. B&B from £22.

For Sleeper Train information, see 'A Fish on the Line'.

The post bus from Lairg to Lochinver (46 miles) cost £4 – which is remarkable. All routes and timetables can be found at www.postbus.royalmail.com/routefinder.asp or by phoning the Royal Mail Customer Service Centre on 08457 740740. There is a Textphone service on 0845 600 0606.

The Duns Tew Snooker Club

Loughs of Ireland by Peter O'Reilly (3rd edition, 1998), published by Merlin Unwin, Palmers House, 7 Corve Street, Ludlow, Shropshire SY8 1DB. Tel: 01584 877803. Fax: 01584 877893. Price £17.99.

Gougane Barra Hotel (Breda and Christopher Lucey) Gougane, Ballingeary, Co. Cork, Ireland. Tel: 026 47069. Fax: 026 47226.

Swansea–Cork Ferries run a daily service from the last week in May to the last week in September (alternate days from mid-March to early November). Tel: 01792 456116, Fax: 01792 644356. Timetables and fares on www.swansea-cork.ie.

We used Ordnance Survey of Ireland maps, Discovery Series (1:50,000) no.s 84 and 85.

From the Ridiculous to the Sublime

The Swan Hotel, Bibury, Gloucestershire GL7 5NW. Tel: 01285 740695. Three rods, dry-fly only fishing on 300 yards single bank of River Coln. Three fish limit (over 2 pounds). Day ticket £47.50, half-day £25 (residents £40, £20).

The Bull Hotel. Fairford, Gloucestershire. Tel: 01285 712535. Four rods per day, catch-and-release, dry-fly and upstream nymph fishing on 1.1 miles single bank fishing on River Coln for brown trout and grayling (barbless hooks, please). No wading. Day ticket £27, half-day £20 (residents £21, £16). Booking recommended especially around mayfly time in late May and June.

The Doonesday Book

Fishing on the west bank of Badgworthy Water, from one field above Malmsmead Bridge, Day ticket-£5, from Mrs Burge, Oare Mead Farm (between Malmsmead and Oare Church). Tel: 01598 741267.

Fishing on East and West Lyn, Watersmeet and Glenthorne Fisheries. Trout day ticket £3, week ticket £10. Salmon day ticket £13.50, week ticket £35. Tickets from Brendon House Hotel (see below).

Brendon House Hotel (Ian and Sandra Rigby), Brendon, Lynton, N. Devon EX35 6PS. Tel: 01598 741206. Charming and friendly and beside the river. Tickets for East Lyn below Brendon. B&B £23 (with dinner £39).

A Fish on the Line

The overnight sleeper from Euston to Fort William can cost anything from an unbelievable £19 (special online offer), depending on how early you book, travel times and class of cabin. A Highland Rover ticket (£59) allows travel on any Highland train (plus buses and some ferries) on four days out of eight – just right for such a trip. Ask ScotRail information and booking on 08457 550033 or visit www.scotrail.co.uk

Alas, The Moor of Rannoch Hotel no longer has fishing on Loch Laidon

The Morar Hotel (A.G. MacLeod), Morar, Mallaig, Inverness-shire. Tel: 01687 462520. The hotel has fishing packages with boats available for residents on Loch Morar. Boats, permits, services for Loch Morar from Ewen MacDonald, 4 St Cummins, Morar. Tel: 01687 462520. Permission to fish the hill lochs from Catchment Superintendent, Viv Defresnes. Tel: 01687 462388.

Inchbae Lodge Hotel by Garve, Ross-shire, IV23 2PH. Tel: 01997 455269. The river runs past the hotel and fishing is free to residents, Day ticket for visitors.

The Garvault Hotel (Tony and Catherine Henderson), by Kinbrace, Sutherland, Scotland. Tel: 01431 831224. Bed and Breakfast £27. The Garvault has fishing on thirteen lochs, large and small, free to residents, and there is also salmon fishing on a mile of the Helmsdale river. Half the lochs have boats (£17 per day) and all fish well from the bank. Bob Beech has written an excellent guide to fishing the Garvault waters.

Boys from the Grey Stuff

Raby Estates has around 7 miles of single bank fishing on the upper Tees above Middleton-in-Teesdale. The Earl of Strathmore Estates has 4 miles on the other bank.

Both permits are fly-only for trout. Day ticket £12 (£6 concessionary) from J. Raines, 26 Market Place, Middleton-in-Teesdale. Tel: 01833 640406.

Upper Weardale Angling Association has 5 miles of double bank fishing (trout, sea trout and salmon) from Westgate to Cowshill. Day tickets £5 from Wearhead Post Office.

The Lost Weekend

The limestone rivers of La Rioja hold some huge and handsome trout. This is not easy fishing but a wonderful place to fish.

There are no private rivers in Spain. All water will be either:

'Libre' – Free and open to anyone holding a fishing licence (around £6) from the office of Caza y Pesca (hunting and fishing) in Logroño, the capital of La Rioja. Trout size limit: 21 cm.

'Acotado' – a *cotos* or reserve where fishing is applied for and allocated by lot each November – this makes it difficult to come by for the casual visitor on the best beats at the best times. Beats are often available later in the season (ends 15 Aug). Size limit: 23 cm. *Cotos* are well marked and fishing between them is free. Several beats (*tramos*) on these rivers are blessed by being 'No Kill' (*sin muerte*), which means nearly what it says: you can take two fish over 40 cm.

'Vedado' – closed to fishing. Most of the smaller tributaries of these mountain rivers are preserved as breeding streams. Fishing prohibited. We stayed at the Venta de Goyo hotel. Tel: 0034 941 378007. Local fishing guides are available and can arrange licences for visitors, saving time and trouble.

I don't remember the name of the bar in Bobadilla.

Things that go Clonk in the Day

Clonks – and advice – are available from J&K Tackle, 62–64 Sheep Street, Bicester, Oxon. Tel: 01869 242589.

Boys' Toys

The Microcat from Angling Technics starts at £595 and stops around £2000, with echo-sounders, TV, solar chargers, the full works. Visit www.angling-technics.com or telephone 01666 575144.

Monnowphil

Kentchurch Court is an impressive, comfortable stately home with a deer park. Bed and breakfast starts at £30 and evening meals are available. Tel: 01981 240228.

Teme Spirit

All these people have fishing on the upper Teme and may, if asked nicely, let visitors fish. The price varies but something between £1 and £5 is normal and will depend on the length of the water, whim and just how nicely you ask. Several farmers have Caravan Club sites. These are not caravan sites with washhouses and a shop and children: they are places where a touring caravan can park for a while.

Several other owners we met that day had fishing and might occasionally allow a casual visitor to fish it but, reasonably enough, did not want this broadcast to the nation.

Mr S. Ruelle, Pound Farm, Llanfair Waterdine. Tel: 01547 510643.

The Red Lion, Llanfair Waterdine. Tel: 01547 528214. This pub has become 'The Waterdine': the pun is intentional and indicates a shift to gourmet meals. They still have accommodation and can point you in the direction of local fishing.

Mr F. Beavans, The Graig, Llanfair Waterdine. Tel: 01547 528516. Caravan Club site.

Maureen Bates, Lower Graig, Llanfair Waterdine. Tel: 01547 528564.

Mrs J. Williams, Monaughty Poeth, Llanfair Waterdine. Tel: 01547 528348. Bed and Breakfast and Caravan Club site.

Mrs G. Evans, Lower House, Knucklas. Tel: 01547 528670.

Milebrook House, Country House Hotel and Restaurant, Milebrook, Nr Knighton. Tel: 01547 528 632. Two rods on one mile (double bank) of River Teme when available.

Mr P. Davies, Bucknell House, Bucknell. Tel: 01547 4248. Bed and Breakfast and Caravan Club site.

Stitched up by the Doctors

The Horseshoe Inn (Dennis and Jessica Plant) Llan-y-Blodwel, Shropshire. Tel: 01691 828969. The inn has accommodation for fishermen and around 1 mile, single bank of the Tanat for a maximum of four rods, all year for trout or grayling and a good run of salmon from late September. £7.50 per day.

Lugg at Last

The Riverside Inn (Liz and Richard Gresko), Aymestrey, Herefordshire, HR6 9ST. Tel: 01568 708440. The inn has nearly a mile of double bank fishing on the River Lugg upstream from the inn by the bridge in Aymestrey and a similar length of the mill leat. The Lugg has a head of resident brown trout and some excellent grayling. The fish are now all wild. The fishing is free to residents; day tickets are sometimes available for non-residents (£10).

Doing it Doggy-Style

I went dog sledding and fishing at Åre Björnens with Kai Westerlund, tel: 0046 647 20164. E-mail: Arebjornens@hundspann.z.se.

Visit http://www.hundspann.z.se/english/hundspann.html for full details of dog sledding in Åre.

River Roo

Berriew lies just off the A483 between Welshpool and Newtown. There is a hotel and restaurant (the Lion) and a small pub (the Talbot) that does B&B.

Berriew Angling Club can be joined at the Corner Shop and post office beside the bridge. Tel: 01686 640477.

For information about the river and its fishing, speak to the Club Secretary, Mr D.J. Beddoes. Tel: 01686 640258.

Opinion varies on the spelling of the name: I have seen Rhiw and Rhiew and I bet there are others.

Fishing with Mr Fernie

The Peeblesshire Trout Fishing Association is exceptional value with a day ticket at £8.00 and a visitor's season ticket at £36. Both available from D.G. Fyfe, 39 High Street, Peebles. Also from tackle shops: Sonny Sports and Tackle, 29 High Street, Innerleithen, Peeblesshire EH44 6HA. Tel: 01896 830806. Tweeddale Tackle Centre, 1 Bridgegate, Peebles EH45 8RZ. Tel: 01721 720979.

And hotels: Traquair Arms Hotel, Innerleithen, Peeblesshire EH44 6PD, Tel: 01896 830229. Tweed Valley Hotel, Walkerburn.

The Gala Angling Association has 13 miles of trout fishing on the Tweed and 4 miles of the lower Gala Water. Day ticket £9, week ticket £17, Season £22 (children below 16 years £2). Tickets from: S. Grzybowski, 3 St Andrews Street, Galashiels. Tel: 01896 755712. Also from the tackle shop, J&A Turnbull, 30 Bank Street, Galashiels. Tel: 01896 753191.

David Norwich makes superb trout and salmon rods at Hillside Works, Fountainhall, Nr Galashiels TD1 2SU. Tel: 01578 760310.

Mustard and the Fisch-Meister

Monschau: day ticket and area licence both available from Frau Brandenberg, Laufenstrasse 66, 5108 Monschau.

Birresborn: day ticket and area licence both available from Josef von Landenberg, Budesheimerstrasse 42, 5535 Birresborn. Tel: 0049 06594 1432.

The Tangle O' The Isles

Information is everything in bagging lochisles. Over the next few months we will be collecting a definitive catalogue of islands: those with trout, those that might, those that look as though they do and don't. We need your help. If you have caught (or stocked) a trout on any island off the British Isles, please let us know which island, and which loch or stream (name or map reference) and when. The smaller islands are particularly valuable. All this information, along with details of ferries, services and permissions, will then be made available to anyone interested in visiting and fishing these magical places. Write to me at *Trout and Salmon*, send me a fax on 01295 758221 or leave your information at the official lochisle website, www.lochisle.co.uk, where you can also see the picture build. Meanwhile, for this trip:

Fishing in the Western Isles – free from tourist offices – lists the principal estates and association with water in the Western Isles.

70 Lochs - A guide to Trout Fishing in South Uist by John Kennedy, £4.95. Indispensable guide to the fishing on Benbecula and South Uist. Available from Bornish General Store, Bornish, South Uist HS8 5SA (add 50p postage).

Rivers and Lochs of Scotland by Bruce Sanderson. Published by Merlin Unwin, £19.99.

The Sports Shop, 1 Francis Street, Stornoway, Isle of Lewis. Tel: 01851 705464. Speak to Donny for invaluable information on fishing in Harris and Lewis.

Caledonian–MacBrayne Ferries run services to virtually every island on the west coast of Scotland. There are Rover Tickets covering all these services or particular groups of islands. For details of routes, fares and timetables contact Caledonian MacBrayne Ltd, The Ferry Terminal, Gourock, PA19 1QP. Tel: 01475 650100. Fax: 01475 637607. They have an excellent website at www.calmac.co.uk.

Snob

Owen Pilkington farms Bank Top Farm, Hartington, Buxton SK17 0AD. Tel: 01298 84205. It is always best to ring first. Bank Top Farm is on the gated road from the centre of Hartington to Pilsbury. It is a massive pain in the neck for a lone driver to approach via Pilsbury, as there are several gates.

Conway Twitter

National Trust, Ysbyty Estate, has four beats on the upper Conwy and the Machno, a Conwy tributary.

All fishing is for small brown trout, fly only (except in flood). Day ticket £5, available from Bob Ellis at 'Bron Ruffydd', Pentrefoelas, Betws-y-Coed, Gwynedd (second house past the café and layby towards Betws-y-Coed). Tel: 0690 710567.

Sea Trout Sampler

The Sea Trout Festival will be returning to the River Annan (where it started) in 2004, 11–18 July. The festival is organized by Anthony Steel, who has excellent fishing and self-catering cottages on his farm at Kirkwood, Lockerbie, Dumfriesshire DG11 1DH. Tel: 01576 510200. Visit www.seatroutfestival.com for details.

Day on the Dee

Watkins and Williams (ironmongers), 4 Berwyn Street, Llangollen. Tel: 01978 860 652. The bloke to speak to is Peter Griffiths. The shop opens at 7.30 a.m., so good for getting a full day on the river. Issues tickets for Llangollen A.A., 14 miles of bank, trout and grayling day ticket £6, week ticket £25. Also tickets for Midland Flyfishers. Four miles from Groeslwyd (above Llangollen water) to Glyndyfrdwy. Trout and grayling day ticket £6.

The Mile-High Club

Fishing on the hotel's 15 km of private fishing is £15 per day. No national licence is necessary. The hotel can arrange fishing at the same cost on about 100 km of private waters, large and small. Most of this is fly-only fishing. The hotel's chef will be happy to prepare your catch for the table, but catch-and-release fishing with barb-less hooks is encouraged.

Hello Dollaghan

Game Angling in the North of Ireland by John Todd. A Blackstaff Guide, price £7.99, available from bookshops or from the Blackstaff Press. Tel: 01232 487161. John Todd runs Gillaroo Angles (02890 862419), which advises on game angling in Northern Ireland.

Hanover House (Merlyn and Trevor), Hanover Square, Coagh, Co. Tyrone, Northern Ireland. Tel: 028 8673 7530. Booking for accommodation is essential.

Fishing on the River Ballinderry at Coagh. Day ticket £7, available from Alex Bradley, 35 Bridgend, Coagh. Tel: 028 8673 7085.

Fishing on the River Main at Shanes Castle. Day ticket £25–£50, available from The Estate Office, Shanes Castle, Antrim BT41 4NE. Tel: 028 9442 8216.